Double-Skin Facades

Integrated Planning

Oesterle · Lieb · Lutz · Heusler

Double-Skin Facades

Integrated Planning

Building Physics
Construction
Aerophysics
Air-Conditioning
Economic Viability

Prestel
Munich · London · New York

Table of contents

Preface

Double-skin facades are assuming an ever-greater importance in modern building practice. They are already a common feature of architectural competitions in Europe; but there are still relatively few buildings in which they have actually been realized, and there is still too little experience of their behavior in operation—a fact that scarcely serves to reduce the skepticism of many clients. First and foremost, clients and developers inevitably see the additional costs associated with multi-layered facades and need to be convinced of the advantages of this form of construction in each specific case. The possible gains for clients, users and even investors usually lie in the combined action of the various properties this type of construction offers, such as improved sound insulation, increased scope for window ventilation and greater user comfort, at least in moderate climates.

Although the basic objectives of the planning are clear, very little has been published on the combined action of the inner and outer facade layers and the intermediate space. Basic research into these aspects is still in its infancy, and a systematic planning approach to implementing requirements that affect a number of trades and disciplines is virtually unknown. The authors wish to remedy these omissions to some extent by describing the main aspects of this kind of construction, based on their long-year experience of planning and building double-skin facades as well as the subsequent measurement and supervision of the developments.

In this context, various aspects will be considered: the basic rules of constructional physics, as well as questions of aerophysics and building construction; the implications of this form of facade for air-conditioning concepts; and the special aspects of tall buildings. In addition to theoretical principles, the book also describes general trends. Simplified procedures for the application of this form of facade will be explained and illustrated by means of practical examples from planning and construction. In an introductory chapter, a summary is provided of the questions that most frequently arise, to which generally valid answers are also given, as well as a description of the most important steps in planning double-skin facades.

Introduction

The evolution of facade construction

Centuries ago, the limited scope for ensuring adequate heating in spaces for human occupation led to the insight that by creating unheated buffer spaces around a room for human occupation, one could perceptibly improve its thermal comfort.

Old farmhouses provide a good example. Usually they are strictly oriented according to the points of the compass, built on the south-facing slopes of valleys, with the stalls and stables for the animals along the north side. A row of coniferous trees may provide further protection against the wind, creating optimum conditions for heating by improving the microclimatic situation. A tiled stove would often be located in the middle of the building, with benches around it on which people could warm themselves. Thermal insu-

0.1 Old farmhouse in Mürren, Switzerland. In summer, it is possible not only to open the box windows, but to remove the outer casements entirely.

lation was not neglected either in view of the timber form of construction and the shutters that could be closed at night.

In Switzerland, one can still find old farmhouses of this kind with box-type windows. These are constructed in such a way that in summer, the inner casements can be opened and the outer layer of glazing removed, thereby allowing a seasonal adaptation of the building skin to the climatic conditions.

The double-skin facades we know today readopt this old tradition of creating a thermal buffer with glazed skins—which may be temporary in part—extrapolating the concept in a modern architectural language. Double-skin facades may be constructed as sophisticated building enclosures that can flexibly adapt to environmental conditions. The construction should allow the regulation of heat, cold, light and wind, as well as external noise, in such a way that optimum comfort can be achieved in the internal spaces without any great consumption of energy. The expression "intelligent facade" that is so much in vogue today might appropriately be replaced with the concept of a flexible facade with intelligent controls.

Developments in facade construction, especially in the use of metal and glass, are a further important factor in the design of double-skin facades. Based on 19th-century greenhouse construction and the evolution of the skeleton frame, in which the outer wall no longer had a load-bearing function but merely that of an enclosing skin, new possibilities opened up for architects in the design of the external skins of buildings at the beginning of the 20th century. The size, form, and number of windows were no longer limited by structural considerations as in the past. As a facade material, glass assumed a new importance in architectural concepts. It was suddenly possible to create dividing elements that were nevertheless transparent, by using room-height glazed walls—something that also furthered the new goals of light and dematerialization in building.

But architectural freedom was—and still is—limited by the constraints of building physics and aspects of comfort. To achieve appropriate internal conditions that meet the needs of users, it became increasingly necessary to resort to technical installations to compensate for shortcomings in the concept and execution of the building skin. The technical means available at the time and the lack of environmental awareness led in many cases to buildings with a high energy consumption and correspondingly great emissions of pollutants.

In the course of time, the sheer technical feasibility of providing ample heating led to the very opposite of the planning philosophy on which the old farmhouses were based; i.e. the way they husbanded energy and resources. Ultimately, the outcome of all this was that people started to seek a way back to these old virtues by designing better-quality facades that provided protection against rain, heat and cold, moisture and noise.

The development of window technology to match specific climatic conditions has its origins in the box-type window. In this form of construction, the traditional single-glazed casement (with thermal transmission coefficients for the glazing of U = 5–6 W/m²K) is supplemented by a glazed outer window. As a rule, the frame construction consists of two opening casements which are set in front of each other and have a coefficient of thermal transmission of roughly U = 2.5 W/m²K. With this type of construction, natural ventilation is possible only if both casements are opened. This form of window can still be found in a lot of houses dating from the turn of the 19th and 20th centuries, especially in central European cities such as Berlin, Wroclaw, Vienna, Prague and Budapest.

At the end of the 1950s, the double-glazed window was developed, based on the box window. In the new form of construction, the inner and outer casements are mechanically connected and can be opened together like a single window light to ventilate the internal space. What is more, only one window frame is necessary instead of two. In some cases, louvered blinds were inserted between the panes of glass as a means of sunshading or as a protection against glare. The thermal insulation is not as good as with the box window, since the distance between the panes is smaller and the frame itself provides less insulation. The two parts of the casement can be separated if required: to clean the panes of glass, for example. With the development of insulating double-glazing elements (U = 3.0

W/m²K) and thermally divided metal and plastic frames in the 1970s, box and composite forms of window construction were largely ousted from the market.

As a reaction to the oil crises, there was an increased interest in energy savings and environmental protection.

Parallel to this, in the U.S., there was a growing awareness in the field of solar architecture of the importance of good physical properties in the outer skins of buildings, of the potential of exploiting structural mass, and of the role played by variability in ventilation and sunshading. These developments were based on studies of traditional forms of construction in regions with a hot climate. In Europe, too, the passive use of insolation as a means of saving energy was increasingly discussed, and well-insulated window shutters were advocated as a form of short-term thermal insulation.

Encouraged by a growing awareness of environmental issues, the building materials industry was not idle either, and a number of rapid developments ensued, particularly in the field of glass technology. Illustration 0.2 shows in diagrammatic form the development of the various types of glazing which have led to constant improvements in thermal insulation values over the past decades.

A similar development has taken place in respect of the total energy transmission factor g (the standard for the solar protection quality of glazing in summer). Set against this tendency towards ever lower U and g values is the need for a maximum degree of light transmittance in order to reduce the consumption of power

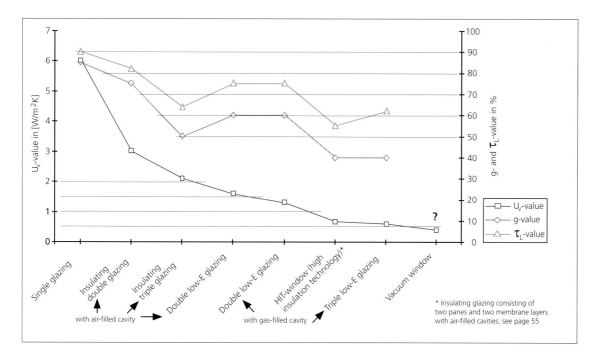

0.2 Development of physical values of various kinds of glazing down to the present day.

U = coefficient of thermal transmission of glazing
g = total energy transmission factor
τ_L = light transmittance (for daylight)

* Insulating glazing consisting of two panes and two membrane layers with air-filled cavities; see page 55

for artificial lighting to a minimum. Light transmittance is described in terms of the value τ_L. Only in the 1990s was a breakthrough achieved with the development of special types of neutral sunscreen glass with a high degree of selectivity (i.e. great light transmittance, yet at the same time, a low total energy transmission factor). These kinds of glazing offer a solution in situations where it would not be possible, or acceptable, to install high-quality adjustable shading devices.

Further developments towards achieving better values in the constructional physics of a building combined with great selectivity of the facade properties include light-deflecting systems and systems where direct light is screened off; e.g. transparent thermal insulation, mirror louvers and grids, and prisms. In view of their ability to reproduce forms graphically, holograms can also be used to create three-dimensional images of such systems. In terms of light deflection or screening out direct sunlight, holograms have the same optical properties as the various systems they reproduce and are referred to as holographic optical elements (HOE).

Electrochromic, thermochromic, and photochromic panes of glass employ a different technique. Their optical properties change according to climatic or environmental conditions. Materials of this kind are based on the wish for variability. With a controlled change of individual physical parameters, it is possible to adapt the function of the facade to specific uses.

All these developments are extremely promising, but they have one thing in common: only in the future will they be available in large enough quantities to make them competitive and more economical in use.

In contrast, double-skin facades achieve a quality of variability through a coordinated combination of components which are both known and available. Furthermore, they also provide a degree of acoustic insulation and usually allow natural window ventilation. The latter is achieved through an intake of air into the cavity between the two layers of the facade, a process that

can be controlled if required and can meet a large part of the total ventilation needs. Free ventilation in combination with increased sound insulation is a quite obvious way of saving energy if it allows mechanical forms of room ventilation to be obviated for at least part of the time.

In Europe today, users are increasingly coming to accept natural ventilation concepts. This has already led to many demands for free ventilation via windows that can be opened. In part, this phenomenon may be seen as a reaction to wrongly dimensioned and badly maintained air-conditioning systems, which are frequently named as one of the causes of the infamous sick building syndrome.

In the variable properties of double-skin facades, one can see a visual correspondence to the constructional physics and ventilation technology of human clothing, which can be adapted to seasonal requirements. Innovative systems, such as electrochromic panes of glass, can certainly be integrated into two-layer facades; but if one adheres to the analogy of clothing, they are more like special suits that can change in transparency and modify their thermal insulation properties at the press of a button.

Experts differ greatly in their assessment of the functional qualities of double-skin facades and their economic viability. In the authors' experience, based on the planning, construction, and operation of various two-layer facade projects, good results are always achieved when the type of building and the specific form of construction are attuned as closely as possible to the respective conditions. A sound knowledge of the basic principles and the way different specialist areas impinge on each other is necessary for this.

One of the aims of this book is to extend this knowledge by making it accessible to others.

0.3 The underlying concept of the variable facade is that it should be able to react to the weather as flexibly as human beings can with their clothing. Are double-skin facades a solution in this respect?

1 | Types of Construction

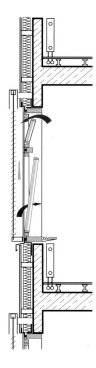

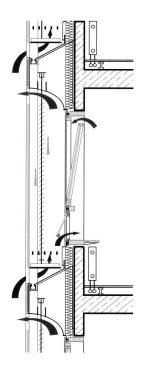

Double-skin facades are based on a multilayer principle. They consist of an external facade, an intermediate space and an inner facade. The outer facade layer provides protection against the weather and improved acoustic insulation against external noise. It also contains openings that allow the ventilation of the intermediate space and the internal rooms. The flow of air through the intermediate space is activated by solar-induced thermal buoyancy and by the effects of the wind. To achieve greater adaptability in reacting to environmental conditions, it may be possible to close the openings in the outer facade layer.

Up to now, the external skins of this type of facade have generally been constructed as a layer of single

glazing in toughened safety glass or laminated safety glass. An adjustable sunshading device is usually installed in the intermediate space to protect the internal rooms from high cooling loads caused by insolation. As a rule, the inner facade will consist of a supporting framework with a layer of double glazing, which provides the necessary protection against thermal losses in winter. In almost all cases, the inner facade can be opened to permit natural ventilation.

The term "double-skin facade" has not yet been clearly defined /C1, C2/. An appropriate classification could be made according to the form in which the intermediate space is divided and according to the desired ventilation function.

Box windows

The box window is probably the oldest form of a two-layered facade. Box windows consist of a frame with inward-opening casements. The single-glazed external skin contains openings that allow the ingress of fresh air and the egress of vitiated air, thus serving to ventilate both the intermediate space and the internal rooms.

The cavity between the two facade layers is divided horizontally along the constructional axes, or on a room-for-room basis. Vertically, the divisions occur either between stories or between individual window elements. Continuous divisions help to avoid the transmission of sounds and smells from bay to bay and from room to room.

Box-type windows are commonly used in situations where there are high external noise levels and where special requirements are made in respect of the sound insulation between adjoining rooms. This is also the only form of construction that provides these functions in facades with conventional rectangular openings. Each box window element requires its own air-intake and extract openings, which have to be considered when designing the outer facade.

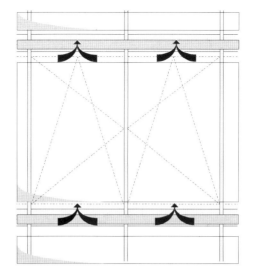

1.2 Elevation of box-window facade. The divisions between each bay mean that an opening light is also required for each bay.

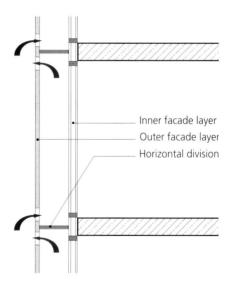

1.3 Section through typical box-window facade with separate ventilation for each bay.

Inner facade layer
Outer facade layer
Horizontal division

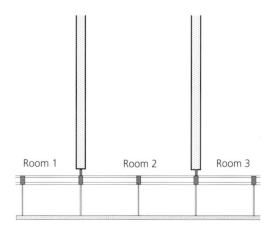

Room 1   Room 2   Room 3

1.4 Plan of box-window facade. The divisions of the facade intermediate space are set on the construction axes.

1.5 High-rise block, Potsdamer Platz 1, Berlin. Architect: Hans Kollhoff, Berlin. Completed in 2000.

Built example: High-rise block, Potsdamer Platz 1, Berlin

This roughly 90-meter-high office building by the architect Hans Kollhoff, Berlin, has a traditional engineering-brick facade with rectangular window openings. There are no suspended ceilings in the rooms, which are equipped with only an ancillary ventilation facility with scope for cooling (three air changes per hour). The proportion of the window area to the total facade area is roughly 35–45 percent. In view of the high external noise levels (71–75 dB(A)) along Neue Potsdamer Strasse, a box window construction was developed. The building was taken into occupation in the summer of 2000. In order to exploit industrial know-how to a maximum, the specification for the box windows was formulated in terms of the function they had to fulfill, stating the required properties in respect of the architecture and constructional physics. The competition was won by the Bisping company from Munster, Germany.

The internal window is designed as a side- and bottom-hung casement with low-E glazing in an oak frame and with aluminum cover strips externally. The entire element, including the frames, is fitted into a prefabricated timber surround built into the carcass structure in advance, with all requisite sealing. The intermediate space between the facade layers is roughly 22 cm deep and houses a louvered blind, the location of which was optimized in respect of its rear ventilation by designing the upper louvers to be fixed at a flatter angle, so that they remain permanently open, even when the blind is lowered. In conjunction with a corresponding gap below the bottom rail, this facilitates a good through-flow of air.

The outer pane of glass sits in a side-hung casement, allowing it to be cleaned from the inside. The ventilation of the intermediate space and the internal rooms is effected via a gap 6 cm high beneath the outer pivoting casement. At the top of the outer skin, there is a 5 cm horizontal slit within the opening light as well as a 1 cm gap above the casement. In order to exploit the collector effect of the cavity more efficiently in winter, the outer pane is equipped with a lifting gear that permits users to close the slit partially or completely by raising the pane.

The simulations carried out at the planning stage show that the combination of window ventilation with additional mechanical support under extreme weather conditions allows a very high degree of thermal comfort to be achieved.

1.6 Internal view of box windows in high-rise block at Potsdamer Platz 1

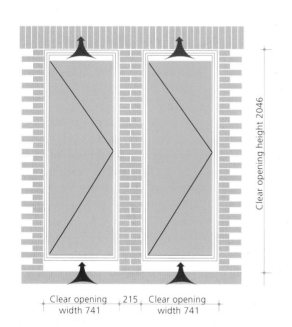

Clear opening width 741 | 215 | Clear opening width 741

Clear opening height 2046

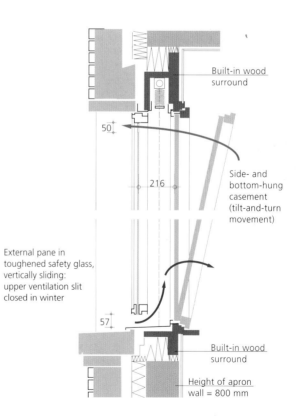

Built-in wood surround

50

216

Side- and bottom-hung casement (tilt-and-turn movement)

External pane in toughened safety glass, vertically sliding: upper ventilation slit closed in winter

57

Built-in wood surround

Height of apron wall = 800 mm

1.7 Potsdamer Platz 1: diagrammatic section through and elevation of box window, showing route of airstream.

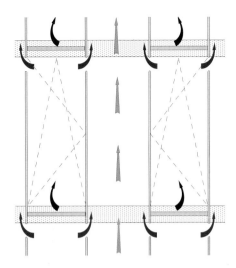

1.8 Elevation of a shaft-box facade. The arrows indicate the route of the airstream.

Shaft-box facades

The shaft-box facade is a special form of box window construction. It is based on the "twin-face" concept developed by the Alco company in Munster and consists of a system of box windows with continuous vertical shafts that extend over a number of stories to create a stack effect. The facade layout consists of an alternation of box windows and vertical shaft segments. On every story, the vertical shafts are linked with the adjoining box windows by means of a bypass opening. The stack effect draws the air from the box windows into the vertical shafts and from there up to the top, where it is emitted. As a means of supporting the thermal uplift, air can also be sucked out mechanically via the vertical shafts.

Shaft-box facades require fewer openings in the external skin, since it is possible to exploit the stronger thermal uplift within the stack. This also has a positive effect in terms of insulation against external noise. Since, in practice, the height of the stacks is necessarily limited, this form of construction is best suited to lower-rise buildings. An aerodynamic adjustment will be necessary if all the box windows connected to a particular shaft are to be ventilated to an equal degree.

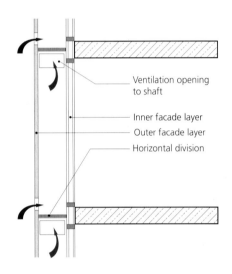

1.9 Section through a shaft-box facade. The arrows indicate the route of the airstream flowing through the box windows into the common ventilation shaft.

Ventilation opening to shaft

Inner facade layer
Outer facade layer
Horizontal division

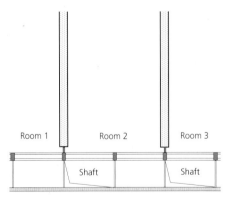

1.10 Plan of a shaft-box facade There are side openings in the shaft divisions in the facade intermediate space.

Room 1   Room 2   Room 3

Shaft   Shaft

Built example: ARAG 2000 tower, Düsseldorf

Designed by RKW Architects, Düsseldorf, in collaboration with Norman Foster in London, this roughly 120-meter-high office tower was divided into four eight-story tiers for servicing reasons. In each tier, the shaft-box facade extends over six to seven stories of offices and terminates in front of the eighth (services) story—or a garden story situated on the seventh and eighth levels. The internal spaces are equipped with supporting ventilation (2.5 air changes per hour) as well as cooling soffits. Because of the extremely high external noise levels (70–78 dB(A)) from the "Mörsenbroicher Egg"—an inner-city traffic junction—and in view of the strong uplift within the shafts, the facade was designed as a shaft-box system. The building was taken into occupation at the end of 2000. Between 1992 and 1994, as part of the development of the shaft-box facade system, extensive trials were carried out on models (up to scale 1:7) to test the main functions and the requisite aerodynamic adjustment.

The inner facade layer was constructed with conventional vertically pivoting aluminum casements with low-E glazing. The windows on the shaft axes can be opened only for maintenance purposes. Louvered blinds were installed in the outer third of the roughly 70-cm-deep intermediate space between the facade layers. Each of the box windows has its own 15-cm-high air-intake opening in the form of a closable flap. Vitiated air is extracted into the exhaust-air shaft via a bypass opening, the size of which is determined according to its position in the shaft. The shaft, in turn, is ventilated via an area of louvers in front of the services story. In order to exploit the collector effect of the facade intermediate space more efficiently in winter, the air-extract shaft is also designed to be closed if required. In addition, the facade flaps can be set in a throttling position with a roughly 10 percent degree of opening. With increasing wind speeds, this facility can be used to reduce the effects of drafts. Where wind speeds exceed 8 m/s, the facade is closed for safety reasons on the windward face of the building.

The simulations carried out during the planning stage showed that free window ventilation is possible for 50–60 percent of the year. During periods of extreme weather conditions, a high level of thermal comfort can be attained with mechanical ventilation.

1.11 Photo of model of ARAG 2000 tower in Düsseldorf. Architects: RKW, Düsseldorf, in collaboration with Norman Foster, London.

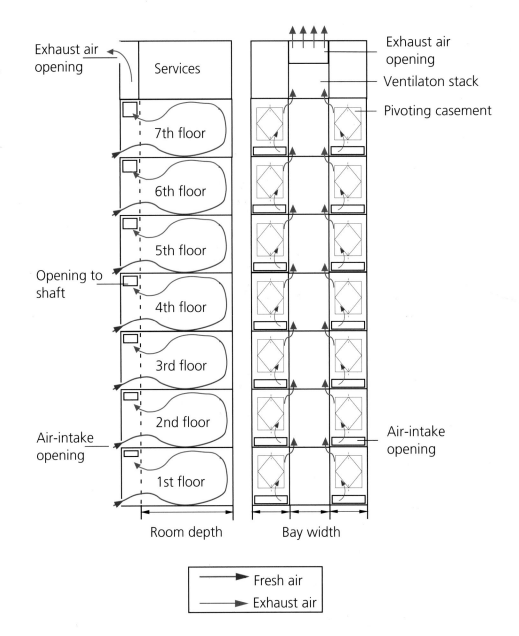

1.12 Diagram of ventilation principle in the 8-story-high shaft-box facade sections of the ARAG 2000 building.

Exhaust air opening

Services

7th floor

6th floor

5th floor

Opening to shaft

4th floor

3rd floor

2nd floor

Air-intake opening

1st floor

Room depth

Exhaust air opening

Ventilaton stack

Pivoting casement

Air-intake opening

Bay width

Fresh air
Exhaust air

1.13 View of mock-up facade for ARAG 2000 building. The shafts occupy single bays between pairs of box windows.

1.14 View along intermediate space between facade layers in mock-up facade construction. In every third bay, there is an extract shaft, which is open at the top.

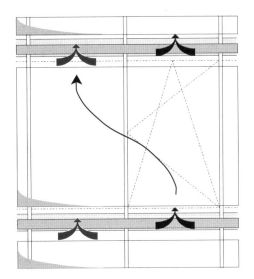

1.15 Elevation of corridor facade. Air flows on the diagonal to prevent vitiated air from the lower story being sucked in with the air supply of the floor above (recontamination).

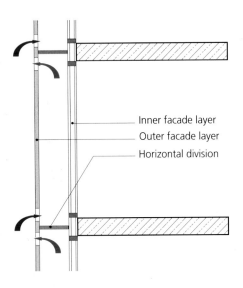

1.16 Section through a corridor facade. Separate circulation for each story.

Inner facade layer
Outer facade layer
Horizontal division

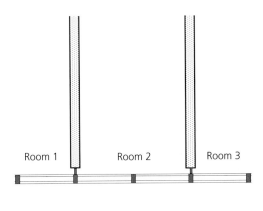

1.17 Plan of a corridor facade. The intermediate space is not divided at regular intervals along its horizontal length.

Room 1   Room 2   Room 3

Corridor facades

In corridor facades, the intermediate space between the two skins is closed at the level of each floor. Divisions are foreseen along the horizontal length of the corridor only where this is necessary for acoustic, fire-protection or ventilation reasons. In the context of ventilation, this will usually be necessary at the corners of buildings where great differences in air pressure occur, and where openings in the inner facade layer would result in uncomfortable drafts from cross-currents. This problem can generally be avoided by closing off the corner spaces at the sides. In the rest of the corridor, there are likely to be only relatively small differences of air pressure, and these can be used to support the natural ventilation.

The air-intake and extract openings in the external facade layer should be situated near the floor and the ceiling. They are usually laid out in staggered form from bay to bay to prevent vitiated air extracted on one floor entering the space on the floor immediately above. Where a corridor-facade construction is used, the individual spatial segments between the skins will almost always be adjoined by a number of rooms. Special care should, therefore, be taken to avoid sound transmission from room to room.

Built example: Düsseldorf City Gate

The 80-meter-high "City Gate" structure in Düsseldorf by the architect Prof. Petzinka was erected directly above the entrance to the road tunnel along the Rhine embankment. The rhombus-shaped building consists of two 16-story towers built over the outer tubular road tunnels and linked at the top by a three-story attic bridging structure. The entire building is enclosed in a glass skin, so that a 50-meter-high atrium space is created at the centre, thereby lending the structure its gateway character. Wrapped around the towers and the attic stories is a corridor facade, the intermediate space of which is 90 cm and 140 cm deep. The temperatures in the office spaces are regulated by means of heating/cooling soffits; and at the height of summer and in winter, a mechanical installation provides the rooms with two air changes per hour.

The facade corridor is divided into 20-meter-long sections by the escape staircase, the atrium and divisions at the corners of the building. The inner facade consists of a framework in laminated construction board with low-E glazing. Incorporated in every second bay are pivoting glass doors that serve to ventilate the offices. These openings also provide access to the corridor space, which therefore functions as a kind of balcony. The high-reflection aluminum louver blinds in the intermediate space of the facade are set close to the outer skin, so that the corridor remains freely accessible and the pivoting doors do not intersect with the blinds.

The outer facade skin consists of a 12 mm layer of toughened safety glass, point fixed at the level of the handrail and held in position at the top and bottom by the continuous ventilation boxes. The boxes also perform important load-bearing functions and house the sunblinds as well as a closable flap. The free width for the airflow in the box is 30 cm. The openings are staggered. In drawing up the concept, extensive computer-aided airflow calculations were made to optimize the system and to achieve an even flow of air through the boxes. The first years of operation show that the building can be naturally ventilated for roughly 70–75% of the year. The reactions of users to the ventilation system are extremely positive.

1.18 South face of "City Gate" in Düsseldorf, with the entrance to the Rhine embankment tunnel beneath.
Client: Engel Projektentwicklung GmbH. Architects: Karl-Heinz Petzinka at Ingenhoven, Overdiek, Petzinka, Partner; later Petzinka, Pink + Partner, Düsseldorf.
Completed in 1998.

1.19 Section through and elevation of the corridor facade, "City Gate", Düsseldorf. A uniform "ventilation box" was used for all air-intake and extract elements.

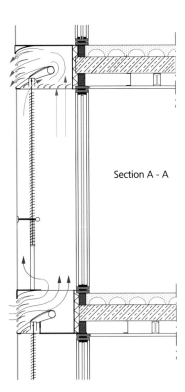

Section A - A

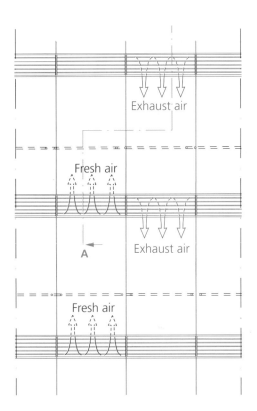

Exhaust air

Fresh air

Exhaust air

A

Fresh air

1.20 View along facade corridor in "City Gate", Düsseldorf. The corridor is 1.4 m wide on this face. The staggered air-intake and extract gratings can be seen in the floor and soffit.

Multistory facades

In multistory facades, the intermediate space between the inner and outer layers is adjoined vertically and horizontally by a number of rooms. In extreme cases, the space may extend around the entire building without any intermediate divisions. The ventilation (air-intake and extract) of the intermediate space occurs via large openings near the ground floor and the roof. During the heating period, the facade space can be closed at the top and bottom to exploit the conservatory effect and optimize solar-energy gains.

Multistory facades are especially suitable where external noise levels are very high, since this type of construction does not necessarily require openings distributed over its height. As a rule, the rooms behind multistory facades have to be mechanically ventilated, and the facade can be used as a joint air duct for this purpose. As with corridor facades, attention should be paid to the problem of sound transmission within the intermediate space.

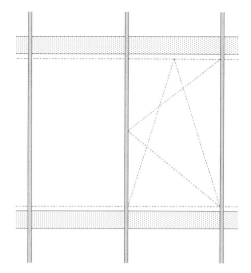

1.21 Elevation of part of a multistory facade. The arrangement of the casement opening lights depends on the ventilation and cleaning concept chosen for the facade.

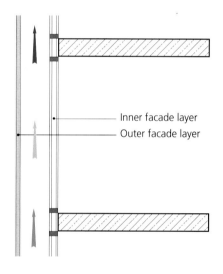

Inner facade layer
Outer facade layer

1.22 Section through a multistory facade. The external skin is set independently in front of the inner facade. The intermediate space can be ventilated in all directions.

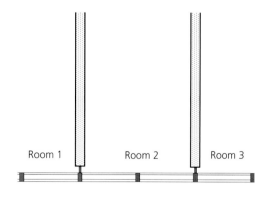

Room 1   Room 2   Room 3

1.23 Plan of a multistory facade. The intermediate space is undivided and can be freely ventilated.

Built example: Victoria Ensemble, Cologne

The Victoria Ensemble by the architect van den Valen-tyn is situated on the Sachsenring in Cologne, an inner-city ring road subject to heavy traffic. The ensemble consists of three volumes, the largest of which is known as the "conical building". Its name is a reference to the form of the structure—a 21-meter-high block with a double-skin facade splayed outwards from bottom to top at an angle of 2.6°. The internal spaces are mechanically air-conditioned, so that the facade can be used exclusively as a means of regulating thermal insulation for different weather conditions.

Continuous strips of flaps were installed around the entire building at the foot and the top of the facade to control temperatures. The flaps can be opened or closed according to needs. A central control system keeps the flaps closed when external temperatures are low, so that the layer of air trapped between the two skins of the facade ensures maximum thermal insulation. When external temperatures rise, the flaps are opened to allow the ventilation of the intermediate space and to prevent it overheating. The facade thus provides the building with variable thermal protection that can be adapted, as required, to ambient conditions.

The illustrations show the impressive overall visual effect of the continuous glazed external skin, which was made possible by the ventilation openings: the intake of air is via a trench at the foot of the building, while vitiated air is extracted at roof level. At the same time, the position of the openings screened from the street ensures a high degree of sound protection, even when they are open for ventilation.

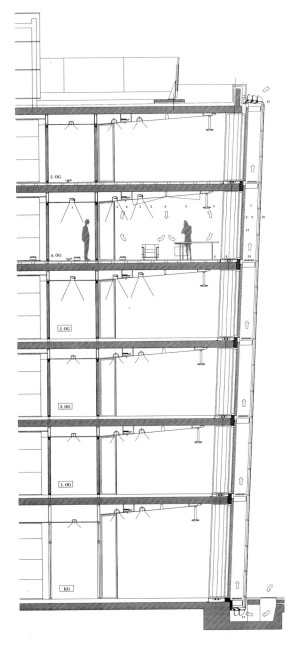

1.24 Section through the multistory facade of the Victoria Ensemble, Cologne. Air streams into the intermediate space via a trench at the foot of the facade, ascends over the height of the building and is emitted at roof level.

1.25 View of corner of "conical building", forming part of the Victoria Ensemble, Cologne. Architect: Thomas van den Valentyn, Cologne. Completed in 1996.
The use of a multistory facade obviated the need for openings distributed over the entire height of the building.

1.26 View along the intermediate space in the multistory facade of the "conical building", Victoria Ensemble, Cologne.
The internal rooms are mechanically ventilated, as a result of which, it was possible to position the sunblinds close to the internal skin.

2　Questions and Answers on Double-Skin Facades

To provide the reader with a quick grasp of the main issues involved in double-skin facade construction, this chapter contains a number of generally applicable questions and answers, together with other relevant information. For those who wish to deepen their knowledge of the subject, there are also cross-references to the relevant specialist chapters.

The steps that are fundamental to planning double-skin facades are treated in a separate section.

For what kinds of building are double-skin facades suitable?

Generally speaking, double-skin facades are appropriate when buildings are subject to great external noise and wind loads. This can apply both to high-rise and to lower-rise structures. If the buildings are to be naturally ventilated via the windows for as great a part of the year as possible, the double-skin construction offers distinct advantages in practice. In this context, see also the question below: "When is window ventilation possible?", as well as the basic principles described in the chapter "Aerophysics".

A further area of application is in rehabilitation work—when existing facades cannot be renewed, or where this is not desirable. In such cases, the second skin provides protection against the elements and also allows the facade to be designed in a modern form.

Double-skin facades have a special aesthetic of their own, and this can be exploited architecturally to great advantage. The visual impression of transparency and depth, often in conjunction with a frameless form of construction in the outer skin, opens up new design paths.

When are double-skin facades economically viable?

The construction of a second facade layer has its price, of course. The additional costs involved compared with single-skin facades have to be offset by lower costs achieved through greater functional efficiency and more effective operation of the building. This can be illustrated in the following example.

An office block located on a busy main road is subject to external noise levels of 70 to 75 dB(A). With a single-layer facade, it would have been necessary, in compliance with most European standards, to design a sound-insulating form of glazing and to install air-conditioning plant as well. With a double-skin facade, it was possible to do without air-conditioning altogether, in view of the scope for window ventilation. Thanks to the favorable physical conditions provided by the construction, a mechanical form of ventilation with a cooling facility (two air changes per hour for the internal spaces) was sufficient. The second, outer skin allowed the sound-insulation requirements for the inner skin to be reduced to normal standards, which it was possible to meet simply by using panes of insulating double glazing.

Taking account of investment and ongoing costs, a comparison of the two alternatives showed that the combination of a two-layered facade with supporting ventilation was ultimately more economical than a single-layer facade with internal air-conditioning. Further aspects of constructional physics are discussed in the chapter "Sound Insulation"; for cost comparisons, see the extensive examples of calculations in the chapter "Economic Viability".

What is the most appropriate kind of double-skin facade construction?

According to the details given in the chapter "Types of Construction", the main aspects influencing the use of a specific facade type can be summarized as follows:

■ Box windows are suited for solid facades with punched openings and where greater importance is attached to privacy between rooms.

■ Because of the smaller size of the external openings, shaft-box facades are suited where particularly high levels of sound insulation are required.

■ Corridor facades are especially effective with regard to ventilation; on the other hand, they limit the sound insulation between rooms.

■ Multistory facades are most commonly used where, for other reasons, it is not possible to do without a mechanical form of ventilation or where a glazed facade without openings is required.

The choice of facade construction has far-reaching implications for the planning, of course. The choice of a particular type of double-skin facade is, therefore, a crucial one. It determines a particular line of development for a project which is scarcely sensible to change subsequently.

Can double-skin facades save energy?

The answer is yes, in principle. But it should be said at the outset that the economic significance of facades of this kind and the level of savings that can be achieved with them are often wrongly assessed. A broad discussion is taking place at present—in the form of specialist articles, for example—about the scope for reducing heating energy and the size of the savings that can be achieved. In many cases, comparisons are being drawn with insulating standards for single-skin facades that are antiquated in terms of modern energy saving. The reason for this is that the poorer the original level of insulation is, the more impressive the savings that have been achieved with a second skin will appear. For buildings with a high level of thermal insulation based on low-energy or zero-energy construction standards, the energy savings achieved through a second facade layer will be quite limited. In this respect, reference should also be made to the chapter "Thermal Insulation".

Assuming average heating costs in Germany of 2–3 € per m^2 gross heated floor area per year—of which no more than 20 percent can be saved under favorable circumstances—it is clear that no substantial amortization of the addition costs for the double-skin facade (in the order of 100–150 € per m^2 gross floor area) can be expected. In this context, see also the chapter on "Economic Viability".

The expected energy savings may also be reduced by the fact that double-skin facades result in poorer light transmission values because of the additional external layer of glass. In most cases, a larger area of glazing will compensate for this; but where the areas of glazing are relatively small (e.g. solid walls with conventional window openings), reduced light transmission will result in the internal lighting being switched on for longer periods. Under certain circumstances, the increased power costs resulting from this can exceed the savings in heating costs.

Significant energy savings can be achieved only where double-skin facades make window ventilation possible or where they considerably extend the period in which natural ventilation can be exploited. By obviating a mechanical air supply, electricity costs for air circulation can be reduced. This will greatly exceed the savings described above. Furthermore, by doing without air-conditioning, the costs for heating, cooling and water can also be cut proportionally. Alone with a 2.5-fold air change per hour in offices, provided by a central mechanical ventilation plant, roughly 15–25 kWh of energy will be consumed per square meter of ventilated floor area per year to power the fans. This is equivalent to about 1.5-2.5 €/m^2 per annum.

What level of sound insulation do double-skin facades provide?

The degree of sound insulation provided by double-skin facades depends largely on the size and position of the openings in the outer layer. In addition, sound insulation can be influenced to a limited extent by absorbent surfaces in the facade intermediate space. Assuming an external skin with a total opening area of 10%, the sound-insulating quality of the inner skin can be improved by roughly 3-6 dB. Where the opening area is only 5 percent, an improvement of nearly 10 dB can be achieved, although this may mean that the opening area is too small to ventilate the internal spaces adequately.

As a rule, this means that requirements made on the inner facade layer can be reduced by one to two sound insulating classes. Care should be taken, however, not to provide too great a degree of sound insulation in buildings that are not subject to high external noise levels. This can result in reduced contact with the outside world, and it can also mean that operating or other noises within the building can become unpleasantly overpowering. In this context, see also the basic principles described in the chapter on "Sound Insulation".

Does a double-skin facade reduce the effects of wind pressure?

It is often claimed that double-skin facades around high-rise buildings can serve to reduce the effects of wind pressure. This is only half the truth, however. With double-skin facades, it is certainly possible to reduce short-term pressure fluctuations—caused, for example, by gusts of wind. This is facilitated by the buffer effect of the intermediate space.

Constant (static) pressure on the facade, however, can spread unhindered into the intermediate space and—if the windows are open—into the rooms beyond. Static pressures may be caused by constant winds flowing round a structure with an almost constant angle of incidence. For that reason, two terms have been borrowed from the language of seafaring to describe the situation around buildings: the windward face is the side facing the wind and subject to excess pressure, while the leeward face (facing away from the wind) is subject to negative pressure.

If the internal layout of a building permits a clear separation of the windward and leeward facades, static pressures are, as a rule, unproblematic, as long as they do not exert a force on doors that prevents them from being opened—or only with great difficulty. Depending on the form of the building, however, an optimum windward/leeward separation for all or at least the most important wind directions can be a complex task. It should be taken into account at an early stage of the planning before the volume and layout of a building have been determined. Further information on this subject can be found in the chapters "Aerophysics" and "High-Rise Buildings".

When is window ventilation possible?

Free ventilation via windows makes sense only when the air outside a building is of adequate quality. In inner-city locations near traffic junctions, this is an aspect that needs to be investigated. In Western Europe, various regulations also exist that specify minimum opening sizes and maximum room depths to ensure a hygienic change of air in the internal spaces. These regulations preclude many open-plan spaces in office buildings where the distance from the ventilating windows would be too great. Regulations of this kind also provide useful reference values in the design of double-skin facades (cf. "Aerophysics").

Other limitations on free window ventilation exist when external noise levels exceed about 75 dB(A). In view of the length of time the windows have to remain open to ensure a hygienic standard of natural ventilation, it may no longer be possible to provide an adequate mean level of sound insulation throughout the day even with a two-layered facade. This can prove decisive in respect of the sound level that has to be maintained for workplaces—which may not exceed 55 dB(A) for mental work. Experts, in fact, recommend a limit of 50 dB(A) or even lower.

The room temperatures that can be achieved in conjunction with window ventilation are not a criterion for excluding this form of construction, but they should be considered in terms of acceptance on the part of users. Since the external air temperature and humidity will rarely coincide with the conditions required internally, provision should be made for an intermittent, dosed form of ventilation and an appropriate air-conditioning plant. In this context, it may be necessary to consider the efficiency of window ventilation in terms of the energy balance, especially under extreme external temperature conditions. (See also "Air-Conditioning")

Do double-skin facades necessitate mechanical cooling?

In some buildings, the extraction of heat from double-skin facades does not function ideally. This has quickly led to the conclusion that two-layered forms of construction tend to cause overheating. Without trying to analyze the vague term "overheating" more precisely at this point, one may say quite categorically that the ventilation of internal spaces via external windows—irrespective of the type of facade—can be effected only by wind movement or by differences of temperature between the internal rooms and the surroundings. At the height of summer in moderate climatic zones, however, there are usually only weak winds, so that non-mechanical forms of ventilation will depend largely on thermal uplift. Without an active or passive cooling of the internal spaces, the room temperature —especially in offices where considerable internal heat loads occur—is usually higher than the external temperature, since the heat loads warm the incoming air even further.

In double-skin facade construction, the air in the intermediate space between the facade skins is also heated. This is caused especially by non-transparent surfaces and by lowered sunblinds. How quickly the external air enters the internal spaces and to what degree it absorbs heat on the way depends largely on the nature of the openings in the inner skin and on the route the air takes. The remaining heat gain then acts as an additional external cooling load that exerts an influence on the cooling needs.

At the same time, double-skin facades often afford better solar protection than other forms of construction, and this can help reduce the effect of external loads as well as cooling needs. The additional external layer of glazing alone reduces the insolation by a minimum of 10%; and a louver blind in the intermediate space between the two facade skins results in a further reduction of around 50-60% compared with internal blinds.

When can air-conditioning plants be reduced in size or omitted altogether?

Basically, this is possible only where there is adequate window ventilation, which refers back to the earlier question: "When is window ventilation possible?" This, in turn, involves aspects such as the quality of the air supply, adequate sound insulation, adequate opening areas in the facade, and the air change in the rooms. Mechanical air-conditioning of the internal spaces is necessary when the windows cannot be used for ventilating purposes because of any one of the above factors.

If it is possible to meet all these conditions, however, air-conditioning only need be restricted to certain partial functions. For example, by continuing to heat and cool the air, it will not be humidified and dehumidified. This means that certain sections of the plant may be omitted or at least reduced in size, which in turn results in a reduction of investment and maintenance costs.

In order to do without air-conditioning plant entirely, window ventilation should be possible throughout the year, and an adequate conditioning of the internal spaces should be provided by other systems (e.g. radiators and/or cooling soffits). These systems should be designed in such a way that the air entering the rooms via the windows is neither so cold in winter nor so hot in summer as to cause discomfort. For further requirements and for details of the suitability of innovative air-conditioning systems (e.g. heating/cooling soffits or thermal activation of the solid elements of a building), reference should be made to the chapter "Air-Conditioning", which contains a description of the reciprocal effects of the various properties of a facade.

3 | Ten Planning Steps

Drawing on their experience in planning various types of double-skin facades, the authors have compiled a list of ten steps that should be taken to achieve an all-embracing planning concept. These steps may serve as a guide for clients and planners in drawing up their own proposals.

1st Step   Checking the constraints

At the beginning of this process, the basic constraints determining the suitability of window ventilation should be checked. This will quickly reveal the suitability and the limitations of the respective systems, as well as the properties that will be required of the double-skin facade. At the same time, an analysis of this kind will provide some idea of the economic viability of the proposed form of construction, in terms of reductions of the additional costs that would otherwise be incurred if a single-skin facade were used.

2nd Step   Determining the type of construction

Once the constraints that have to be observed to achieve adequate window ventilation and sound insulation are known (the latter may also preclude the use of window ventilation), the architectural and air-conditioning concepts can be addressed. In this way, a matrix of requirements can be established that will help to decide the appropriate form of double-skin facade construction. This step is extremely important, since the basis for the subsequent dimensioning will be determined at this stage, and any later changes may necessitate a whole new planning process for the facade and the air-conditioning installation.

3rd Step   Ensuring a good fresh-air supply

Once the type of double-skin facade has been determined, the dimensions of the openings and the air-flow routes into the rooms themselves can be planned. It should not be forgotten what users expect of natural ventilation: namely that, when the inner windows are fully opened, sudden ventilation will occur with a perceptible air change. A change of air may be measurable and even adequate, but if it is not perceptible, users will experience a sensation of discomfort. The impression that no air change is occurring is known as the "aquarium effect" and can be critical in a sensitive environment.

4th Step   Avoiding overheating in the intermediate facade space

In dimensioning the openings, care should be taken to limit heat gains in summer in the space between the two facade skins, so as to ensure thermal comfort in the rooms and to avoid increased cooling loads. With single-story-type double-skin facades, the air temperature stratification in the intermediate space can mean that the extract-air temperature and the layer of warm air beneath the ceiling internally have virtually no effect on the adjoining space. The air flow must be designed in such a way that the heat gain does not increase upwards from floor to floor. With multistory facades, the temperature stratification results in a critical load on the topmost story, so that measures will have to be considered to minimize the extract-air temperature and the warm-air buffer.

5th Step   Optimizing the flow of air

The following basic parameters determine how the airflow can be optimized and excess temperatures limited:

■ size and position of the openings
■ appropriate aerodynamic design of the narrowest cross-sections through which the airflow must pass
■ additional propulsion where required.

In the authors' experience, the permanent, self-regulating forces of thermal uplift are sufficient in themselves if a low-resistance airflow route with large cross-sections can be constructed. Wind forces can provide a welcome form of support in this respect; but in central and northern Europe, they are not a reliable motive force in extreme conditions at the height of summer. Fans used as a mechanical means of propulsion would have to move large quantities of air to make any significant contribution. In seeking to minimize the excess temperature within the facade, the scope for heat recovery will be reduced, although there is scarcely any further use for the warm air that is sucked out.

6th Step   Planning the conditions for operation

To provide acoustic insulation and thermal insulation in winter, the openings in the facade should ideally be small—the very opposite of what is needed for good ventilation and low thermal gains. Both sets of requirements can be met under certain circumstances by openings that can be varied in size or closed altogether. But that, in turn, raises the question of their operation, activation and control. Examples range from openings that can be adjusted according to the season, to flaps that respond flexibly to wind pressure. At all events, concepts of this kind should be subject to close scrutiny at an early stage, not only in respect of their economic viability, but above all in the context of operating conditions over the course of the year and in special situations. This will allow the links with other functions of the building to be recognized in good time. At present, it is not uncommon for systems of this kind to be installed without specifying the means of control and the main values or a complete classification of of the main functions. This can lead to elaborate and expensive subsequent installations in the form of sensors to help distinguish between various operating conditions.

7th Step   Exploiting the construction to the full

The facade planner or consultant should be invited at an early stage of the scheme to participate in discussions on the airflow, and, where appropriate, the aerodynamic optimization of the design. Only through a process of mutual coordination of concepts can detailed solutions be found that will be constructionally practical and economically acceptable and that will not have to be revised in the course of the subsequent planning. One of the main purposes of this process of collaboration is to ensure that the conclusions reached in the field of aerophysics are not just theoretical and that the functions do not ultimately prove disappointing. This process also presents a major opportunity: the breakdown of the structure into its basic elements can lead to the design of qualitative, standardized details and a large measure of prefabrication which are likely to offer economic advantages.

8th Step   Putting the dimensions to the test

Once the basic characteristics of the facade are known in terms of building physics and ventilation technology (and when they have been structurally verified if necessary), the data should be integrated into the existing air-conditioning concept, so that the dimensions of the mechanical services can be determined. In most cases, this will be practicable only with the help of simulation tests, since the special advantages of two-layered facades often lie in the variability and coordination of certain parameters.

If the combined effect of the proposed measures successfully passes the test in computer calculations, a major step will have been taken towards coordinating them with each other. In most cases, however, the required optimization is a much longer process and continues in a series of iterative steps carried out in an exchange between the various partners in the planning, until the best possible overall solution has been found. The duration of this process should also be taken into account in drawing up the planning schedule.

9th Step   Integrating clients and users into the planning process

In all these steps to optimize the ventilation and air-conditioning, it is essential to reflect the needs of the client and, if possible, the subsequent users, so that there will be no false hopes or expectations in respect of the functioning of the window ventilation in a double-skin facade. One common expectation, for example, is that window ventilation can replace a cooling system in summer—something that is, of course, physically impossible.

On the other hand, greater optimization of the joint effects of the facade and air-conditioning can be achieved only with the understanding of the client, since savings resulting from a simplification of the air-conditioning can impose certain limits on user comfort. An example of this may be seen in the omission of radiators under windows where heating and cooling soffits are installed. Given favorable U-values, this may be acceptable; but it may lead to stronger air currents at floor level. Aspects of this kind are of importance both for owner-occupiers and for investors who may later wish to sell or lease their property. As a rule, the adjustments that have to be made to coordinate the various systems do not pose any great problem if the effects can be foreseen clearly and in good time. That is why a process of overall optimization will require all parties involved in the planning to assume a share of the responsibility.

10th Step   Taking the control mechanisms into operation

Double-skin facades are still a relatively young technology. Their construction is more or less new ground for everyone in the building sector. That is why it has proved sound policy to ensure a close collaboration between planners and construction firms. This applies equally to aspects of aerophysics as to the control of active components of the facade and their interaction with the internal air-conditioning.

Model facades play a crucial role in this respect. Prior to the release of the design for serial production, they allow clients, architects, facade planners and facade construction firms to make a final joint check to determine whether the design, construction and technical goals have been achieved and optimized. At this point, it is often a good idea to take validating measurements of data relating to the constructional physics and aerophysics. This will allow the go-ahead to be given for production on the basis of a comprehensive and mutually agreed decision.

Parallel to this, it will be important to coordinate the adjustment of the facade functions and the air-conditioning as well as the process of taking the control mechanisms into operation. The variable properties of double-skin facades allow a number of innovative air-conditioning concepts, but these can be successfully implemented only if one ensures that they engage smoothly with the control process like the teeth of two cogs. One of the basic conditions for the acceptance and success of concepts of this kind is that the tuning process should take place in good time, so that teething troubles do not have to be eliminated, to the annoyance of users, after they have moved in.

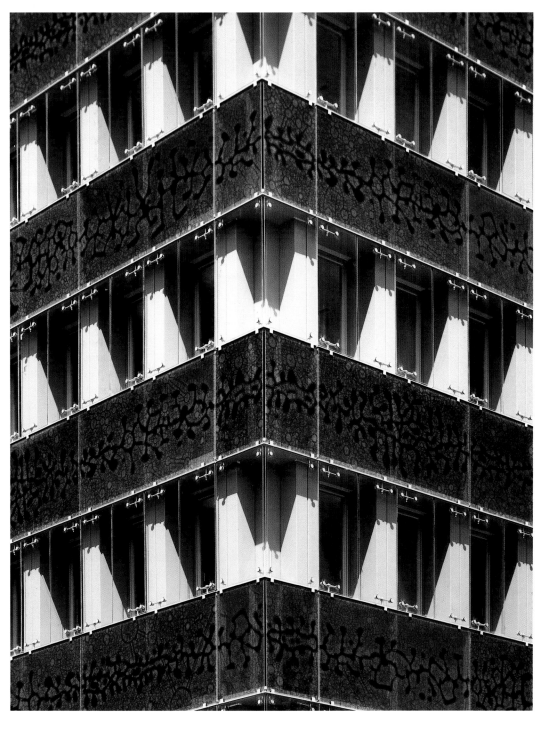

3-01 Close-up of the realized box-window double-skin facade used for the refurbishment of the Federal German Ministry for Food, Agriculture and Forestry (BML headquarters building), Bonn

Client: Federal Republic of Germany
Project management: Federal German Office for Building and Regional Planning
General planners and architects: Ingenhoven Overdiek Kahlen und Partner

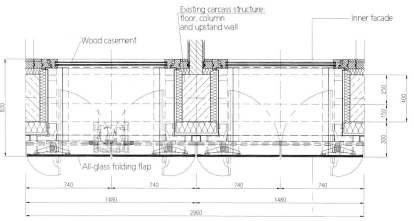

Existing carcass structure:
floor, column and upstand wall

Inner facade

Wood casement

All-glass folding flap

3-02 Plan of box-window for refurbishment of BML, Bonn.

The inner facade skin was designed in wood; the outer facade with all-glass pivoting casements. For a closer description of this project see pages 127 and 144/145.

4 Sound Insulation

The functioning of the outer facade skin

This chapter, which describes sound insulation in the context of double-skin facades, is the first of a series of sections in which specialized aspects are explored in greater depth. There is a good reason why this subject should stand at the beginning of the exploratory sequence. In the view of the authors, sound insulation is the most important single reason for the use of double-skin facades. The application of this form of construction in buildings that are not subject to external noise pollution—in the country, for example—can be justified only in exceptional cases. A description of the contingent conditions and the criteria for the use of double-skin facades is given below.

An additional, external facade layer can considerably improve the sound insulation of a building, partially screening off external noise like a protective wall. It might be described as an acoustic screen set in front of the windows. The provision of openings to ventilate the facade intermediate space does not contradict the idea of sound insulation, although they obviously have an influence on the effect. A sound-insulation wall does not extend up to the sky. Normally, a height of only a few meters is sufficient.

4-1 Acoustic screening wall in front of Neven-DuMont-Schauberg publishing house, Cologne.
Architects: Hentrich Petschnigg und Partner, Düsseldorf.
Completed in 1998

The external plane screens off noise by reflecting it back in the direction it has come—with three main results.

■ The noise level from external sources is lower behind the outer skin, which means that the sound insulation of the facade as a whole is improved. If the windows in the inner skin are opened, they are exposed to only this reduced level of external noise, so that the sound insulation is improved internally even when the windows are open.

■ Sound cannot be reflected back by the opened areas of the facade. The size of these areas, therefore, determines the potential screening effect of the outer skin. Since the openings are also crucial for the ventilation of the intermediate space, however, there is a reciprocal relationship between the level of sound insulation that can be achieved and the needs of ventilation.

■ Sounds from internal sources will be reflected back partially into the interior of the building by the outer facade skin. In certain situations, this may lead to an undesirable transmission of sound or information from room to room.

Double-skin facades are certainly a valid response to the constantly increasing levels of traffic noise in city centers, providing a greater degree of sound insulation than single-skin facades. In some situations, a double-skin facade will make window ventilation possible where it would otherwise not be acceptable, since the noise level at the workplace would be too high. In this case, the use of a double-skin facade may obviate the need for an air-handling unit which would otherwise be necessary as a result of non-openable windows; or it may at least result in a reduction of the annual operating time of such a unit by switching over to natural ventilation. In both cases, this depends on the external air being of an adequate quality to allow direct ventilation via the windows.

A number of questions have to be answered at the planning stage.

■ How great is the sound-insulating effect of the outer skin, or how great should it be optimally?

■ What is the level of sound transmission from room to room, and what measures should be taken to reduce it to an acceptable level?

■ Is the investment in a second facade layer worthwhile in order to achieve this?

The first two questions are related to the acoustic dimensioning of the double-skin facade and will be dealt with at length later in this chapter. The third question refers to aspects covered in depth in the chapter on "Economic Viability". To allow readers an insight into the subject of sound insulation and to acquaint them with the technical language of acoustic engineers, a series of basic terms is explained at the outset.

The following brief summary is provided for those not requiring in-depth information. Window openings can be incorporated in double-skin facades where the external noise levels are around 68–75 dB(A). This would not be possible with other forms of construction. These conditions apply to a wide range of inner-city properties.

As a rule, sound transmission from room to room via an open facade corridor or a multistory facade space is a problem only where the level of external noise to which the facade is exposed is too low (less than 60–65 dB(A)), or where the sound-screening effect of the external skin is too great. Otherwise, the external noise in the intermediate facade space drowns out most sounds from internal sources. In practice, sound transmission is more likely to be accepted by users than the sacrifice of window ventilation.

Noise and its evaluation

The constantly increasing volume of road traffic is one of the main causes of noise pollution in our cities. This may be compounded by further sources near railway lines or in industrial areas; but in nearly all projects in which the authors have been involved, it was street noise that predominated. The noise level is determined by factors such as the following:

- proximity of the road to the facade of the building
- distance from the nearest traffic lights
- nature of the road surface
- number of vehicles per hour at peak periods and the mean figure per day
- speed of the vehicles and
- proportion of heavy vehicles.

The noise level is measured as L_A in dB(A). The index "A" for the noise level L_A and for the unit dB(A) means that measured noise levels are evaluated in relation to their frequency in order to match the frequency-related sensitivity of the human ear.

The noise level of street traffic varies constantly and should be measured over a period of at least one day. This will allow the *median noise level L_{eq}* to be determined for the whole day (6 a.m.–10 p.m.) and for the loudest hour during the night. Allowing various additions and deductions for specific situations, the evaluation level L_r and the so-called *relevant external noise level* can be defined. These form the basis for further calculations and evaluations, as defined in the relevant standards and guidelines in most countries (see /S1,S2/).

If no measurement data is available, the anticipated evaluation level L_r can still be determined in its spatial distribution, using a special calculating method based on actual or predicted traffic data. In complex assignments, this may require a computer-aided simulation of the noise diffusion and reflection. It should also be remembered that, since the automobile industry is developing ever quieter vehicles, the results may tend to be higher than comparable measured data. The reason for this is that the principles for calculation are based on the technical standards existing at the time of publication.

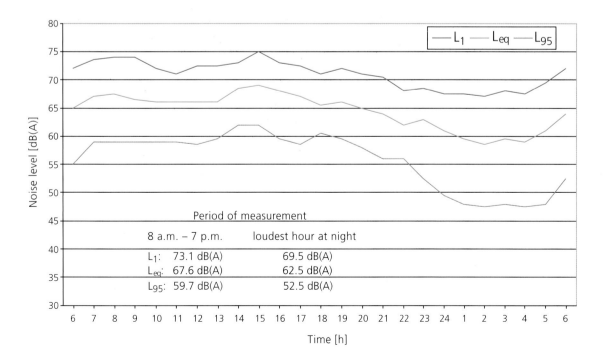

4-2 Graph of external noise levels on main radial route in Hamburg over a period of 24 hours.

L_1 = frequently recurring peak noise levels (1% level)
L_{eq} = equivalent permanent noise level (integrated hourly mean)
L_{95} = constant background noise (95% level)

Standards relating to sound insulation in buildings permit a statistical evaluation, not only of the mean noise level, but of the range of fluctuations. These may be referred to as level L_1, for example, (the noise level that was exceeded for only 1 percent of the period of measurement), or as level L_{95} (the noise level exceeded for 95 percent of the time). In practice, therefore, measurements that also take account of traffic data are recommended as reference values wherever possible. These can then be used as a basis, to which the acoustic simulation of a changed situation—resulting from new buildings or increased traffic—can be related. The simulation also supplements the measurement process by providing the spatial distribution of noise at all points of interest—information that it would be far too laborious to measure.

Simulations should not be challenged, therefore, in their function as the main instrument for extrapolating data and for the planning process. It may be useful to augment this information with measured values, though, especially where one is concerned with obtaining precise decibel figures in the context of double-skin facades and window ventilation.

For a quick assessment of the noise situation all round a building or in an urban context, the relevant external noise levels in dB(A) may be classified into noise-level ranges with a width of 5 dB(A) each.

Sound-insulation requirements

It has long been known that noise can impair health and concentration, and this knowledge has led to many mandatory regulations relating to sound-insulation standards. These are not always implemented in everyday building, however, with the result that in Europe, the list of complaints about the quality of buildings is headed by those involving a lack of adequate sound insulation /S4/. There are two main approaches to the definition of acoustic insulation:
■ via standards and regulations that define the sound-insulating quality required for building components that separate areas subject to noise from areas to be protected;
■ via standards and regulations that define the maximum permissible noise levels for the areas to be protected. The noise may be caused by sound transmission from other areas; or it may be in the form of external noise or noises generated within the building (e.g. from technical installations or working processes). The defined limits may possibly be related to the effects caused as a result of only one or more of these noises.

Depending on the brief, these two approaches are to be drawn into the acoustic planning to provide specified limiting values.
■ *The value (R) for the requisite degree of sound insulation* of a building component is obtained by means of the first approach. This value describes the sound-insulation quality of a wall, a floor, a window or a door as a dividing element between two acoustically discrete areas. In accordance with the definition given in the relevant standards and the value obtained by means of technical measurements, this sound-insulation value is referred to as the (frequency-related) sound insulation value R or R'. The latter (with the apostrophe) is applicable in constructional situations where part of the effect is caused by so-called "typical constructional sound bypasses" and is used only in certain countries as the given standard value.

In defining the requisite values, the additional terms "necessary" and (where a number of components result in a combined effect) "resultant" are used. Where a building component possesses proven qualities based on trials and a testing certificate, the supplementary terms "tested value" and "calculated value" may be used. The tested value is the actual value measured under test conditions and will usually consist of a mean value derived from several test samples and trial measurements. The calculated value is derived from the test value by making further reductions to provide a safety factor. The calculated value is usually the only value that may be used for extrapolatory calculations in planning and should not be confused with the measured values often given in producers' catalogues.

Further mandatory values of this kind exist, for example, for the lateral sound insulation of an adjoining building component and for the impact-sound insulation of a floor or staircase. At this point, suffice it to say that all these values based on standardized processes force the sound-insulating quality obtained via the sound frequency spectrum into a single value, although in reality the sound insulation effect obtained via the frequency spectrum can reveal various patterns and certain characteristic irregularities. As a result, depending on the noise acting upon a structure (i.e. the make-up of the frequencies), the sound-insulating effect can vary somewhat. In extreme cases, an evaluation will have to be made for all the frequencies separately if accurate results are required.

In the second approach based on the use of standards and regulations, as described above, the admissible values for the level of noise acting on a room or workplace are defined. They are often applied, for example, when determining the admissible noise levels for workplaces. These describe the permissible noise from external sources measured in the course of a working day. They help to define a mean assessment level that may not be exceeded (in many countries, for example, $L_r = 55$ dB(A) for mental work). In case of doubt, a carefully conducted and evaluated measurement at the workplace might determine that a particular location is too loud for mental work.

At the planning stage, therefore, values are to be specified in order to achieve a mean assessment level of 50–52 dB(A), for example, for the working day. These measures are supported by the knowledge that a reduction of the noise level acting on a certain situation to below 55 dB(A) helps to increase concentration considerably.

The effect of sounds with an information content

Whether or not a sound is perceived as disturbing will depend not only on the volume—i.e. the sound level—but on its information content. The constant humming of ventilation plant or the buzz of street noise is more likely to be tolerated than other noises at the same level such as conversation, a prolonged sound at a single frequency, or clearly identifiable working noises. Special consideration should be given to sources of this kind where sound transmission is likely to occur via the open intermediate space between the skins of the facade.

In specialist literature, the term distance from background noise is used /S6/, which refers to the subjective disturbance of noise with an information content. The distance from the background noise is defined here as $\Delta L = L_1 - L_{90}$. L_1 and L_{90} refer to the peak noise levels that are exceeded for 1 percent of the period of measurement; or the basic noise level that is present for at least 90 percent of the period of measurement (L_{95} is often used in this context, in which case the values given below will shift accordingly). The following table by Schmidt /S6/ shows how a spoken text can be understood when the distance between the speech signal level L_1 (spoken text) and the background noise level L_{90} attains certain dimensions for the hearer.

If the distance from the background noise has a positive value, the disturbing noise will be louder than the background noise itself. If it has a negative value, the reverse will be the case. The relationships are shown in ill. 4.3 on the following page.

These illustrations demonstrate that sounds with an information content can be identified even when they are at a considerably lower volume than the ambient background noise level. Where double-skin facades are used, the predominantly higher frequencies of the sounds with an information content in the facade intermediate space will be transmitted more distinctly than lower frequencies and, therefore, accentuated along this route.

In addition, one has to consider the psychological element on the part of the user in conjunction with the scope for window ventilation. Everyone is familiar with disturbances entering a room through an open door, where the general reaction would be to close it, while the window can remain open to provide continuous contact with the outside world as well as resulting in a higher level of background noise in the room. Contact with the environment plays a role that is often underestimated in terms of the positive psychological sensation of being at peace with oneself and one's surroundings and not being disturbed so much by others. The latter applies, of course, to unit offices, although it may also play a role in group offices when a workplace is close to a window.

If the noise disturbance enters via the window, one can, of course, close it like a door; but part of the desired contact with the environment will then be lost, while the background noise level is lowered within the room. In other words, the noise disturbance in the room will be reduced, but the distance from the background noise does not decrease to the same degree, so that the remaining noise elements seem subjectively more pronounced.

Sound transmission via the intermediate space between the facade skins can, therefore, be perceived as more disturbing than the transmission of sound at a technically equal level via partitions or doors. In the acoustic planning of double-skin facades with scope for window ventilation, special attention should be paid to the subject of "disturbances caused by noises that fluctuate over a period of time or that have an information content".

Distance from background-noise	Degree of disturbance	Comprehensibility
10 dB	great	good, effortless
5 dB	small	(still) good with familiar texts
0 dB	scarcely perceptible	difficult with familiar texts
-5 dB	minimal	fragmentary with unknown texts
-10 dB	none	fragmentary with familiar texts usually impossible

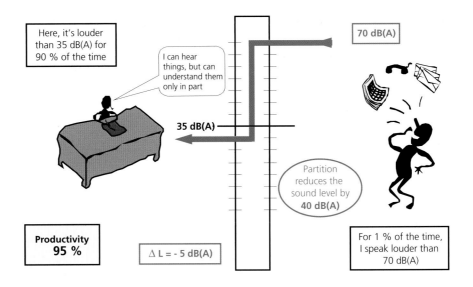

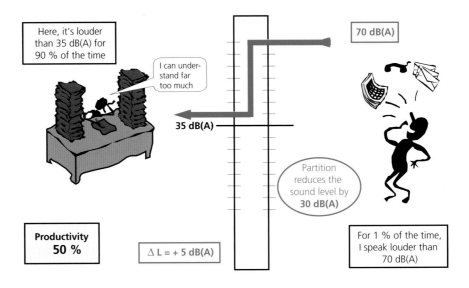

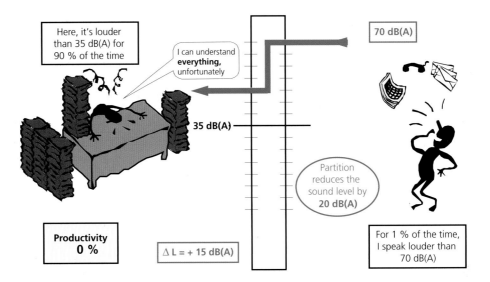

4-3 Influence of sound insulation on audibility and intimacy in adjoining room.

The percentages given for productivity are exaggerated to underline the effect.

Sound insulation against external noise

The first question raised at the beginning of this chapter was: how great is the sound-insulating effect of the external skin; or, how great should it be optimally? Requirements for the overall sound-insulation of a facade depend on the level of external noise and are defined in most national building regulations for the facade as a whole. The design of a sound-insulating single-skin facade can follow established practice and rules of construction. The question then arising concerns improvements in the sound insulation resulting from the screening effect of the second, outer facade layer.

Once the improvement in the sound insulation is known, it is easy to furnish proof of the required degree of sound-insulation, since standard values are based on a situation with closed windows. The screening effect of the outer facade skin can, therefore, be used to reduce the sound-insulating requirements for the inner skin. At the same time, it is also possible to determine whether window ventilation is permissible or acceptable in accordance with the assessment levels at the workplace. This could also be determined by assuming a mean level over a given period during which the windows are open for part of the time.

If the outer facade is permanently open, the sound-insulation properties for a non-hermetic building element used for ventilation purposes have to be determined. This may also be necessary where the outer skin of a facade can be closed, but where there is an automatic opening function. In such cases, where the user is not in a position to control the opening movement, building standards require any calculations for proof of sound insulation to be based on the facade in an open state.

The same applies in determining the degree of sound insulation for facades with intermittent window ventilation. In this case, the task is complicated by the fact that during the process of ventilation, both facade skins may be open over part of their area and for part of the time. In this context, though, the element of time does not pose any basic problems, since there are known and reliable methods for calculating sound levels that fluctuate over a given period, and for converting them to obtain a mean assessment level.

The partial opening of a window, e.g. in a tipped or pivoted position, has to be related to the specific degree of opening that is required to provide adequate ventilation. It is necessary, therefore, to define the various opening positions of windows with different movements—side-and-bottom hung, vertically pivoting, sliding casements, etc.—to provide a basis for any statement on sound insulation. In the case of single-skin facades, more or less precise values can be found in the relevant literature (e.g. /S9/) and by known

measurement values obtained by specialists in this field. Very little empirical data and even fewer theoretical findings exist for the role these values play within the overall system of double-skin facades.

The authors, therefore, present their own calculating method, which can be theoretically confirmed if certain assumptions are made. The results achieved with this method also correspond to a large extent with existing measured values for comparable situations. The authors offer this method to professional circles as a basis for discussion, since the method will possibly need to be elaborated for special situations.

Window ventilation and sound insulation

The noise level at the workplace can be calculated according to generally recognized principles of technology if certain parameters are known or can be defined. For example, a single-layer facade with
- 50 percent window area
- sound insulation in the non-transparent outer skin amounting to R = 50 dB
- sound insulation of the window when closed: R = 37 dB
- sound insulation of the window in a tipped position: R = 10 dB
- a relevant external noise level of L_A = 70 dB(A), will provide the following data:

During an eight-hour working day, the window may be tipped open for a total period of 150 minutes if an assessment level in the workplace of L_r = 55 dB(A) is to be maintained. The window may be tipped open for only 48 minutes in eight hours if a workplace assessment level of 50 dB(A) is required.

A workplace assessment level of 55 dB(A), caused by noise sources extraneous to the workplace, is the upper limit defined for office workplaces in most relevant standards /S10,S11/. If one considers that traffic noise entering from outside is not the only external source of noise at the workplace and that 55 dB(A) is recognized as the minimum quality for concentrated work, it is essential in planning modern office buildings to aim for an assessment level for external noise of well below 55 dB(A); i.e. closer to 50–52 dB(A) would be appropriate.

Given the parameters described above, i.e. where L_A = 70 dB(A), adequate window ventilation is scarcely acceptable with a single-skin facade. The windows could be opened in a tipped position for only six minutes per hour; alternatively, the peak ventilation periods would not be counted as working time. This demonstrates that window ventilation with single-skin facades is reasonably possible in terms of the assessment levels only where the relevant external noise level is well below 70 dB(A), or, depending on the required degree of comfort and the facade concept, up to about 68 dB(A). The various sets of relationships involved here are shown in the nomogram 4-4, which also contains initial information on the additional sound insulation provided by a second facade skin. In other words, there is a strong argument for a second facade layer in the form of a vented "noise screen". Every decibel screened off by the second skin permits a greater degree of window ventilation through the facade with correspondingly higher external noise levels. If this function is to be a criterion of the design, it will be necessary to calculate the improvement in sound insulation resulting from the external skin, as mentioned at the beginning.

The calculation method applied by the authors, together with the theoretical analyses and empirical experience on which it is based, are described in the two following case studies. The description addresses especially readers with a knowledge of sound insulation, since it would not be possible to explain all specialist terms in a generally understandable form without exceeding the scope and the purpose of this book. The known limits to this approach are also described and discussed.

4-4 Nomogram for resultant noise assessment level in room in relation to duration of ventilation and relevant external noise level.

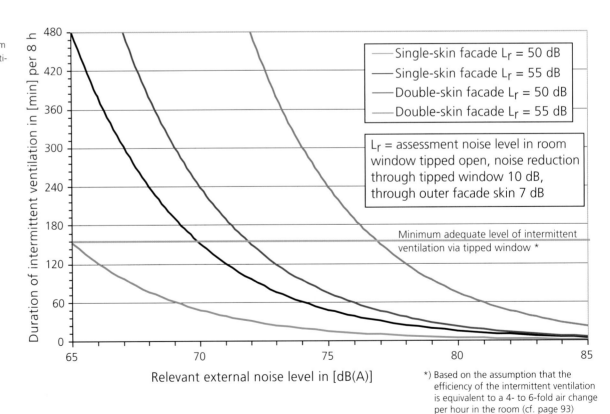

Single-skin facade L_r = 50 dB
Single-skin facade L_r = 55 dB
Double-skin facade L_r = 50 dB
Double-skin facade L_r = 55 dB

L_r = assessment noise level in room window tipped open, noise reduction through tipped window 10 dB, through outer facade skin 7 dB

Minimum adequate level of intermittent ventilation via tipped window *

Duration of intermittent ventilation in [min] per 8 h

Relevant external noise level in [dB(A)]

*) Based on the assumption that the efficiency of the intermittent ventilation is equivalent to a 4- to 6-fold air change per hour in the room (cf. page 93)

Case study 1: Calculation of sound-insulating effect of a second facade skin

The cavity between the two skins of a facade can be regarded as a space with a sound-insulating value x for the outer enclosing layer and a sound-insulating value y for the inner enclosing layer. In accordance with this, the sound insulation would be calculated in the form of the reduction of the level of external noise entering the facade intermediate space and proceeding from there into the internal space. But this approach, taking into account the separate factors, is appropriate only where the facade intermediate space is really a space in which a more or less diffuse sound field can develop: in other words, where the distance between the outer and inner skins is sufficiently great. Where the depth of the intermediate space is relatively small, however, this method is questionable. The calculation of the reverberation radius in the facade space can serve as a test criterion for this.

The reverberation radius will depend on the reverberation time T_N in s, or on the equivalent sound-absorption area A in m^2 in the facade intermediate space. In principle, these values can be simply calculated from each other using the sabin formula.

$$A = 0.163 \cdot \frac{V}{T_N} \quad [m^2]$$

where V is the volume of the facade space in m^3. In the present case, though, the values have variable properties. The reverberation times and absorption areas will differ, depending on whether the facade skins are closed or partially opened. Theoretically, therefore, the sound insulation should also have variable properties in relation to the facade skins calculated in this way; but this is not much help in the planning process.

Following these preliminary remarks on the problems of theoretical analysis, the methods of calculation will be presented, based on the assumption of a diffuse sound field. It was possible to check the results empirically in part, and the respective measurements are given at the end of this section. Further theoretical investigations can and should be carried out on this basis.

In specialist literature on the subject, a calculation model is provided that will help to determine the sound insulation properties of partially opened building elements (see /S13/):

$$R_{res} = R_1 - 10 \lg (1 + f \cdot (10^{0.1\,R_1} - 1)) \quad [dB] \quad (S1)$$

where
R_{res} is the resultant overall sound insulation
R_1 is the sound insulation of the closed element, and
f is the proportion of the open area to the total area.

Applying the equation (S1), for a facade with an opening area of 10 percent (f = 0.1) and a sound-insulation value of $R_1 = 30$ dB, the overall sound insulation will be 10 dB. A value of $R_1 = 30$ dB corresponds, for example, to a pane of glass 10–12 mm thick. Values above 30 dB have no further influence on the result. This example is based on a reception space with a diffuse sound field; i.e. a normal, furnished room with an average sound absorption. The situation corresponds roughly to that of a double-skin facade where the inner skin is completely opened; e.g. via room-height, side-hung or vertically pivoting casements.

This analysis is confirmed by measurements. The outer facade skin of the DB Cargo building in Mainz, erected for the German railroad organization, was designed as a glass curtain-wall screen with continuous, 10-cm-high air-inlet and air-extract slits. Above the apron wall in every facade bay are openable side-/bottom-hung casements. Using loudspeakers as sources of external noise, acoustic measurements were taken in a four-bay room with four fully opened windows. The results showed a sound-insulation value from outside to inside of R = 15 dB.

According to equation (S1), assuming 2-meter-high windows and an opened area of 10 percent, the sound insulation value would be 10 dB in the window area. In the present example, measurements were taken not only for the window areas, but for the entire facade, including the solid upstand walls. If the sound insulation they contribute is taken into account, the measured value of 15 dB is confirmed by the calculations. The validity of equation (S1) is, therefore, demonstrated in this case. The various relationships that exist are more complex with double-skin facades, since there is an additional intermediate space.

4-5 Acoustic measurements of double-skin facade of DB Cargo building, Mainz.
Activation by means of external loudspeakers.

If one wishes to calculate the screening effect of the external facade layer with respect to the intermediate space (as described above), the acoustic-power levels of the various areas of the outer facade have to be added together and converted to obtain the sound pressure level in the intermediate space. The expressions

$L_{P1} = f(A_1, (L_A - R_1))$ for the closed areas and
$L_{P2} = f(A_2, L_A)$ for the open areas

are then integrated into the equation (S1). After a number of conversion stages, the equation for the sound-insulating effect of the external facade is obtained:

$$\Delta R = -10 \lg \left[\frac{f \cdot (1 - 10^{-0.1 R_1}) + 10^{-0.1 R_1}}{A} \right] \text{ [dB]} \quad (S2)$$

Equation (S2) is, therefore, a version of equation (S1), corrected to take account of absorption in the facade intermediate space. Identical results are obtained if a value of 1 m² is substituted for A in (S2). In this form, the equation is always related to a one-meter-long section of the facade.

Case study 2: Experience with measured results
Equation (S2) is to be applied to two selected examples, for which extensive measurements were taken by the authors' office.

Measurement 1: City Gate, Düsseldorf

The "City Gate" in Düsseldorf, described earlier in the chapter on "Types of Construction", is an 80-meter-high structure with a corridor facade. The space between the two facade layers is 0.9 m deep in part and 1.4 m deep in other areas. The facade corridors are divided into sections about 20 m long. The openings in the ventilation boxes mounted on the ceiling are 60 cm high in elevation and, when open, have a clear opening height of 30 cm—determined by their internal geometry. The story height is 3.6 m. The value f, therefore, is 0.083.

The equivalent sound absorption area is based on a one-meter length of the facade. In order to substitute the correct value for A in the calculation for this example, a measurement of the reverberation time in the facade intermediate space was also made—with open external flaps and a closed inner skin. The outcome of this was an equivalent sound-absorption area per meter length of the facade of A = 0.42 m², or a mean sound-absorption level of $\alpha = 0.0776$ for all surfaces in the intermediate space.

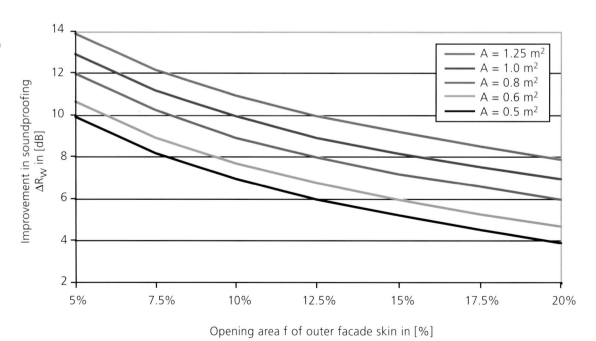

4-6 Nomogram for improving sound insulation ΔR_w in relation to f and A,
where
f is the proportion of the open area in relation to the entire facade and
A is the equivalent sound-absorption area in the facade intermediate space.

Improvement in soundproofing ΔR_w in [dB]

A = 1.25 m²
A = 1.0 m²
A = 0.8 m²
A = 0.6 m²
A = 0.5 m²

Opening area f of outer facade skin in [%]

Using equation (S2), $\Delta R = 6.9$ dB.
In 1998, acoustic measurements of traffic noise were taken on the 17th floor. The relevant external noise level was $L_A = 67$ dB(A). The following data were recorded for the inner facade skin in a closed state and opened to various degrees:

■ inner facade closed: $\Delta R = 6$ dB
■ inner facade open by 5°: $\Delta R = 6$ dB
■ inner facade open by 45°: $\Delta R = 7$ dB.

These data reveal two things. In the present case (with a closed inner facade layer), equation (S2) provides figures that correspond closely with the measured results (deviation only 1 dB). The tendency towards better figures for the outer facade layer where the absorption area in the intermediate space is larger (as a result of the greater degree of opening of the inner facade) is also confirmed. For a description of the influence of traffic noise as a sound source, see the section "Sound frequency spectrum" on the following page.

Measurement 2: DB Cargo, Mainz

The DB Cargo building in Mainz, described above, is a five-story linear office development. A glass acoustic insulating screen was erected outside the inner facade skin, with a spacing of 25 cm between the two. Above the parapet walls and below the floors are 10-cm-high horizontal ventilation slits. There is also a narrow vertical slit on the axis of each facade post, although this is ignored here, since the slit is largely covered by the geometry of the post itself. The internal facade was designed with a solid parapet wall and conventional rectangular openings, with windows divided vertically into three sections. Only the middle section—a bottom-/side-hung casement—can be opened. The external and internal openings are, therefore, vertically offset to some extent. Although the facade intermediate space is not divided, the window axes are constructed in a form resembling that of a box window, since the cavity is largely obstructed at regular intervals by the facade sections. In view of the 2-m-high windows, f can be calculated with a value of 0.1. Assuming a mean sound-absorption value of $\alpha = 0.08$ (analogous to example 1, but with a more effective external opening), the equivalent sound-absorption area A is calculated as 0.36 m² per meter length of window. Applying equation (S2), $\Delta R = 5.5$ dB.

In 1997, when the building was nearing completion, acoustic measurements were taken before and after the assembly of the outer glazed screen (with sound penetrating from below, using a loudspeaker at an angle of 45°; see ill. 4-5). The difference between the measured values for the sound insulation of the windows with and without the screening skin (R = 38 dB and R = 44 dB) was $\Delta R = 6$ dB. In other words, the calculated results were consistent with the measured values.

Important ancillary aspects
■ Equivalent sound-absorption area
One general remark should be made on the subject of the equivalent sound-absorption area A. Errors can easily occur in this context, since the surface areas of the facade intermediate space are, as a rule, largely sound-reflecting and have only minimal sound-absorbing properties. Even small changes in the assumed absorption areas can have an effect on the results. But it is not possible to give exact data for some of the surfaces, since the absorbent properties resulting from various degrees of opening, the presence of ventilation boxes and other factors are not precisely known.

The selected area of the facade can also have a significant effect on the outcome of the calculations. Our analysis is again based on one meter length of the facade. Otherwise, a correction factor would have to

4-7 View into facade intermediate space in DB Cargo building, Mainz. The cross-section of the posts of the outer facade skin creates a deep division in what is essentially a continuous intermediate space. In view of its low height, the ground floor window shown here is not divided into three parts as the windows on the upper stories are.

be added to (S2). In example 1, the calculated reverberation time in the facade intermediate space and the equivalent sound-absorption area derived from this are both related to a one-meter length of the facade corridor. The theoretical surfaces dividing one length from the next are assumed to be completely sound-reflecting, since the same noise level exists in both spaces.

The data for the reverberation time in the facade intermediate space given in measurement 1 above and shown in diagram 4-8, can be used as a point of reference for other examples. These measurements provide information about the sound-absorbing effect of the largely glazed surfaces and the ventilation openings in relation to sound frequencies. For professionals in this field who may be interested in other applications of these data, one should say that the sum of the surface areas was 169 m² in this case. The total ventilation area visible in the facade intermediate space was roughly 10 m², of which only half may be assumed to be open, on account of the geometry of the ventilation boxes.

■ Sound frequency spectrum

The acoustic measurements made in the two examples above incorporated traffic noise (example 1) and loudspeaker noise (example 2) as sound sources. One knows that these two kinds of activation are not directly comparable because they are composed of different spectra. The traffic noise spectrum usually produces "poorer" measured results than the spectrum of so-called "pink-noise" used in acoustic tests on buildings. International standards take account of this discrepancy by providing spectrum adjustment values (see /S14/). The spectrum adjustment value for traffic noise C_{tr} usually leads to reductions in the R-values.

In the case of the two examples described above, this would mean that the value $\Delta R = 6$ dB recorded in measurement 1 with traffic noise would have to be improved to make it comparable with the results obtained in measurement 2, as the calculated values indicate. Questions of dependence on sound frequencies and frequency adaptation will not be considered further at this point. It suffices to mention the influence these factors can have on the results.

■ Diffuse sound field

Reference should again be made to the necessary limitations on applying equation (S2). The equation is based on a space with a diffuse sound field. It is necessary, therefore, to test whether these conditions actually exist in a facade intermediate space. By definition, the diffuse sound field predominates outside the radius of reverberation. The latter defines the interface at which the direct and diffuse sound fields are of equal intensity. In the diffuse sound field, the sounds reflected from the enclosing surfaces of the space which effect a listener dominate; the sound level remaining more or less constant and not decaying continuously with distance as it does in the open air.

The reverberation radius can be calculated relatively simply with the equation $r_H = \sqrt{A/50}$ [m] from the equivalent sound-absorption area. But this formula for the reverberation radius applies only to a sound source that radiates equally in all directions of a space. With a double-skin facade, however, this is not the case. Here, the sound source is the opening in the outer skin; i.e. at one edge of the space. If one follows the description contained in /S16/, the boundary radius for a sound source radiating in a semi-space may be taken as the beginning of the diffuse sound field:

$$r_g = \sqrt{A/25} \ [m] \quad (S3)$$

4-8 Reverberation time T_N in the intermediate space of a corridor facade in the City Gate building, Düsseldorf. Measured values with opened and closed flaps in outer skin of facade.

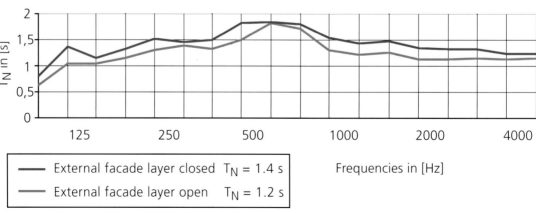

In this context, Fasold/Veres /S17/ give, as a further differentiation, a sound source with a pronouncedly directional character, such as the sound vector of a loudspeaker. A situation of this kind would seem to be the closest approximation to a slit opening in the facade as a noise source for the facade intermediate space. This is more difficult to calculate, since a directional factor Γ (large Greek gamma) and a degree of focusing γ (small gamma) have to be taken into account. The directional range to be incorporated is defined as $r_r = \Gamma \sqrt{\gamma A/50}$. In our opinion, though, it need be considered only in the case of sound elements of a relatively high frequency, since for spherical sound diffusion it is transformed into equation (S3). We shall, therefore, ignore it here and use the concept for the boundary radius derived from equation (S3) (the sound source radiating into a semi-space) in considering the facade intermediate space.

The question of the volume that should be taken into account may be answered as above: an effective meter length may be assumed with sound-reflecting side boundaries. In view of the linear structure of the facade intermediate spaces, it would be unnecessary and confusing to consider the entire, possibly elongated, volume. For measurement 1, therefore, a boundary radius of 13 cm is calculated; for measurement 2, a boundary radius of 12 cm. In measurement 1, where the facade intermediate space is 90 cm deep, the result is not so important as in example 2, where the intermediate space is only 25 cm deep: in this case, the diffuse sound field can be regarded as of only limited relevance. Further consideration will, therefore, have to be given to this subject.

Generally speaking, before applying equation (S2), one should check what the boundary radius will actually be, calculated in accordance with equation (S3). The greater the equivalent sound absorption area, the greater the boundary radius will be. Especially where the distance between the facade skins is small, the existence of a diffuse sound field, and thus the general validity of equation (S2), is questionable.

■ Direct sound field

Near the openings in the external facade, there will always be a direct sound field, which, beyond a certain distance (the boundary radius in accordance with (S3)) will become the diffuse sound field within the facade intermediate space—if there is sufficient room for this. If this is not the case for large parts of the facade cavity, one should consider what conditions exist in the direct sound field.

The sound-pressure level at a distance s (L_{Ps}) in the direct sound field can be obtained from the appropriate description in specialist literature (see /S18/ or /S19/, for example):

$$L_{Ps} = L_W + D_i + K_0 - D_S - \Sigma D \quad [\text{dB}] \quad (S4)$$

where
L_W = the sound level at the source
D_i = the value for the directional effect for assessing the direction of travel of sound
K_0 = the steradian value of the source radiating in a full, semi- or quarter-space (i.e. 0, 3 or 6 dB)
D_S = the distance parameter in relation to the surface radiating into the full, semi- or quarter-space; i.e. 11, 8 or 5 dB, plus $20 \lg (s/s_0)$, with a distance s in meters, and $s_0 = 1$ m
ΣD = factors influencing the propagation of sound, such as air absorption, floor damping, plantings, weather, obstacles, etc. These factors, derived from the application of this equation to greater distances, are here taken as zero.

In this context, the opening in the outer facade through which sound flows into the intermediate space is regarded as the sound source. The sound level L_W is derived from the sound-pressure level L_P outside the outer facade and the opening area S in the outer facade, based on $L_W = L_P + 10 \lg (s/s_0)$. At this juncture, reference is expressly made to the fact that in using these methods, no generally applicable theory is being advanced for the interaction of the direct and diffuse sound fields in the facade intermediate space. The relationship between the two will depend to a large extent on the facade geometry. Moreover, for a closer examination, they will have to be calculated in the context of the relevant frequencies, since the input values—especially in the case of equation (S4)—will vary considerably for different frequencies. Comparative investigations of various geometries for double-skin facades should be made on the basis of measured results if one wishes to determine the appropriate values with sufficient accuracy. This applies in particular to forms of facade construction with a relatively shallow intermediate space.

Conclusions on the calculation of sound insulation provided by a second glazed facade layer with a ventilated rear space

It is difficult to calculate the sound-insulating effect of an outer facade skin when it is partially opened for ventilation purposes. The authors recommend the following procedure:

■ One should ascertain whether the geometry of the facade intermediate space and the design of the surface areas result in a largely diffuse sound field, or whether—in view of the smaller dimensions between the two skins—a direct sound field is relevant in an evaluation of the inner skin. Equation (S3) may be used for this purpose. As a rule, the direct sound field will be significant where the facade intermediate space is very shallow and where the openings in the inner and outer skins are close together.

■ Where a diffuse sound field clearly exists (i.e. where there is a great distance between the facade skins in relation to the boundary radius), equation (S2) will ensure theoretically based results that have been confirmed empirically in other schemes. The equation contains a somewhat uncertain input value in the form of the equivalent sound absorption area A. The measured values shown in fig. 4-8 provide a useful reference in this respect. The sets of relationships discussed in the context of equation (S2) for the diffuse sound field are shown in nomogram 4-6 for various common areas of application.

■ In all facade intermediate spaces, a direct sound field exists around the external opening. Equation (S4) provides a theoretically proven method for calculating the decrease in the sound level in the direct sound field. The application of this equation in the case under discussion here is unusual, though. A number of input values can only be estimated. Above all, with shallow facade intermediate spaces, prior to the application of (S4), a further theoretical elaboration is to be recommended on the basis of extensive empirical material.

■ An evaluation of the typical sound frequency spectrum for traffic can be undertaken—as for all other external construction elements—in accordance with /S20/, using the spectrum adjustment value C_{tr} if the sound insulation value R for the external facade skin (R_1 in equation (S2)) is known in relation to the frequency.

Empirically, one knows from the measurement practice described here as well as from other measured examples that external facade skins which ensure an adequate fresh-air supply (i.e. usually with an 8–10% opening area) can improve the sound insulation by roughly 5–8 dB. The opinion sometimes expressed in other publications /S21/ that reductions in the sound level of more than 4 dB are possible only where the opening area is smaller than 5% or only where additional sound absorbers are installed cannot be confirmed.

Internal sound insulation

The nature of sound transmission

If a number of rooms next to or above each other are linked via an undivided intermediate space between the facade skins, the problem of undesirable sound transmission from one room to another can arise. The sound insulation provided by the divisions between the rooms will be diminished because the sound can take an alternative route via the facade space. At first glance, the situation would not seem to be much different from that of a corridor that links adjacent rooms acoustically when the doors are open. The situation nevertheless differs in the following respects:

■ A corridor will usually provide greater acoustic damping, so that when the doors are open, more absorption will occur along this route than in the case of sound transmission via glazed facade spaces, where there is usually a minimum of sound absorbence.
■ In many cases, the double-skin facade functions as a means of free ventilation for the internal rooms. The windows will, therefore, have to be open for at least part of the time to allow a change of air. In contrast, a corridor door can be kept closed the whole time if required.
■ As a building element, the window has a special psychological function for a person within a room. Users identify it more closely with their individual space and expect less disturbance of their sense of intimacy from this source than when they open the door.
■ Where high external noise levels exist, caused by traffic, for example, they will usually result in a stronger masking sound in the intermediate space. This applies even when the double-skin facade functions as a form of sound insulation against external noise. The level of disturbance from room to room will thereby be reduced.

Calculating sound transmission

How can these various factors be quantified and evaluated for the planning process?

In contrast to the question of sound insulation against external noise, reliable methods of calculation exist for sound transmission. These can be borrowed from a different technical field and may be usefully applied in this context: guidelines for noise reduction in air-conditioning installations /S22/ exist in most countries and recognize the case of sound transmission via a network of ducts that link adjacent rooms. In this respect, the two different situations must be differentiated, depending on whether a continuous duct has openings into the rooms or not. In the present context, the case of a duct opening into adjoining spaces is of special interest. The German guideline VDI 2081

is taken as an example here; but ASHRAE or CNBSC guidelines give similar figures. Fig. 27 in section 8.5.2 of VDI 2081 shows an example of this kind and cites the following equation:

$$L_3 = L_1 + 10 \lg \left[\frac{(S_1 \, S_2 \, S_3)}{(S_0 + S_2) \, (S_3 + S_4) \, A_3} \right] + 6 - \Delta L_W$$
$$[dB(A)] \quad (S5)$$

where
L_3 = sound level in the recipient space
(related to L_1 as the source)
L_1 = sound level in the transmitting space
S_1 = opening area to duct in transmitting space
S_3 = opening area to duct in recipient space
S_0, S_2, S_4 = cross-sectional areas of duct
A_3 = equivalent sound-absorption area in recipient space
ΔL_W = reduction in sound level as a result of absorption by duct, changes in cross-section, deflections, corrections at junctions, outlets, etc.

If this equation is applied, for example, to a continuous facade corridor divided floor by floor, but without changes in cross-section, the expressions S_0, S_2 and S_4 will be identical, so that the equation can be written as follows:

$$L_R = L_T + 10 \lg \left[\frac{(S_1 \, S_2 \, S_3)}{2 \, S_2 \, (S_2 + S_3) \, A_E} \right] + 6 - \Delta L_W \quad [dB(A)]$$
$$(S5a)$$

Here
L_R = sound level in the recipient space (related to L_T as the source); this corresponds to L_3 in equation (S5)
L_T = sound level in the transmitting space; this corresponds to L_1 in equation (S5)
S_1 = opening area to corridor in the transmitting space
S_2 = cross-section of corridor
S_3 = opening area to corridor in the recipient space
A_R = equivalent sound-absorption area in the recipient space
ΔL_W = reduction in sound level as a result of absorption in the corridor, and possible changes in the cross-section of the corridor, deflections, confluence corrections, etc.

In applying equations (S5) and (S5a), reference should be made to /S23/, especially in respect of the expression ΔL_W. Sample calculations were carried out for the facade corridor from case study 1. A brief comparison with measured results is given, since an opportunity arose during the work executed in 1998 on the Düsseldorf City Gate to take acoustic measurements and to verify the calculations.

Sound measurements were made for various situations in immediately adjoining spaces, in which the pivoting lights in the inner facade layer were closed, as well as opened in a 5° and 45° position. Measurements were also taken for the corridor with the doors to the rooms in an open position. In a 5° opening position, a difference in sound level of 28 dB was recorded for the windows; and for a 45° opening position, there was still a sound-level difference of 19 dB.

These measured data reveal a close approximation to the figures obtained with equation (S5a).

For casement doors opened at a 5° angle (vertical pivoting):
area S_1 0.05 m x 2.82 m = 0.141 m²
area S_3 0.05 m x 2.82 m = 0.141 m²
area S_2 2.82 m x 0.90 m = 2.538 m²
A_E = 12.4 m² (where V = 61 m³ and T_N = 0.8 s)
L_S = 70 dB(A)
ΔL_W = approx. 1 dB, damping of "duct length"

$$L_E = 70 + 10 \lg \left(\frac{0.141 \cdot 0.141 \cdot 2.538}{2 \cdot 2.538 \cdot (2.538 + 0.141) \cdot 12.4} \right) + 6 - \Delta L_W$$

$$= 70 + 10 \lg \left(\frac{0.0505}{168.62} \right) + 6 - 1$$

$$= 70 - 35 + 6 - 1$$

$$= 40 \text{ dB(A)}$$

The calculated difference in sound-level ($L_S - L_E$) from room to room resulting from the transmission via the facade intermediate space is thus 30 dB(A). Measurements revealed a difference of 28 dB(A) (see ill. 4-9). Taking into account that at the time of measurement, the continuous dividing wall had an R value of only 33 dB because it had not been sealed, the R value of 37 dB which may normally be expected for a dividing wall without openings would have given a measured value 1 or 2 dB higher.

For casement doors opened at a 45° angle (vertically pivoting):
area S_1 0.46 m x 2.82 m = 1.30 m²
area S_3 0.46 m x 2.82 m = 1.30 m²
area S_2 2.82 m x 0.90 m = 2.538 m²
A_E = 12.4 m² (where V = 61 m³ and T_N = 0.8 s)
L_S = 70 dB(A)
ΔL_W = approx. 7 dB (5 dB for deflection; 1 dB for cross-sectional change; 1 dB for damping)

$$L_E = 70 + 10 \lg \left(\frac{4.29}{241.57} \right) + 6 - 7$$

$$= 70 - 17.5 + 6 - 7$$

$$= 51.5 \text{ dB(A)}$$

The calculated difference in sound level ($L_S - L_E$) from room to room is thus 18.5 dB(A). Measurements revealed a difference of 19 dB(A) (see ill. 4-10).

Here, too, a careful consideration of the geometry is crucial. If, as in the case of the Düsseldorf City Gate, vertically pivoting casements are used, the change in cross-section and above all the resultant deflection have to be taken into account. VDI 2081 /S24/, as applied here, provides useful values for these influences in ΔL_W.

4-9, 4-10 Measurement of sound transmission from room to room via the facade corridor in the City Gate building, Düsseldorf.

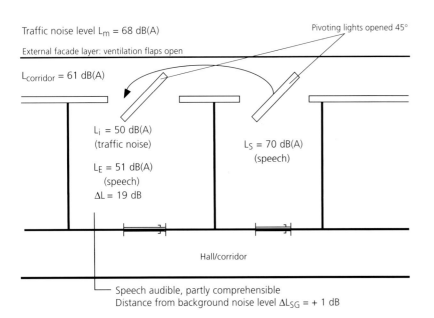

Traffic noise level L_m = 68 dB(A)

Pivoting lights opened 5°

External facade layer: ventilation flaps open

$L_{corridor}$ = 62 dB(A)

L_i = 45 dB(A) (traffic noise)

L_E = 42 dB(A) (speech)

ΔL = 28 dB

L_S = 70 dB(A) (speech)

Hall/corridor

Speech audible, but scarcely understandable
Distance from background noise level ΔL_{SG} = -3 dB

Traffic noise level L_m = 68 dB(A)

Pivoting lights opened 45°

External facade layer: ventilation flaps open

$L_{corridor}$ = 61 dB(A)

L_i = 50 dB(A) (traffic noise)

L_E = 51 dB(A) (speech)

ΔL = 19 dB

L_S = 70 dB(A) (speech)

Hall/corridor

Speech audible, partly comprehensible
Distance from background noise level ΔL_{SG} = + 1 dB

In complex geometric situations, such as stack systems with partially divided intermediate spaces, the equation will have to be applied with the appropriate modifications. Where there is only a shallow facade intermediate space, it may be worthwhile to make an evaluation related to the relevant frequencies as well, since lower frequencies with greater wavelengths may possibly be filtered out by the narrow facade space. VDI 2081 /S25/ also provides different values for ΔL_W for a frequency-related investigation. In general, therefore, equation (S5a) is a useful tool for calculating the sound level transmitted through a facade corridor.

Evaluation of sound transmission

Of greater interest than the results themselves is the way they are interpreted. What does it mean when the noise from an adjoining room is perceived in one's own room reduced in level by 28 dB or by 19 dB? To evaluate this, various parameters have to be taken into account:

- the intensity of the transmission level (here L_1 or L_T)
- the intensity of the basic sound level in the recipient space
- the constancy of this noise level over a period of time
- the information content of the noise transmitted.

The intensity of the initial transmission level was assumed here for speech raised in pitch at times: L_1 = 70 dB(A). This is by no means a maximum level; the volume of the human voice can be even greater when a person is excited. On the other hand, a quiet conversation may be at a level of around only 60 dB(A). The background-noise level in one's own room will depend, among other things, on the volume of traffic noise and the degree to which the window is open. The wider it is open, the greater will be the level of noise transmitted from the adjoining room as well as the background noise level from traffic.

All these noise levels are more or less variable over a period of time. What is possibly a disturbing noise transmission from an adjoining room may coincide with a loud or soft level of traffic noise or with loud or soft self-generated noise within one's own room. The transmission and reception situations will also be subject to constant fluctuations, since the two parties in adjoining rooms can cause and suffer disturbance, depending on their respective working situations (see also illustration 4-3).

In view of these imponderables, if an evaluation is to be made, one should assume the worst possible situation. This would comprise a realistically low background-noise level in one's own room, resulting from street traffic (where the inner and outer facade skins are open); and self-generated working noises, including those caused by technical apparatus. Above all, it is important to consider the information content of the noise disturbance. Since one can hear and partly understand speech even when it is at a lower sound level than that of background noise with little information content, a target should be set for the distance from the background noise source at roughly ΔL = -10 dB in order to eliminate disturbances or to ensure a relatively safe degree of intimacy.

Generally speaking, this sense of intimacy will be possible only to a limited extent if the inner facade skin is open. This condition in a double-skin facade differs only minimally from that of quiet urban situations where there is no double-skin facade. Here, again, if a degree of intimacy is required, the windows will generally have to be closed. In the case of double-skin facades, however, there is a tendency for noise with an information content to be accentuated through the reflection within the facade intermediate space. This occurs because the relevant frequencies are easily transmitted; and that, in turn, results in a worse situation than in a house with open windows in a quiet location without a double-skin facade.

Experience in operating the City Gate in Düsseldorf shows that users value the scope for personal control of windows much more highly than the exclusion of objectively measurable noise disturbance. People seem prepared to put up with the latter. This applies even to leased office space, where immediately adjoining rooms are occupied by the staff of different firms. At the planning stage, it is certainly advisable in situations of this kind to allow for the subsequent installation of screening elements within the facade intermediate space, so as to be able to respond to user requirements after the building has been taken into use.

One difference that should be heeded is in buildings where the double-skin facade does not have a sound-insulating function against external noise. In this case, a situation may arise where the sound-insulating qualities of the building in respect of internal disturbances may be worse than if there were no second facade skin.

Effects on the sound insulation of internal partitions

The case mentioned at the end of the previous section draws attention to a phenomenon that is often neglected. Double-skin facades are conceived not only for the sound insulation they provide. They may be installed for design reasons and to save energy. In this respect, it may be sensible to design the facade so that it can be closed. If the external noise level decreases appreciably for a time, however, or if the sound insulation is greatly improved temporarily by closing the openings in the outer skin, the facade may prove to be overdimensioned at times and the background noise level will be reduced even further.

A facade that can be closed will have not only a variable U-value (thermal insulation), but a variable R-value (sound insulation), too. The range of variations in the latter case will be considerably broader than that for the U-value. Sound insulation values can vary by as much as 10 dB with a closed or open outer facade. Is that desirable, and how should this be handled at the planning stage?

In addition to the facade as an external building element and the facade corridor as a transmission duct, internal construction components will also be affected. The dimensions of partitions and doors or dividing floors are based on the assumption that in office buildings there is a background noise level of at least 35 dB(A). Where the sound insulation against external noise is "unnecessarily" increased, this assumption may be erroneous, since the background-noise level is likely to be lower. However welcome this may be, one has to consider that the sound insulation provided by internal constructional elements such as partitions will have to be correspondingly higher if the generally expected quality is to be achieved. If the background-noise level sinks to 30 dB(A), a wall with a good standard quality R = 42 dB will seem only as good as a wall with R = 37 dB with a background noise level of 35 dB(A). (In this context, see also ill. 4-11.)

To maintain the desired quality, the wall would have to be dimensioned to achieve a value of R = 47 dB. This would necessitate not only a quite different cross-section, but also different abutment details between the wall and adjoining elements. At this level of quality, continuous, slenderly dimensioned inner facades, certain hollow-floor systems, "system partitions", etc. soon reveal their limitations. Standard building components are no longer automatically appropriate, and what might subjectively be called a "higher" level of sound insulation in the internal building elements may be jeopardized.

In such a situation, the case under discussion would not pose a problem if, for example, background noise were to be caused by a ventilation system during the periods when the centrally controlled outer facade was closed. The background noise level of a ventilation system of this kind will usually be around $L_A = 35$ to 40 dB(A). Aspects of this kind should be investigated in the planning. A more common problem is that facades are often designed for acoustic loads that occur on only one side of the building, but which, for architectural reasons, are applied without more ado to the other faces, where the actual loading is lower.

To recognize this and to take the appropriate steps in the planning is a complex task that will have to be resolved individually for each specific project.

Note: If a housing block is designed with a double-skin facade, these problems are likely to be intensified, since the internal components for dwellings are subject to higher sound insulation standards. In such cases, therefore, it is essential to check what background noise levels may be expected during the day and at night, so that the planning may satisfy occupants' expectations in terms of internal sound insulation.

4-11 Potential degree of intimacy dependent on the acoustic insulation values of partitions and the background noise level in the room.

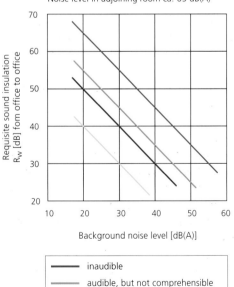

Sound insulation dependent on background noise level and on degree of intimacy required
Noise level in adjoining room ca. 65 dB(A)

Requisite sound insulation R_W [dB] fom office to office

Background noise level [dB(A)]

— inaudible
— audible, but not comprehensible
— audible, but difficult to understand
— easily understood

Conclusions on internal sound insulation

A double-skin facade will have a number of different effects on the internal sound insulation of a building.

■ If a double-skin facade is designed with (partially) non-divided intermediate spaces, undesirable sound transmission can occur when the inner skin is open; e.g. via an open facade corridor. Equation (S5a) provides a suitable means of calculating the anticipated noise-disturbance level.

■ The evaluation of the potential causes of disturbance can be carried out according to the criteria stated at the beginning (see the section "The effect of sound with an information content"). When the inner facade and the facade intermediate space are open, one can avoid overhearing and understanding information from the adjoining room only when the degree of opening is limited and the noise from external

traffic creates an adequate blanketing sound. One cannot expect intimacy when the windows are open, however.

■ A double-skin facade that has no insulation function against external noise and in which the facade intermediate spaces are open should be subject to critical scrutiny.

■ In view of the fluctuations in external noise levels over a period of time, and in situations where the external noise level is low, the construction of a double-skin facade can result in an acoustic overdimensioning of the external element and an underdimensioning of the internal construction. Even where a double-skin facade does not have to guarantee a specific sound-insulation quality, it will always have a sound-insulating effect, which should not be ignored in respect of the internal constructional components.

4-12 DB Cargo building, Mainz: corridor facade to end face.
Architects: INFRA group, Mainz, in collaboration with RKW, Düsseldorf. Completed in 1998. Adjoining rooms are located acoustically next to a common glazed "balcony". Decreasing levels of external noise result in increased awareness of sound transmissions from room to room.

Opportunities for improved sound insulation and the risks involved

In the context of sound insulation, double-skin facades are complex constructional elements that require very careful planning. They offer advantages, but there are also risks attached to them.

The main advantage is the additional protection they provide against external noise on sites subject to high noise levels. As a result, it may be possible to incorporate window ventilation—in office developments, for example—where this could not otherwise be implemented without exposing the workplaces to unacceptably high noise levels. Whereas window ventilation can be provided in single-skin facades up to a relevant external noise level of ca. 70 dB(A), a properly designed double-skin facade can permit window ventilation up to a relevant external noise level of about 75 dB(A).

Where the noise levels are higher, no known facade system will allow workplaces to be naturally ventilated via the windows. For housing, higher sound-insulation values are required and, depending on the traffic situation (especially at night), the critical external noise levels are likely to be lower. At all events, where a property is subject to noise loads, the sound-insulating effect of the double-skin facade will allow the dimensions of the inner facade to be reduced.

Our knowledge of the sound-insulating effect of non-hermetic external facades has been based hitherto primarily on empirical measurements. Equation (S2) now provides a simple calculating method that allows predictions to be made which may serve as a basis for the planning process. A definition of those areas to which these methods apply and of the relevant input values has already been given, but further empirical and theoretical evaluation is desirable.

Risks are involved when double-skin facades are constructed where they have no insulating function against external noise, since they automatically result in lower background noise levels in the interior spaces. This may mean that increased demands will be made on the internal sound insulation of a building. Where the intermediate space between the facade skins is open, greater attention will have to be paid to the question of sound transmission between rooms. In such cases, a new situation arises within the building, and this may prove problematic in terms of the expectations of users.

Equation (S5a) allows the sound transmission via the facade intermediate spaces to be calculated in relation to the background-noise level. An assessment of the disturbance effect will be necessary especially in respect of the information content of the sounds transmitted between adjoining spaces, although in such cases it is easy for the users to take remedial action themselves by individually operating the windows in the inner facade skin.

The double-skin facade is still a relatively young building component. It affords interesting new scope to planners, among other things, in the realm of acoustic design and the optimization of buildings, provided the overall concept is carefully developed. For acoustic engineers, this form of construction also contains fascinating theoretical aspects that have already been explored, in part, but that also require further investigation.

5   Thermal Insulation

One argument frequently put forward in favor of double-skin facades is that the outer skin provides greater thermal insulation both in summer and winter. The buffer effect, with which one is familiar from conservatories and glazed loggias, can result in a considerable saving of energy. Similarly, it is argued, the facility for accommodating sunshading in a protected position in a well-ventilated intermediate space between the inner and outer skins means that the construction of all-glass facades presents no problems. The authors cannot substantiate these claims without major reservations, however.

It is true that double-skin facades improve the thermal insulation of a building in winter; but this has only a limited effect on heating-energy needs, since current regulations governing thermal insulation in most European countries already ensure an adequate quality for the inner facade layer. The effect may be greater in refurbishment schemes; but even here, a second skin is not as effective as an additional layer of insulation. At best, it can be regarded as a welcome side effect where an outer skin has to be constructed for some other reason.

In summer, a double-skin construction offers certain advantages if the winds acting on a high-rise building or on a particularly exposed situation do not permit external sunshading. An adequately ventilated sunshading system in the intermediate space of the double-skin facade can have almost the same effect as an external installation; and it will be much more efficient than internal sunshading behind solar-control glass. There will, however, be an adverse increase in the temperature of the air required for ventilation in the intermediate space.

A double-skin facade also provides a means of night-time ventilation that is both burglar-proof and protected against the weather. With single-layered facades, this is usually possible only with motor-operated opening lights. Compared with single-layered facades, therefore, the double-skin construction can achieve a comparable degree of thermal insulation in summer; but when two-layered facades are planned with fully glazed inner skins, the cooling loads will increase in proportion to the larger area of glazing.

The airtightness of a facade also contributes to its thermal insulation qualities. With double-skin facades, special conditions arise if the openings in the outer skin are in the form of closable flaps. The combined effect of two sealed layers increases the hermetic quality of the joints of the building, which can lead to a reduction of heating needs especially in high-rise buildings. On the other hand, it can also result in condensation on the inside face of the outer skin if air from the internal spaces with a higher moisture content enters an inadequately ventilated intermediate space between the facade skins. In such cases, it will be necessary to consider what action can be taken; for example, an appropriate reaction of the flap mechanism should be planned, as will be described below.

To provide readers with a quick grasp of the complex processes involved in thermal insulation, the basic concepts of the transport of heat will be described at the outset, together with the most important values in the field of building physics. Elaborating on this information, further aspects will be discussed, from the improvement of thermal insulation in winter to the layout of the heating plant. Simulation calculations show the energy savings that can be achieved by these measures in the course of a year. The effects of thermal insulation in summer are treated in a separate section.

Heat and its transmission

It is not as simple as it may seem to explain the terms "heat" and "temperature" in a generally understandable form, although everyone is familiar with them and has a concept of what they mean. Every substance, whether a solid, liquid or gas, can emit or absorb heat, depending on the temperature of the substances with which it is brought into contact. We have all experienced this. But what is the phenomenon we call "heat", which is perceived in the temperature of a body and which may be stored, liberated, transmitted or lost (wherever it may go)?

In double-skin facades, all kinds of heat-transmission mechanisms come into action simultaneously and overlap with each other. To make these invisible processes more easily comprehensible, it will be necessary initially to look at the constituent atoms.

Atoms form solid bodies, liquids or gases, depending on their cohesive forces. All atoms oscillate backwards and forwards to some extent—except at absolute zero temperature, which lies around -273.15 °C or 0 kelvin. All solids, liquids and gases with temperatures above absolute zero possess an inner heat. This is contained in the oscillations—not visible even under a microscope—of the individual atoms and molecules. As well as the so-called *thermal capacity* of a material, the temperature is also a measure of this innate heat.

In addition, heat can also be bound up in the links between the atoms themselves. This applies, for example, to the melting heat of ice or the vaporizing heat of boiling water. In these cases, one speaks of *latent heat*, since the heat is not continuously absorbed or liberated in relation to the temperature, but is suddenly available at a certain point when the atomic structure breaks up.

The temperature also describes the inclination of the atoms to pass on their heat. If two neighboring atoms have different temperatures, they will oscillate at different rates; and they will have a reciprocal influence on each other until a temperature equilibrium has been attained. The warmer atom will cool down and yield heat to the cooler atom, which, in turn, will heat up. This process will continue until both atoms have the same temperature (and oscillation rates), at which point they will cease to influence each other.

If a body is heated on one side, the atoms on this side will continuously yield heat to their cooler neighbors. If the other side is cooled, no thermal equilibrium can be achieved. Nevertheless, heat will continue to be transmitted from the warmer to the cooler side. In this case, one speaks of *heat conduction*.

Conduction occurs wherever there are neighboring atoms. If the atoms are situated far apart, there will be a low degree of conduction. If the atoms are in close contact with each other (in an undisturbed crystal lattice, for example), high conduction values will occur. For that reason, gases are relatively poor heat conductors, which is why enclosed layers of air provide good thermal insulation. The complete isolation of heat is not possible, though, because a certain amount of heat will always be transmitted when atoms adjoin each other.

In the case of fluids and gases, there is a further mechanism for heat transmission. The atoms are able to move and thus transport their heat to other locations. This process is referred to as *convection*.

Since warmer liquids or gases are usually lighter than cold ones, they rise towards the top of a volume. This phenomenon is known as *free convection* in contrast to *forced convection*, where the movement of the atoms is caused by outside forces such as wind.

Within a pane of insulating double glazing, where different temperatures prevail inside and outside the building, the air in the cavity between the panes of glass will be warmed on one side and cooled on the other. The heated air rises upward, while the cooled air sinks to the bottom. The result is a cyclical motion, whereby the heated molecules of air are initially borne upward before giving off their heat to the cooler pane of glass and sinking again. To reduce this transport of heat through free convection, double glazing units are no longer filled with air nowadays, but with inert gases.

5-1 Left: the principle of conduction, resulting from an exchange of energy between atoms of different temperature.

5-2 Right: the principle of convection, caused by the movement of atoms of different temperature.

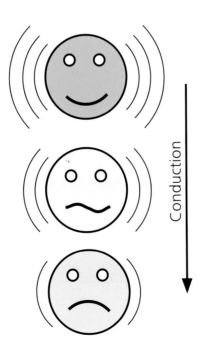

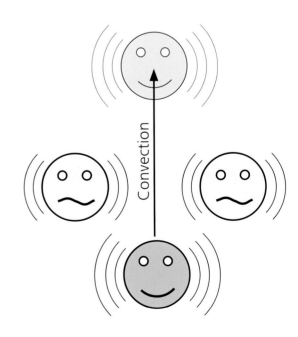

If one wishes to increase the thermal insulation of the glazing even further, a number of intermediate spaces can be created between the panes, so that the heat has to be transported several times by means of convection. This is the case with triple glazing and with so-called "HIT glass". HIT (high-insulation technology) glass is a development in insulating glazing dating from the 1980s: two plastic membranes are inserted into the space between the inner and outer panes of glass, thereby creating three cavities. In an analogous way, the thermal-insulating properties of single-glazed windows can be temporarily improved by stretching a plastic film over the casement frame parallel to the plane of the glass. If the film has a tight seal all round, a closed cavity will be created, and the thermal insulation value will be almost that achieved with insulating double glazing.

In addition to thermal conduction and convection, heat can also be transmitted by *radiation*. Radiation is the only possible form of heat transmission through a vacuum. It is in this form that most of the heat from the sun reaches us; in other words, by means of electromagnetic radiation. This radiation is emitted by all bodies with a temperature above absolute zero; but only above a temperature of about 550 °C is it visible in the form of light. That is the point at which an iron hotplate on an electric cooker will slowly begin to glow red. Objects at a lower temperature emit radiation in the infrared range that is invisible to the human eye. This could be described as "thermal light". The range and distribution of the wavelengths emitted from a body—and especially the shortest, which are also the most energy-intensive ones—will depend on the temperature of that body. This radiation can be measured with special infrared cameras in a process referred to as "thermography". In this way, the surface temperature of a body can be determined without having to make contact with it.

In the visible-light range, different materials have quite different visual characteristics, such as a special color, a shine or a state of transparency. In the infrared range of thermal light, on the other hand, almost all materials appear black, apart from bare metals; in other words, they are wholly absorbent. This quality can be usefully exploited for windows. The *conservatory effect*, to which reference is often made, is based on the fact that glass is permeable to visible light, but largely black in the infrared range. The visible light of the sun can, therefore, pass unimpeded through glass into the internal space beyond, warming the surfaces onto which it falls. These surfaces then yield the heat by various kinds of transmission—in the form of infrared light, for example, which is unable to escape through the window again.

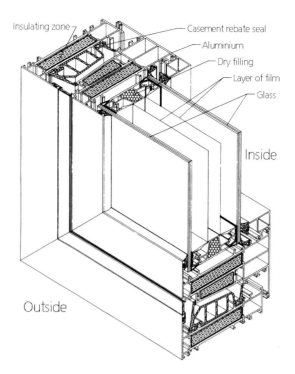

Insulating zone — Casement rebate seal — Aluminium — Dry filling — Layer of film — Glass

Inside

Outside

5-3 Isometric cutaway section through HIT glazing; system developed by Geilinger company, Switzerland.
Parallel to the two panes of glass are two intermediate layers of plastic film, which divide the space into three air cavities.

In the case of *low-E glazing*, one takes this a step further. With the aid of a metallic film applied to the surface of the inner pane, the glass acquires a mirror-like reflecting quality in the infrared range (but not for visible light). As a result, the exchange of heat between the panes by means of radiation is greatly reduced, since mirrors reflect the light that falls on them, but can scarcely emit light themselves. The film-like layer emits little heat and is known as a low-emission or low-E layer. Without technology of this kind to limit the transmission of heat, the development of thermal insulation with ever-improved glazing, as described at the beginning of this book, would not have been possible.

Logically enough, developments have continued in the direction of vacuum glass. By pumping out the gases from the intermediate space of a pane of insulating glazing, a more or less perfect vacuum is created, a void (almost) without atoms. As a result, heat conduction and convection between the panes of glass can scarcely contribute to heat transport any more. This principle has been exploited in solar collectors for some years now, but it has its price. Technically, the main difficulty lies in providing mutual support for the panes of glass, since without a gaseous filling,

5-4 Principle of heat transmission through an exchange of electromagnetic radiation in the infrared light range.

Radiation

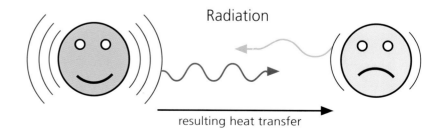

resulting heat transfer

there is no counterpressure internally to the air on the outside. Furthermore, every strut-like supporting member forms a path for heat conduction. This is known as a *thermal bridge*. The degree of thermal insulation that can be attained with vacuum glass is, therefore, still unclear.

Standard values of thermal insulation

To find a simpler approach to the processes of thermal transmission in everyday practice, various standard values are used in building physics, such as the *coefficient of thermal transmission (U-value) in W/m²K*. (The U-value laid down in European standards /T1/ is also known in some countries as the "k-value".)

The U-value describes the transmission of heat through a construction element in relation to the ambient temperature difference on both sides. The entire path traveled by the heat—from the room air into the building component and out again into the air on the other side—is described in terms of the standard value 1/U: the resistance to thermal transmission. This value is obtained by adding all resistances along the path of the heat transmission.

$$1/U = R_{Si} + s/\lambda + ... + R_{Sa} \ \ [m^2K/W] \quad (T\ 1)$$

where
1/U is the resistance to thermal transmission
R_{Si} is the heat-transfer resistance; i.e. the resistance to the transfer of heat from the air in the room to the building component
s/λ is the resistance of the first component layer to heat conduction, resulting from the thickness (s) in [m] of the layer and the conductivity λ in [W/mK] of the material
... is further possible layers of the building component with s/λ or heat transfers R_S; e.g. for a cavity between panes of glass
R_{Sa} is the resistance to the transfer of heat from the building component to the external air.

The outer heat transfer, at least, is characterized by free or forced convection, which is strongly influenced by the air speed on the surface of the component. To calculate the U-value, however, uniform standard values for the heat transfer are used. Although these are determined individually in different countries, the values are broadly similar /T2/. The actual thermal insulation may, therefore, be somewhat better in situations sheltered from the wind or somewhat worse in situations exposed to the wind than the figures obtained with the U-value.

5-5 Construction of typical low-E insulating double glazing. The low-E coating is applied to the inner pane in the cavity between the two layers of glass. In the case of triple glazing, a low-E layer is inserted in both cavities.

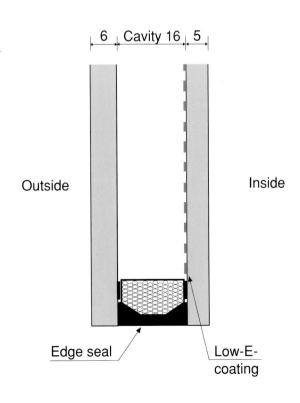

6 | Cavity 16 | 5

Outside

Inside

Edge seal

Low-E-coating

As already described, the thermal insulation provided by multilayer insulating glazing will depend largely on the heat transfer that occurs in the cavity spaces, which is a product of the processes of convection and radiation. In particular, the radiation increases more than proportionally to the difference in temperature. Since the U-values are usually measured with a temperature difference of 10 kelvin, the real thermal transmission for greater temperature differences (30–35 K) will be somewhat less favorable than is indicated by the U-value.

As a result of the additional resistance to thermal transmission in the intermediate space between the layers of a double-skin facade, the effective temperature difference for the pane of glass will be proportionally reduced, so that the thermal transmission also appears proportionally somewhat more favorable. The magnitude of this effect is shown in diagram 5-6 for double and triple low-E glazing. The latter exhibits the same rising characteristics in principle; but because of the two intermediate spaces between the panes of glass, each with a low-E layer, the relevant temperature difference is halved for each cavity.

Depending on the type of building component, special indices are attributed to the U-values: U_{AW}, for example, stands for a wall, and U_w for a window. The latter comprises the effect of the glazing (U_g) and the frame (U_f). For example, U_f = 1.5–1.7 W/m²K is the relevant value for wood and plastic. Good aluminum frames achieve a value of $U_f \approx$ 2.0 W/m²K, followed by typical thermally divided metal frames with $U_f \leq$ 2.8 W/m²K. Since modern low-E glazing provides a better degree of thermal insulation than all standard frame materials, the U_w-value of windows today is, as a rule, worse (greater) than the U_g-value of the glazing.

Windows and glazing are transparent building elements, so that, in addition to the thermal insulation qualities defined by the U-value, permeability to light and solar heat gain are important. These properties are described by the so-called τ_L-value for light transmittance (measured in the daylight range /T5/) and the total energy transmission factor g /T4/ for heat gains. The g-value includes not only the directly transmitted element of insolation, but also the so-called secondary thermal yield, which can be caused by a heating-up of the sunshading or the panes of glass. Heat gains in the facade intermediate space also lead indirectly—via the U-value of the inner facade layer—to a secondary yield, which forms part of the g-value.

The g-value and the τ_L-value are given as percentages and are related to the respective insolation of the sun. Both values are dependent on the optical properties of the glass and the angle of incidence of the sun; they decrease with the flatness of the angle of incidence, since the reflected proportion of light increases. As standard values, however, they are always based on an incidence of light at right angles to the pane of glass /T4, T5, T6/ and applied in this form in calculations.

For a description of the reciprocal effects of heat loss and heat gain through a window, the expression equivalent thermal-transmission coefficient U_{eq} has been introduced in certain regulations covering thermal insulation /T11/ but is not used anymore in modern European standards. The coefficient is calculated by deducting a certain proportion from the thermal transmission values for solar gains (in relation to the g-value) during the heating period. The U_{eq}-value is thus a fictitious calculating value in the context of the annual energy requirements, forming part of the calculating process laid down in some thermal insulation regulations. As such it cannot actually be measured in a building.

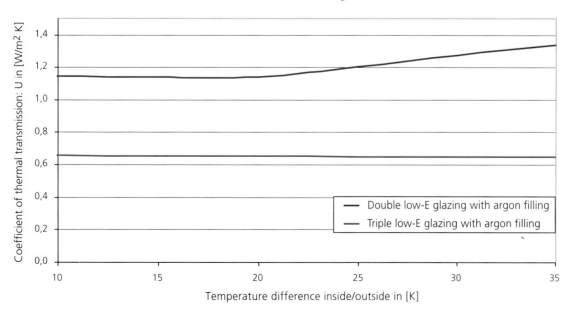

5-6 Relation between U_g-value and temperature difference between inside and outside.

In accordance with its function, *sunscreen or solar-control glazing* has specially low g-values. In the past, this automatically implied a great reduction in the transmission of light as well, and a more or less strong coloration. In the mid-1990s, so-called "neutral" solar-control glass types were developed. Through a combination of functional principles, they achieve low g-values and a high degree of light transmission. The phenomenon is referred to as *selectivity* and describes the relation between light transmission τ_L and the g-value. Glass types with a great selectivity attain values of up to almost 2.0, which means that practically only the visible portion (approx. 47%) of the daylight is allowed to enter, while infrared thermal radiation is largely filtered out. Typical standard values for neutral solar-control glass are $\tau_L \geq 60\%$ (for light transmission) with a total energy transmission factor of $g \leq 40\%$.

5-7 Relation between degree of solar heat transmission and angle of incidence of sun to the outer pane of glass.
In comparison with the nominal light transmission of the outer pane (ca. 85% where the incidence of light is at right angles to the glazing), the measured values for the west face reveal considerably lower energy gains, despite the low elevation of the sun.

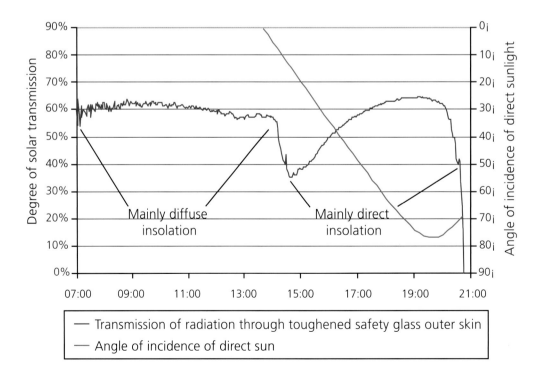

All tightly sealed?

The definition of the U-value as a measure of thermal gains or losses implies a well-sealed form of construction for the facades. If there is some degree of permeability, additional losses will occur as a result of convective heat transmission. This corresponds to the thermal transmission through a window opened for ventilation purposes, through which warm air can escape in winter and unwanted warm air can enter the internal spaces in summer. In addition to the concept of heat losses as a result of thermal conduction in the closed elements of a building, thermal-insulation regulations also include the term "ventilation heat loss". As a rule, though, this does not include losses through poorly sealed joints, cracks, etc.

For losses through the latter, building regulations /T7, T8/ provide only general overall requirements; for example, in the form of so-called *joint permeability coefficients a*, which are given for a unit of one linear meter (of window sealing). Technically feasible a-values for single-skin facades in modern forms of construction can be assumed at around
$a \approx 0.5$ [m³/(h m (daPa)$^{2/3}$] for opening lights, and
$a \approx 0.1$ [m³/(h m (daPa)$^{2/3}$] for joints in fixed glazing.

The significance of the permeability of joints is shown in diagram 5-8 below. This describes the heat losses through a window in terms of the U-value plus the heat losses through the peripheral joints (for a window 1.2 m wide x 2 m high) and in relation to wind speed and the a-value of the joints. It should be noted that the mean wind speed in moderate climatic zones in Europe, for example, lies predominantly between 2.5 and 4.5 m/s, so that the effective thermal insulation of a window may be limited if it is exposed to wind.

These additional heat losses also have to be taken into account in planning the heating installation /T10/. Related standards may use the a-values given in the unit [m³/(h m (Pa)$^{2/3}$], instead of [m³/(h m (daPa)$^{2/3}$] as in thermal insulation regulations. In the denominator, the factor *decca*$^{2/3}$ is therefore missing (= 10$^{2/3}$). If one compares the German standard values for joint permeability given in different regulations with varying units, one will see that the factor 0.3 was used for the conversion (not the mathematical factor $1/10^{2/3} = 0.215$). The authors of these standards evidently erred on the side of safety here in determining the heating demand, and also provided a simpler factor for the conversion.

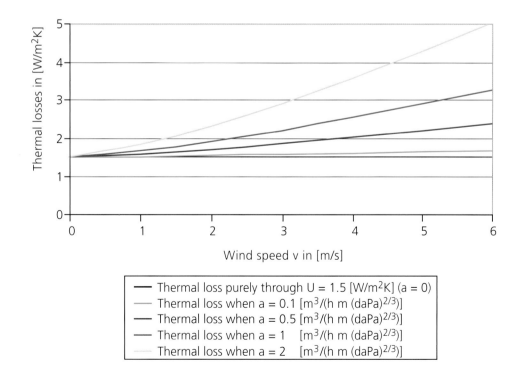

5-8 Heat losses resulting from thermal transmission (corresponding to U-value) and from ventilation through non-airtight joints (corresponding to a-value).
The mean annual wind speed in central Europe and similar continental areas is between 2.5 and 4.5 m/s at a height of 10 m above ground level. A relative pressure difference of $\Delta cp = 1.3$ was assumed for the calculation; in other words, the example window was subject to the full wind pressure.

— Thermal loss purely through U = 1.5 [W/m²K] (a = 0)
— Thermal loss when a = 0.1 [m³/(h m (daPa)$^{2/3}$)]
— Thermal loss when a = 0.5 [m³/(h m (daPa)$^{2/3}$)]
— Thermal loss when a = 1　[m³/(h m (daPa)$^{2/3}$)]
— Thermal loss when a = 2　[m³/(h m (daPa)$^{2/3}$)]

Thermal insulation in winter

Improving the thermal transmission coefficient U

In calculating the improved U-value of a double-skin facade (compared with the inner skin alone without an outer layer and rear-vented cavity), one is tempted to apply a greater *external heat transfer resistance value R_{Sa}* (R_{Sa} = 0.08 m²K/W instead of R_{Sa} = 0.04 m²K/W), as appropriate for rear-ventilated cladding. This would seem to be only logical, since an external facade layer represents an additional protection against rain and wind, and it forms a barrier against heat emissions through radiation when the sky is clear. In calculating the equivalent U-value (U_{eq}) /T11/, the additional outer pane of glass certainly results in a lower total energy transmission factor g for the double-skin facade as well. In conjunction with the scarcely improved U-value, the Ueq-value for a permanently ventilated facade intermediate space will, in part, be poorer than that for a single-skin facade. The results will be somewhat better where the intermediate space can be closed. If the ventilation concept requires the facade to remain closed for a large part of the heating period (with the provision of alternative mechanical ventilation), a special bonus for the "closed glazed extensions" might be claimed when calculating annual heating demands /T11/, thereby taking into account solar gains and the conservatory effect of a closed facade. For an outer skin in single glazing, this permits the previously calculated U_{eq}-value to be reduced by a fixed amount (e.g. 30 percent. The conditions obtaining with and without a closable outer skin are shown in diagram 5-9 for different points of the compass.

To provide a comparison, the authors have carried out simulations for thermal transmission through all-glass double-skin facades in a number of different situations. The simulations showed that the specification of a higher heat-transfer resistance R_{Sa} is justified even for permanently ventilated facade spaces. Calculations yield a value of R_{Sa} = 0.10 m²K/W for a facade outer skin with a permanently ventilated space to the rear, with a 10% opening area (5% air-intake; 5% air-extract) and with story-for-story divisions of the intermediate space. If the proportion of the opening area is increased to 25%, the improved thermal-insulation values will be lost. In other words, there is a critical limit to the opening area. The improvement of the U-value of a well-insulated apron panel is also negligible. The improvement of the U-value for window areas has also been confirmed by research carried out in Switzerland /T12/. The findings show that for different forms of glazing to the inner facade layer and different air-circulation heights in the intermediate space, improvements of the thermal resistance values of about 0.06 to 0.09 m²K/W can be achieved for the same sizes of window opening; in other words, R_{Sa} = 0.10–0.13 m²K/W. Under optimum conditions, using triple glazing, this means an improvement from U_w = 1.20 W/m²K to U_w = 1.08 W/m²K. For conventional low-E double glazing, the authors have calculated an improvement from U_w = 1.50 W/m²K to U_w = 1.38 W/m²K. The relative values are shown in diagram 5-10.

In the case of a facade intermediate space that can be closed, the Swiss study assumes a reduction of only the air-extract area by about 90%. This results in an improvement in the resistance to thermal transmission of between 0.09 and 0.16 m²K/W, which would corre-

5-9 Equivalent U-value as defined in the thermal insulation regulations currently valid in Germany /T16/, dating from 1995. The coefficient of thermal transmission for a single-skin facade or for the inner layer of a double-skin facade is U_w = 1.5 W/m²K.

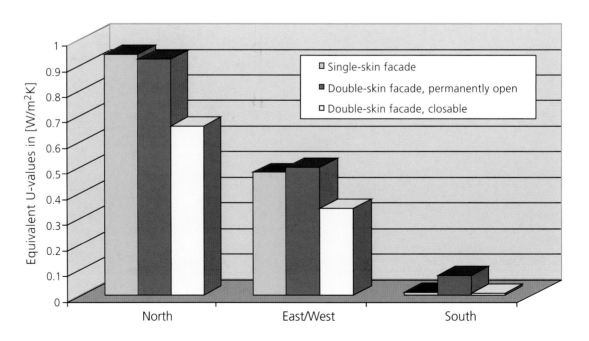

spond to a simple, not particularly airtight flap in the air-extract opening. In view of the remaining 10% of the air-extract area, the flap could remain closed for the entire heating period if only to maximize solar gains. A flap of this kind could be operated by hand twice a year. The improvement achieved with a triple-skin facade is expressed in the value $U_W = 1.0$ W/m^{2}K instead of $U_W = 1.2$ W/m^{2}K without the outer skin. In the case of sealed air-intake and air-extract areas with a residual permeability of around 0.7% of the original openings (e.g. as a result of drainage holes), the authors calculated improvements in the resistance to thermal transmission of roughly 0.20 m^{2}K/W where there were low external temperatures. For the situation described above, low-E double-glazing would achieve an improvement from $U_W = 1.50$ W/m^{2}K to $U_W = 1.10$ W/m^{2}K. With triple glazing, a value of $U_W \approx 0.95$ W/m^{2}K could be expected instead of $U_W = 1.20$ W/m^{2}K.

This is consistent with theoretical calculations of convectional heat transfer and radiation in accordance with /T13/, which give a resistance to thermal transmission for the facade intermediate space of roughly 0.22 m^{2}K/W for these situations. It is interesting to note that the heat transfer resulting from free convection through the circulation of air within the closed facade space is virtually independent of the depth of this space. The heat exchange through radiation α_r, on the other hand, is a dominant factor at roughly 3.5 W/m^{2}K for normal panes of glass. Only when a low-E layer is used, is this value perceptibly reduced (by 2.5–3 W/m^{2}K). Since this low-E layer would be subject to the usual soiling and would require cleaning if applied to an exposed surface, its effectiveness and ultimately its durability would probably be seriously impaired. Furthermore, reducing the heat transfer to this extent would increase the danger of condensation on the outer pane, as will be described below.

Standards applying thermal insulation (see /T14/) also describe the effect of static layers of air. For an air layer 20–500 mm deep (cavity depth), a constant improvement of the resistance to thermal transmission of 0.17 m^{2}K/W is usually given. This is wholly consistent with the knowledge that the depth of the static air layer has only a minor influence on the heat exchange resulting from radiation and convection. As an indication of the improvement of thermal insulation through a closed facade space, this value lies on the safe side in comparison with calculated values. Its application need not be restricted to facade depths of up to 500 mm, though, as diagram 5-11 shows.

The standard values for thermal insulation provided by rear-ventilated external skins and static layers of air would also seem appropriate when dimensioning the heating surfaces behind double-skin facades. On the one hand, these values take account of the tendency to improved values mentioned above; on the other hand they still contain a certain safety margin compared with the calculated values. This safety margin may allow for fluctuations resulting from different forms of construction. Nevertheless, with a permanent opening area in the outer skin of 20% or more, one can no longer speak of a rear-ventilated layer, since the wind penetration will increase considerably. The same applies to corridor and multistory facades where the size and distribution of permanent openings in the outer skin facilitate a cross-ventilation of the space between the facade layers.

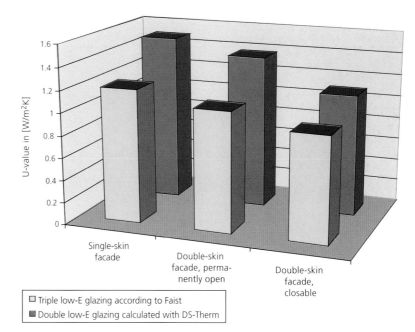

5-10 Improvement of U_W-values for low-E double and triple glazing with ventilated and closable facade intermediate spaces.

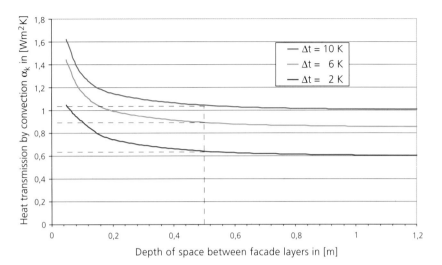

5-11 Reduction of convective heat transfer α_c with increase in width of gap (vertical gap). Together with the heat exchange that occurs through radiation α_r, amounting to 3.5 W/m²K, there is a resultant heat-transfer resistance of $R_{S,fis} = 0.22{-}0.27$ m²K/W.

5-12 Location of measurement sensors in facade of debis headquarters, Berlin.

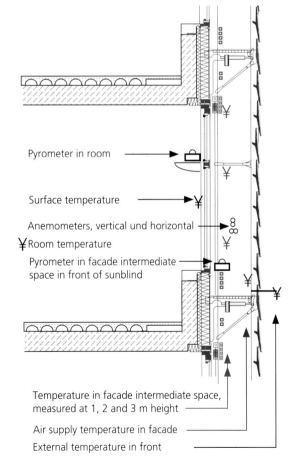

Pyrometer in room

Surface temperature

Anemometers, vertical und horizontal

¥ Room temperature

Pyrometer in facade intermediate space in front of sunblind

Temperature in facade intermediate space, measured at 1, 2 and 3 m height

Air supply temperature in facade

External temperature in front

Measured data in winter: debis headquarters at Potsdamer Platz, Berlin

The debis headquarters will be discussed in detail in the chapter dealing with "Air Conditioning". In the present discussion of thermal insulation, however, it is the temperature data that are of interest. They were measured during the first and second weeks in February 1999 (from Friday, 1/29, to Friday, 2/12—at midday in each case) in the corridor facade on the 15th story at a height of roughly 50 m. Illustration 5-12 shows the positions of the points of measurement in the facade.

Illustration 5-13 shows the external temperatures, the temperatures in the intermediate space (at a height of 2 m), the room temperatures and the surface temperatures internally on the facade posts—all measured during the first week. Reflecting daytime operations and the night-time reduction of the heating, the room temperature fluctuates around a mean value of 20 °C. The aluminum facade posts reveal what appear to be low surface temperatures (12–15 °C); but if one converts these back to the U-value, frame values of roughly $U_f = 2.0$ W/m²K are obtained (including the effect of the double-skin facade), which is good in relation to what is technically possible.

Illustration 5-15 gives a more precise picture of the related temperature curve within the facade. The excess temperatures in relation to the external air were plotted for various positions within the facade cavity. The external, scale-like louvers were kept closed during the period of measurement; but a residual open joint area of 2 to 3% of the elevational area may be assumed as a principle of the construction. The sun-shading system was not activated. The effect of the mainly diffuse solar radiation shown in ill. 5-14 was marginal. The fluctuations in external temperatures were the outcome solely of weather conditions, with the passage of cold and warm air masses.

One striking feature of these graphs, however, is the reduction of excess temperatures in the facade cavity as a result of wind action. Illustration 5-16 shows the horizontal wind-induced and the vertical thermally-induced airflow speeds in the facade corridor during the first week. During the first day or two, the vertical velocity remained at a level of between 0.15 and 0.3 m/s. These airflow speeds were caused by the uplift effect of the heated air next to the inner face. With falling external temperatures, this led to an increasing penetration of air through unsealed openings in the skin. At the same time, considerably greater wind-induced currents occurred in a horizontal direction. If these fluctuate around a mean value of roughly 0.5 m/s, an air-temperature stratification of 2 to 3 kelvin over the height of the facade is still possible. If the intensity of the wind increases, causing

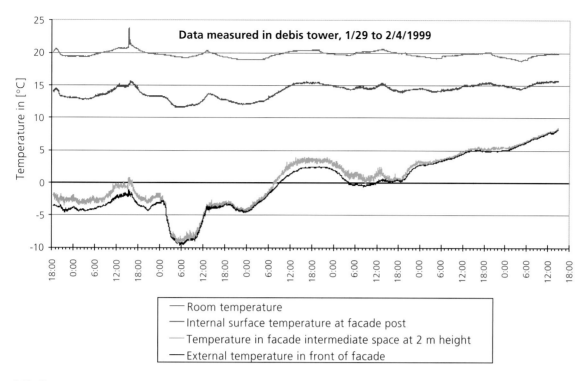

Room temperature
Internal surface temperature at facade post
Temperature in facade intermediate space at 2 m height
External temperature in front of facade

5-13 Above: temperatures internally; in facade intermediate space; and externally.

5-14 Below: insolation in double-skin facade. The sky was overcast for the whole week.

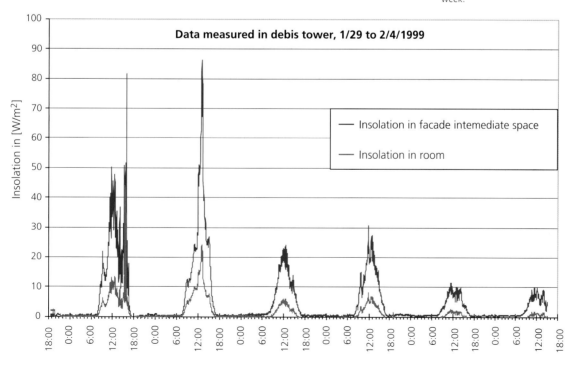

Insolation in facade intemediate space

Insolation in room

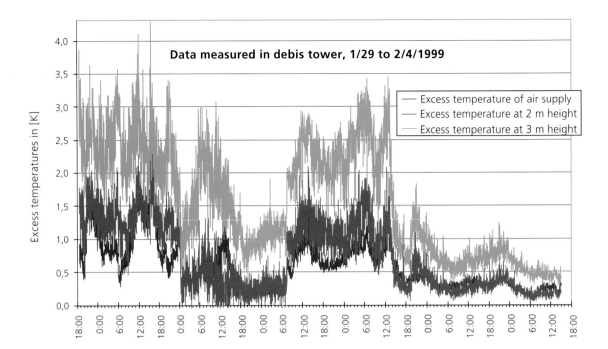

5-15 Excess temperatures in facade intermediate space, calculated in relation to external air temperatures outside facade.

5-16 Horizontal and vertical air speeds in facade corridor.

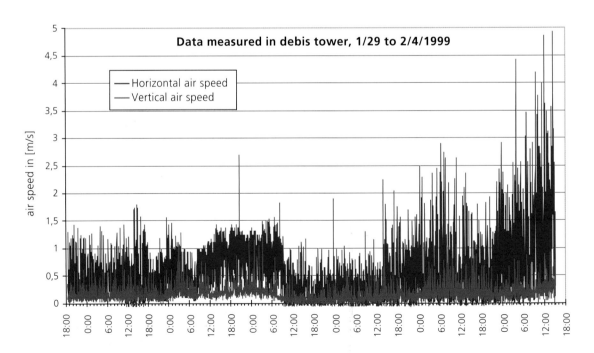

airflow speeds of about 1 m/s or higher in the facade space, the stratification will collapse to around 1 K, as may be seen especially during the last days of the first week.

On a number of days during the second week, the sun broke through and warmed the west-facing facade in the afternoon. Again, the sunshading installation was not activated, since the room in question was not occupied. Analogously to illustration 5-13, figure 5-17 provides a graph of the internal and external temperatures for the second week. During the second half of this week, the weather became colder, but the sky was clearer, so that the sun caused a periodic increase in temperature of around 5 to 10 degrees.

Illustration 5-18 shows the insolation measured for this period. Of special interest is the heating-up of the room behind the facade, a process that lags somewhat behind the heating of the facade itself. The internal surface temperature of the facade is evidently influenced not so much by the increasing room temperature as by the insolation absorbed through the outer face.

In comparison, illustration 5-19 shows the excess temperatures in the facade space. These rise temporarily quite steeply as a result of the insolation absorbed over the closed areas of the facade (apron panels, posts, rails, etc.), but they also sink relatively quickly again. A special feature of the facade design is the incorporation of clay pipes, which provide a number of thermal-storage elements in the intermediate space.

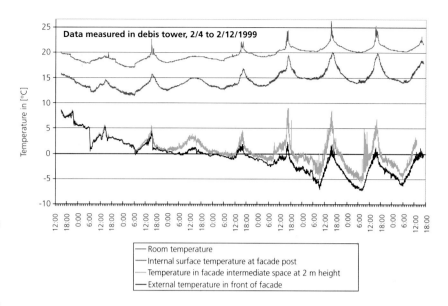

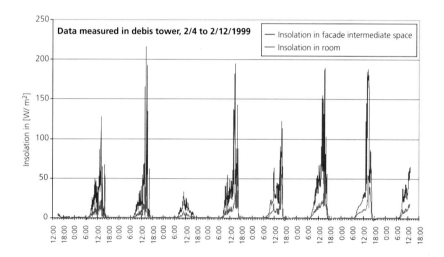

5-17 Top: temperatures externally; in facade intermediate space; and internally —measured in second week in February.

5-18 Center: insolation in facade intermediate space.

5-19 Bottom: excess temperatures in facade intermediate space.

The second week was sunnier than the first.

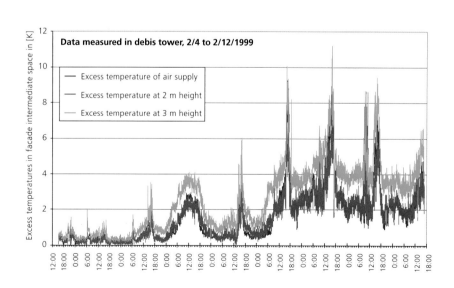

Improving the thermal transmission coefficient U

Improving the sealing quality

In planning heating installations and determining the head loads for each room, heat losses resulting from ventilation play a major role, especially in tall buildings. As proof of adequate thermal insulation, however, only overall requirements apply, which well-built facades may undercut by about 50% at present. If, instead of the standard values contained for example in DIN 4701 for the coefficient of permeability of the joints $a = 0.3$ m³/(h m (Pa)²/³), one applies values that are technically feasible today using closable casement lights at $a = 0.15$ m³/(h m (Pa)²/³), the heat losses resulting from ventilation through joints can be halved. Furthermore, a high sealing quality can be achieved with the closable openings in the external facade, so that the resistance to heat losses through ventilation is cumulative.

Calculations made in accordance with the relevant standards and guidelines to ascertain the combined effect of the two sealed facade skins will initially have to determine the specific volume of airflow leakage $\dot{V}$ through the joints of the inner and the outer facade skins separately. This is achieved by multiplying the coefficients of permeability of the joints by the length of the joints:

$$\dot{V}_{joint} = \Sigma\,(a_i \bullet l_i) \quad [\text{m}^3/\text{h (Pa)}^{2/3}] \quad (\text{T 2})$$

If the specific airflow volume $\dot{V}$ for the inner and outer facade layers is the same, the double resistance value will represent a maximum improvement in impermeability. Illustration 5-20 shows the relationship between the resultant specific overall airflow volume and the specific volume flow through the inner facade layer, which is dependent, in turn, on the relationship between the specific airflow volumes internally and externally. This is obtained from the division of the motive pressure difference acting on the two facade planes. Since the specific coefficients of joint permeability and the specific airflow volume are dependent on the active pressure to the power of two-thirds, the specific overall airflow volume will not be simply halved, but halved to the power of two-thirds. In general, one can formulate this for the specific overall volume flow as follows:

$$\dot{V}_{joint,res} = \cfrac{1}{\left[\cfrac{1}{(\Sigma(a_i \bullet l_i))^{3/2}} + \cfrac{1}{(\Sigma(a_i \bullet l_i))^{3/2}}\right]^{2/3}} \quad \begin{array}{l}[\text{m}^3/\text{h (Pa)}^{2/3}]\\ (\text{T 3})\end{array}$$

When calculating the specific airflow volume in accordance with equation (T 3), point sources of permeability, such as drainage holes, will have to be assessed, particularly with respect to the outer skin. Strictly speaking, a calculation of the airflow should be made for each point of pressure difference. But if one wishes to obtain a pressure-related value to the power of two-thirds (analogous to the a-values), it will be necessary to take account of small pressure differences (e.g. 10 Pa), since a coefficient of permeability of the source point, derived from the area with openings, will diminish with increasing pressure. Based on the system of a-values used in many standards, e.g. /T7, T8/, a basic value can be obtained for small holes (up to a few millimeters in diameter) as follows:
$a_{opening} \approx 0.015$ m³/(h mm² (daPa)²/³).

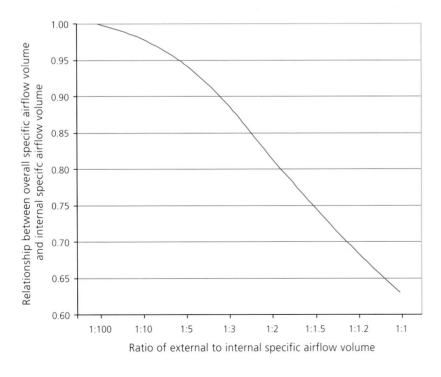

5-20 Reduction of permeability of joints for double-skin facade as a whole compared with impermeability of inner layer alone; expressed as a relationship between external and internal impermeability.

Condensation in the facade cavity

If a closable facade has too tight a seal, condensation can form on the inside face of the external skin for more than just short periods. This can impair the view through the facade in both directions, as if a pane of translucent glass had been installed in the outer skin. The effect is undesirable for a number of reasons, however, not just because of the visual disturbance it causes and the interruption of contact with the outside world. In this section, the factors influencing the formation of condensation will be described, and planning recommendations made.

In principle, condensation can form in the cavity space during the cold periods of the year—independently of the ventilation—when humid air from the internal spaces comes into contact with surfaces whose temperatures lie beneath the dew point of the humid air. The dew point, or rather the dew-point temperature, describes the air temperature at which the moisture contained in the air corresponds precisely with the maximum moisture-absorption capacity of the air; i.e. when the air is saturated with moisture or has a relative humidity of 100 percent. If the air is cooled below this dew point, moisture is precipitated in the form of rain, mist, condensation or frost.

A single-glazed outer facade skin can cool down quite rapidly at night if efficient thermal insulation in the inner facade layer prevents virtually any heat escaping from the building to the outer face and if, at the same time, there is a clear night sky and wind or radiation result in great heat losses. (The temperature of the night sky—i.e. the upper layer of the atmosphere—can easily be 10–20 kelvin cooler than the air surrounding the building.) In the experience of the authors, in such cases, no condensation or frost will be formed on the outer face of the facade—in contrast to the phenomenon observed with cars on clear nights. Evidently the small amounts of heat emitted from buildings are sufficient to prevent the outer skin cooling below the dew point of the external air. Noteworthy, too, is the fact that horizontal surfaces in the surrounding area cool down much more quickly, and moisture is precipitated there before the facade reaches a critical temperature.

The situation is different when humid air from the rooms escapes into the intermediate space between the facade layers. This can occur with intermittent ventilation: when the natural moisture emitted by people during a conference, for example (on average, ca. 50 g per hour per person), is absorbed by the air in the room, and this suddenly escapes through the window into the intermediate space. Humid air can also be produced by a moisturizing facility in the mechanical ventilation system, which may be recommended, for example, to avoid dry room air in winter.

This humid air has a tendency to rise in the intermediate space of the facade. If the space is well ventilated, the stream of moist air will escape quickly, and precipitation will occur on the outer face only in extreme cases. As a rule, this will be a local phenomenon, and any condensation will dry out relatively quickly (see ill. 5-21). As mentioned above, though, the situation will be somewhat different where a facade can be closed and where there is only a minimum degree of ventilation through the residual permeability of the joints. In such cases, the humid air will be unable to escape freely. It will cool down in its entirety, and the moisture it contains will be precipitated in large part on the cold surfaces; i.e. mainly on the inner face of the outer skin (cf. ill. 5-22). This may result in condensation over large areas or indeed over the whole surface, since the moisture will be unable to escape at the top via an upward current and will be distributed over the entire intermediate space.

Once condensation has occurred—most commonly in the early hours of the morning before solar radiation can warm the facade—it may take hours before the surface has dried completely. This can be explained in part by the latent heat of the water which is liberated in the formation of condensation (i.e. in the transition from a gaseous to a liquid state) and which has to be reintroduced before the moisture can evaporate. If the condensation were to run off, the amount of

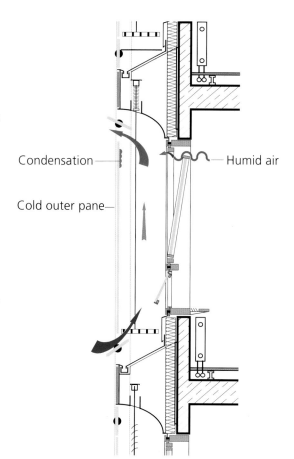

Condensation

Cold outer pane

Humid air

5-21 Route taken by moist room air when the facade intermediate space is ventilated.

water on the facade skin would be reduced, thereby shortening the drying process; but this rarely happens: it would require a very large amount of condensation; in other words, the moisture would have to form droplets large enough to run down the panes of glass.

Once condensation has formed in the early hours of the morning, the heat liberated will usually be immediately transferred to the cold surroundings. The sun will first have to restore the heat necessary for evaporation and also heat up the facade cavity sufficiently for the air to be able to reabsorb the moisture. The second part of this process can be accelerated somewhat if the flaps in the outer facade skin are opened and dry, cold air is admitted. This, however, will slow down the heat intake necessary for evaporation. In terms of thermal insulation, the question arises whether a longer period of ventilation of the facade space—which has been closed to save energy—is acceptable.

In the opinion of the authors, any increase in the moisture content of the air in the internal rooms should be restricted to a necessary minimum. In this context, the external temperature can be taken as a reference for the critical dew-point temperature of the air supply. If heavy condensation is nevertheless repeatedly observed, the source of the moisture should first be clarified. If the moisture source is permanent and unavoidable—for example, through a special use

of the rooms—it may be necessary to open the outer flaps. To avoid condensation, it will be adequate, as a rule, to open the flaps before operations start within the building (i.e. after the preheating of the rooms in the morning) and to leave them open until shortly after sunrise.

For psychological reasons, it would be inappropriate simply to require users to keep the windows closed, and it would probably not be possible to implement this either. Experience shows that users become accustomed to window ventilation to such an extent that they are not consciously aware of the outer facade being closed. When the window in the inner skin is opened, there is always a supply of cool—and presumably fresh—air entering the room. A number of temporarily opened windows in corridor and multistory facades do not play the same role in the overall moisture balance of the intermediate space as they do with box-type windows. In the latter case, however, a user receives direct feedback on personal behavior if the view out of his or her own window is suddenly restricted through condensation on the glass.

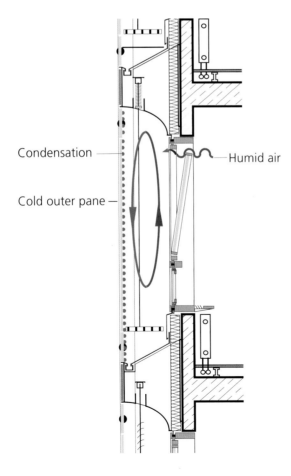

5-22 Route taken by moist room air when the facade intermediate space is closed.

Condensation

Humid air

Cold outer pane

Surface temperatures and thermal comfort

An important argument in connection with closable outer facades and alternative concepts of air-conditioning without radiators in front of windows is the improvement of thermal comfort by means of high surface temperatures along the facade. This is related to the human perception of temperature.

The specific heat of the human body (body heat), means that man is unable to measure the temperature of his surroundings objectively. He simply feels the change of skin temperature caused by heat losses or gains. *Perceived temperature*, as this phenomenon is known, is a product of the air temperature and the temperatures of the surrounding surfaces; and it is, in turn, dependent on the proportions of thermal transmission involved. The perceived temperature is influenced by personal clothing and by the airflow speed and turbulence of the surrounding air (since these enhance the process of heat transfer by convection). These should be compared with the factors that determine sensations of comfort and the relevant standards relating to this subject, as described in the chapter on "Aerophysics".

Through the phenomenon of thermal radiation, the surrounding surfaces have a considerable influence on a person's overall perception of temperatures. In rooms where the surface temperatures of walls and ceilings are low, human beings react unconsciously to these influences by turning up the heating and thus increasing the air temperature. Conversely, high surface temperatures may create a sensation of comfort, even where the air temperatures are low. The coldest wall of a room will usually be the facade, and in particular the windows and glazed areas. An improvement in their U-value, therefore, will have a noticeable effect on the perceived temperature.

A further aspect of comfort is the so-called *radiation temperature asymmetry*. Colder surfaces on one side of a room are less pleasant to the user than generally low room temperatures. Thermal losses on one side are perceived by users as drafts, although these are not necessarily the result of air movements. In this case, they are caused by radiant heat exchange. This phenomenon occurs not only in conjunction with cold facades, but also where the floor or ceiling is too cool. The temperature difference in the front and rear (or upper and lower) halves of a space can be measured with so-called "globe thermometers". Some standards specify limits for this (see /T18/). Differences of more than 8 kelvin horizontally and 3.5 kelvin vertically are regarded as critical and, indeed, unacceptable if prolonged.

Facade surface temperatures $t_{O,i}$ are calculated from an initial approximation based on the U-value and the temperature difference between the room air and the external air. The formula for this is:

$$t_{O,i} = t_i - (t_i - t_a)\, U_w \bullet R_{Si}\ [°C] \quad (T\ 4)$$

where

t_i is the room air temperature or the temperature of the air on the room face of the facade in [°C]
t_a is the external temperature in [°C]
U_w is the U-value of the facade in [W/m²K]
R_{Si} is the resistance to heat transfer from the inner facade to the room in [m²K/W].

In Germany the resistance to heat transfer from an inner wall to a room is assumed to be $R_{Si} = 0.13$ m²K/W, and standards in other countries provide similar figures. Equation (T 4) is relevant only in cases where the thermal transmission through the facade is largely dependent on the room air temperature. Where the U-values exceed ca. 2.0 W/m²K—the standard for windows until only a few years ago and the actual state in most buildings today—this will result in extremely low surface temperatures: down to values below 12 °C. Even today, this phenomenon can occur in the area of the window frames and especially where thermally divided metal frames are used (typically $U_f = 2.0$–2.8 W/m²K). The debis headquarters at Potsdamer Platz described earlier in this chapter (ill. 5-13) is an example of this. For that reason, it would have been unthinkable to omit radiators beneath the windows, since they ensure a high level of thermal transmittance to the window: the resulting veil of warm air in front of the panes of glass has a considerably higher temperature than the room air, thereby increasing the surface temperature.

The excellent U-values of present-day glazing and facades have ameliorated this problem to some extent. With U_w values of 1.0 to 1.5 W/m²K, the mean surface temperatures will not be below 13–15 °C where there is a temperature gradient of -15 °C externally and +20 °C internally. Nevertheless, opinions are divided on the question of whether radiators can be omitted in front of windows. In this context, see also the discussion in the chapter on "Air-Conditioning" and the example given there, with high surface temperatures in conjunction with a heating soffit.

The controversy over whether it is possible to do without radiators beneath windows is related to the phenomenon of cold-air drop, among other things. Cold-air drop occurs as a result of normal convectional air currents passing over a surface that is colder than the air temperature. The air gives off heat to the surface and cools down in the process, thereby becoming heavier and sinking downwards. Depending on the height and the temperature of the cold surface, a large volume of air can be set in motion at a considerable speed as a result of cold-air drop. With 2- to 3-meter-high windows, this will not be a major problem if there is a radiator beneath the window; for this creates a warm current of air that counteracts the cold falling air. The situation is different in multi-story facades (e.g. in halls), where a radiator at the foot of the facade will usually not be adequate to stop the descending current of cold air. The latter will flow over the warm-air current from the radiator in a step-like form. In such cases, heat sources will have to be distributed over the height of the facade; for example, by heating the window frames.

If the radiator beneath the window is omitted altogether or is installed in only every second bay, the cold-air drop will possibly reach the floor, even where the windows are only 2–3 meters high. This will then cause cold-air currents in the room, and these will affect the degree of comfort. The effect will usually be perceived in the form of cold feet and drafts around the legs, caused by the low temperature of the cold-air current itself and the greater thermal transfer resulting from the increased air speed over the skin.

Heating-energy and heating-power requirements
The preceding sections contain a description of how and to what extent a double-skin facade can improve the thermal insulation within the facade itself. These aspects, as well as the question of increased impermeability of the facade (especially in the case of high-rise buildings), are contained in regulations governing heating needs. This will not lead to a proportional reduction in the dimensions of the heating system, however—a factor that would be of economic relevance—since radiators, boilers and pipe runs are available only in sizes based on larger incremental steps.

Using the simplest procedure for calculating the annual heating-energy requirements of a building (the multiplication of the thermal needs by the number of hours of "full use", as described, for example, in the German guideline VDI 2067 /T15/), the reduction of the thermal needs will be reflected in linear form in the estimated annual heating-energy requirements. The energy savings that may be expected in terms of room heating would then be, like the thermal needs, less than 10 percent in most cases.

The calculating method laid down in the European standard EN 832 /T17/ follows a similar procedure. In this process, the heat losses through the outer skin in relation to the U-values of the individual surface areas are added and set off against the ventilation heat losses, solar gains and internal loads. Using given factors, these heat losses and gains are projected to obtain the annual heating needs. Solar gains are either calculated with U_{eq}-values (as described at the beginning); or the figures for all the individual transparent areas are added together. Valid thermal insulation regulations take account of radiation gains from direct and diffuse insolation. For different facade aspects, therefore, there will be different solar gains as well as a prescribed upper limit, since overheating behind large areas of glazing does not result in energy savings. This method does not take account of factors such as the impermeability of the facade or local conditions. The method of calculating thermal losses through ventilation differentiates between only a small range of situations and does not cover different ventilation strategies in office and commercial developments. A detailed estimate of the actual energy needs cannot be expected, therefore. The method is nevertheless well suited to comparing alternative forms of thermal insulation in standard situations where there are few special constraints.

To obtain a more realistic estimate of the annual energy needs of a building, dynamic computer simulations made for a yearly cycle are useful. These calculations usually take the hour weather data of so-called "test reference years" (TRY or TRD) provided by local meteorological authorities as a uniform basis.

Calculations based on thermal simulation provide a picture of the behavior of buildings or sections of buildings in respect of room temperatures and thermal currents from room to room as well as between the rooms and the surroundings, taking account of all important physical parameters. This method reflects the use that is generally defined according to daily, weekly and annual profiles. Individual rooms or sequences of similar rooms grouped into zones are assumed to have uniform temperatures. The various thermal currents originating from the surroundings, from the air-conditioning or from the reciprocal action between neighboring rooms and zones all have an influence on these temperatures. Constructional dividing elements, such as walls and floors, form a barrier to these thermal currents and are also capable of storing heat. In principle, therefore, very precise estimates of both the temperature behavior and the heating- and cooling-energy needs are possible. A large number of contingent factors will have to be clarified first, however, if all the processes involved are to be adequately assessed. Deviations may also occur if, for example, for purposes of simplification, only individual rooms are considered or if the reciprocal effects occurring within a building are ignored.

To ensure maximum comparability between the results of the various simulation programs available, a series of tests was compiled within the scope of the German guideline VDI 6020 /T18/. These were designed to examine and evaluate the main characteristics of the programs and to test the results obtained. In this context, the simulation program DS-Therm /T19/ used in preparing this book was also investigated and revalidated, having proved its efficiency in practice over a period of 15 years.

A special problem arises in the case of double-skin facades: namely that the airstreams within the facade, which are subject to dynamic changes through the influence of temperatures and thermal currents, have to be determined in the simulation in order to obtain precise data. This requires very complex calculations of the multiple optical reflections between the panes of glass and the sunshading; and of the separate thermal and air currents in front of and behind the sunshading layer. The underlying phenomena of thermal buoyancy and wind-induced airflow will be described in the chapter dealing with "Aerophysics".

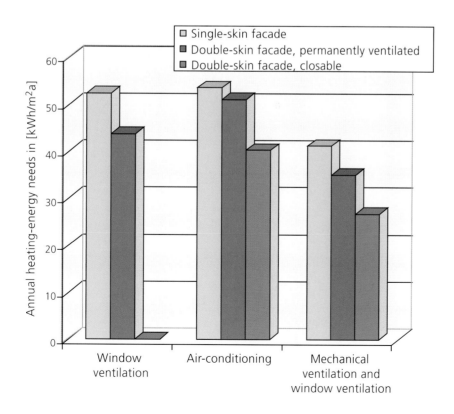

5-23 Data compiled from thermal simulation for building in respect of annual heating-energy needs; calculated as an average for the four faces of the building.

If one wishes to compare the calculated annual heating energy requirements for a number of different cases using thermal simulations, the question arises how the various alternatives are related to each other. If window ventilation is possible with a single-skin facade—taking into account environmental factors such as noise and air quality—this is certainly the simplest and most efficient solution in terms of "natural air-conditioning." On the other hand, the heating-energy needs will be greatest in this case. Moreover, with the improved thermal insulation provided by a double-skin facade and the preheating of the air in the intermediate space between the facade layers (which in this case would have to be permanently ventilated), heating-energy savings of about 15% can be achieved in the course of a year for the middle rooms that were investigated.

The fact that the improved thermal insulation provided by the double-skin facade, with a 9% lower U-value, plays only a minor role in this respect, is shown by comparisons with alternatives using mechanical forms of air-conditioning. In these cases, the heat losses caused by ventilation will not be reduced by the increased temperature in the facade intermediate space. The reduction of the heating-energy requirements—by about 5%—will be considerably smaller.

The scope for energy savings, where double-skin facades with closable windows are used, is demonstrated by a roughly 25% improvement compared with permanently ventilated double-skin facades, and by a roughly 35% improvement compared with single-skin facades. In other words, the potential energy savings exceed those obtained by a mere U-value improvement of 25% compared with single-skin facades. The reason for this is the high level of solar heating that occurs in the facade intermediate space when the sunshading is lowered.

Nevertheless, the absolute savings in heating energy are relatively small, since 36 MJ/a represent a saving in heating costs of roughly 0.25–0.30 euros per square meter per annum. In practice, therefore, greater interest will be focused on a maximum period of natural ventilation over the whole year. If mechanical ventilation is necessary, as, for example, in high-rise buildings, one will attempt to restrict its use to periods of high heating or cooling loads and to manage with window ventilation for as long as possible in the transitional periods. That will increase annual heating-energy needs by 10–15% compared with a fully mechanical system of air-conditioning with scope for heat recovery; but in terms of the overall energy requirements for heating, ventilation and cooling, it will show a roughly 20-percent saving. For a discussion of the overall economics of these alternatives, reference should be made to the detailed example given in the chapter "Economic Viability".

Case study:
contingent conditions relating to thermal simulations

For a neutral comparison of various facade types contained in this book, simulation calculations were drawn up for a theoretical office building under the climatic conditions prevailing in the south German city of Würzburg (weather data: TRY 05). The building has rooms facing all four points of the compass and served by a common access corridor. All offices are three bays wide (3 x 1.35 m bay width x 5.45 m room depth); they have a floor area of roughly 22 m² each and contain two workplaces. The rooms have a clear height in the middle of nearly 3 m and a volume of about 66 m³.

The values calculated are based on middle rooms on a standard story. The heating-energy needs for rooms on the ground floor or in the roof story and at the corners of the building will inevitably be greater. These marginal situations were deliberately not evaluated, since this would have required the size of the building to be determined.

A typical situation in a modern office was, therefore, reconstructed. For interested readers, the contingent conditions are given in detail below, in order to allow a comparison between these results and those of other investigations. The data obtained here formed the basis for the assessment of thermal insulation in winter and summer and for the model calculation in the chapter "Economic Viability". For a fuller understanding of the results presented here, it is not necessary to be familiar with all contingent conditions. The reader may, therefore, omit the following description.

Every workplace is equipped with a PC that emits 130 W in waste heat during its operating period. Together with the heat emitted by people, amounting to 70 W per person (the 50 g/h per person moisture emission will be calculated separately), internal loads of 18 W/m² accrue (excluding lighting) when the user is present. Direct artificial lighting was assumed with a heat emission of 15 W/m². The lighting is turned on and off depending on the level of natural lighting (in relation to the daylight factor).

The building is in operation Monday to Friday from 7 a.m. to 6 p.m. A flexitime use was assumed with a core period from 9 a.m. to 4 p.m. and a lunch break from 12 noon to 1 p.m. The average duration of the presence of staff was thus 8 hours per day plus the lunch hour. Since these simulations serve mainly to allow a comparison between energy-requirement values, an average staff presence of 70% over the whole year was assumed. The figures cannot, therefore, be extrapolated for load calculations without certain reservations.

The facade consists of an 80-centimeter-high apron wall and a continuous 2.2-meter-high strip of windows with a glazing area of 80% and a frame area of 20%. The glazing consists of low-E glass with nominal values of U_W = 1.5 W/m²K, g = 58% and τ_L = 75%. The construction assumed for the double-skin facade consisted of a 12 mm layer of single glazing set in front of the inner layer, with a 60 cm spacing between the two. The g-value of the outer skin is dynamically calculated and is nominally 90% (where the angle of incidence of the light is perpendicular to the facade). The apron panel, with a 12 cm layer of thermal insulation, has a coefficient of thermal transmission of U_{AW} = 0.32 W/m²K. For the single-skin facade, external sunshading in the form of pull-up louver blinds was assumed with a typical factor of z = 0.15. The double-skin facades have a comparable sunblind system in the intermediate space with a solar transmittance of τ_e = 20%. Any secondary heat emission that might occur into the internal space (which, together with the solar transmittance would give the g-value) is calculated with the airflow through the facade cavity as an integral part of the program.

The rooms have a hollow-floor construction with a 3 cm floated screed. On the underside, the solid flat-plate floors (28 cm reinforced concrete) are left exposed over half their area and activated as a storage mass. The other half of the soffit is in the form of a sheet metal sail construction, suspended 45 cm beneath the concrete slab and accommodating the lighting installation. At the same time, the suspended area is used as a cooling soffit. The sail construction also has an acoustic function. The partitions dividing the offices from the corridor and from each other are in the form of 50 mm metal-stud walls lined on both faces with two layers of 12.5 mm gypsum fibreboard. Inserted in the voids between the metal studs are 4 cm mineral-wool insulating slabs over the full area. The partitions thus have a sound-insulation value of $R_{w,res} \geq 42$ dB.

Three different types of facade construction were compared:

■ single-skin facade
■ double-skin facade with permanent ventilation of the intermediate space
■ double-skin facade with closable flaps.

The double-skin facade types have continuous openings 15 cm high at the top and bottom of each story. The story height is 3.65 m, and the height of the thermal uplift in the intermediate space is roughly 3 m. The flaps in the closable facade construction are shut when the external temperature sinks below 5 °C. A closure of the flaps in strong wind conditions, which is often necessary in the case of high-rise buildings, was not taken into account in this simulation.

The three facade types were combined with three different air-conditioning systems:
- window ventilation, radiators and cooling soffits
- mechanical air-conditioning (filtering, heating, cooling, moisturizing and demoisturizing), in conjuction with windows that are assumed to be non-openable and with radiators and cooling soffits
- partially mechanical air-conditioning (moisturizing, heating, cooling and ventilation) under "extreme" weather conditions; otherwise, window ventilation, radiators and cooling soffits.

In all cases, the mechanical ventilation provides a constant airflow volume equivalent to two and a half air changes per hour in the rooms. The ventilation functions as a mixed airflow system, with a maximum temperature difference of 8 kelvin between the air supply and the room air. The ventilation plant incorporates the following functions: filtering, heating, cooling, moisturizing and demoisturizing (also referred to as full air-conditioning) and is equipped with a heat-recovery unit in the form of a regenerator with 75% efficiency. The recovery of cooling energy is not foreseen.

The room radiator is designed with a maximum heating load of 50 W/m². The cooling soffit has a capacity of 35 W/m² for the office areas, with a temperature difference of 10 kelvin between the cooling soffit and the room. The performance of the cooling soffit is calculated dynamically in accordance with the respective temperature differences. The control of the heating and cooling, and of the air-supply temperature, complies with the data contained in German standards /T20/, with a gradual increase of the admissible room temperatures in summer from 22 to 26 °C, when the external temperature is between 26 and 32 °C; and a minimum temperature of 21 °C during working hours in winter.

The window ventilation is assumed to provide an 0.8-fold air change per hour during the heating period. In winter, the windows remain closed at night. A minimum air-change rate of 0.2 per hour occurs as a result of the non-airtight nature of the facade. With increasing room temperatures, the windows may be assumed to be tipped open permanently during the working period from 23 °C upwards. Under these

conditions, there will be between two and four air changes per hour, depending on the external wind speeds and the differences between room temperatures and external temperatures. If the room temperatures rise above 25 °C, a partial opening of the pivoted windows is assumed, and there will be up to six air changes per hour—again depending on the temperature difference and the wind. The dynamic calculation of the air change rate is carried out on the basis of the specific air exchange and in accordance with the conditions described in the chapter on "Aerophysics".

The supporting mechanical ventilation is based on operational strategies that have been developed in combination with a closable double-skin facade construction for high-rise buildings. Accordingly, the mechanical ventilation operates when external temperatures fall below 5 °C and rise above 20 °C. Users should then keep their windows closed to maximize the effectiveness of the heating or cooling of the rooms. In the simulation, "ideal" user behavior was assumed to demonstrate the potential of this form of operation. To obtain a comparison, this concept was also simulated for a single-skin facade and for a permanently ventilated double-skin facade.

5-24 Temperature curve around sunshading in a double-skin facade.
Ventilation of the space behind the sunshading is particularly important to ensure that the air supply to the rooms is not overheated.

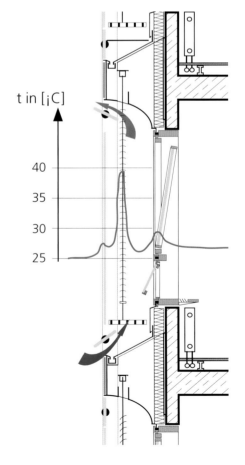

t in [¡C]

40

35

30

25

Thermal insulation in summer

The efficiency of sunshading in the facade cavity

If the sunshading is located in the intermediate space between the facade skins, it enjoys greater protection against wind and weathering. By screening off the effects of the wind, the sunshading is less exposed to external loads and will hardly ever have to be drawn up simply to protect it from damage. This applies especially to locations subject to very strong winds, e.g. on the coast or around high-rise buildings. This lower wind loading may, in turn, allow a simpler form of construction for the sunshading and guide tracks.

This aspect of protection against the elements applies especially in the case of rain. Placing sunshading systems in the intermediate space also slows down the process of soiling, which can occur very quickly with blinds situated on the outside of the facade. That, in turn, improves the long-term appearance of the sunshading within the facade cavity. The sunshading in double-skin facades plays a crucial role in absorbing heat from sunlight and liberating heat within the intermediate space—regardless whether the shading is in the form of pull-up louvers or a blind. In fact, this is likely to be the main cause of the air in the facade space heating up—an aspect that is directly related to the ventilation of this space.

Basically, one can assume that, as a result of their mainly absorbent properties in the infrared light range, strongly reflecting white or metallically shining surfaces will absorb at least 30 to 35 percent of the insolation and will convert this into heat, which will then be transmitted to the surrounding air and to adjoining surfaces by means of radiation and convection.

The facade space is divided into two parts by the sunshading. The position of the shading within this space, therefore, plays a major role in the distribution of the heat gains in the intermediate space. The smaller space will heat up to a greater extent than the larger. If the sunshading is situated just in front of the inner facade and if the air space between the two is not optimally ventilated, the air in front of the window can heat up considerably—an unsatisfactory phenomenon, regardless whether the windows are open or closed. When they are closed, a secondary heat emission occurs (excess temperature times U-value); when they are open, the situation is even worse, since there will be a direct inflow of heated air.

The sunshading should, therefore, be positioned in the outer half of the intermediate space—ideally at roughly a third of the depth of the facade cavity, with good ventilation to the outer space above and below the sunshading. It should not be too close to the outer pane of glass, either, so as to avoid excessive heating up and thermal loading of this layer. For these reasons, the Institute for Window Technology in Rosenheim /T21/ recommends a minimum distance of 15 cm between the sunshading and the external skin of the facade. The authors also regard this spacing as necessary for ventilation purposes. The section through the intermediate space (see ill. 5-24) shows a typical horizontal temperature curve in such a situation.

Determining the effective characteristics of the sunshading in each case poses a special problem at the planning stage, since the properties can vary considerably, according to the type of glazing and the ventilation of the sunshading system. But these conditions are not reflected in most standardized codes of measurement. According to DIN 67507 /T4/, for example, each layer is measured separately. The sunshading provides either a complete screening of the area behind it or, in the case of louvers, it may be in a so-called "cut-off" position. This is the angle of the louvers at which the blind allows no direct radiation to penetrate it. Applying the above-mentioned DIN standard, all values are calculated on the basis of a perpendicular incidence of light, so that the cut-off position for louvers will usually be 45°. Data for permeability to light and energy are also based on this. Where the louvers are set at a steeper angle, there will be a greater degree of shading, but a reduced rate of light transmission as well.

For large-scale projects, it is worth investigating the precise characteristics of the combination of glass and sunshading, as well as the proposed ventilation of the intermediate space in relation to the angle of the louvers. This can be done either in a mock-up facade or under laboratory conditions. So far, however, no standard method of measurement has been established that embraces all these factors, although steps in this direction are being taken. For the present, the method will have to be agreed from case to case to obtain the necessary information.

The effect of night-time ventilation

On hot summer days when external temperatures are over 26 °C, it is quite normal—in accordance with strict air-conditioning criteria—to allow room temperatures to rise above a range of 22–24 °C. In rooms with window ventilation, this increase in temperature is anyway unavoidable, although it will not necessarily be perceived as uncomfortable. As long as the room temperature remains a few degrees below the external temperature, particularly in the hot hours of the afternoon, it is regarded as acceptable.

In both cases, however, the rise in temperature will affect not only the air in the rooms; after some delay, the temperatures of the furnishings, ceilings, walls, etc. will also rise. These objects and constructional elements absorb and store heat in proportion to their mass and storage capacity. After working hours, a large proportion of this stored daytime heat will still be present in the room and the objects within it. If the windows and doors are now closed and if the mechanical ventilation and cooling systems cease to operate at night, the heat will be trapped inside. As a result of the conservatory effect, the heat can hardly escape through the windows as radiation, and efficient thermal insulation incorporated for the winter prevents a rapid cooling of the interior.

5-25 Temperature curves in the course of a week: externally; within the facade (mean temperature); within the room; and on the surface of the heat-storage soffit.

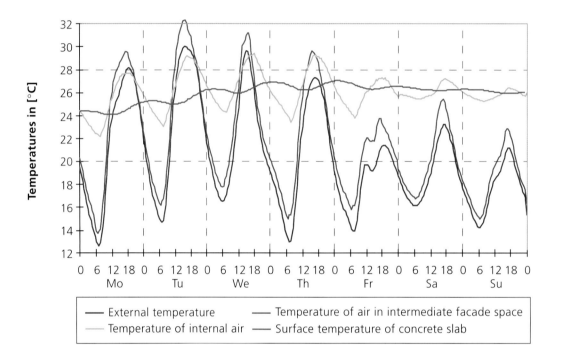

5-26 Thermal currents in the course of a week: caused by insolation, ventilation and heat storage.

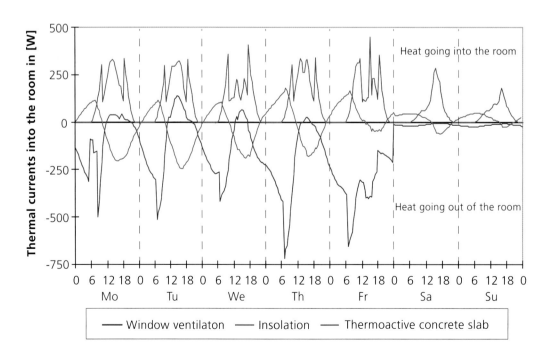

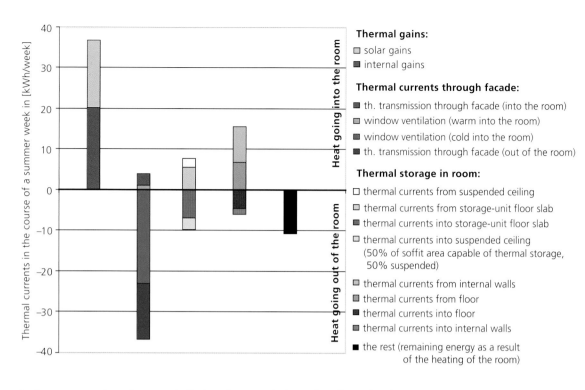

Thermal currents in the course of a summer week in [kWh/week]

Heat going into the room

Heat going out of the room

Thermal gains:
☐ solar gains
■ internal gains

Thermal currents through facade:
■ th. transmission through facade (into the room)
■ window ventilation (warm into the room)
■ window ventilation (cold into the room)
■ th. transmission through facade (out of the room)

Thermal storage in room:
☐ thermal currents from suspended ceiling
☐ thermal currents from storage-unit floor slab
■ thermal currents into storage-unit floor slab
☐ thermal currents into suspended ceiling
   (50% of soffit area capable of thermal storage,
   50% suspended)
■ thermal currents from internal walls
■ thermal currents from floor
■ thermal currents into floor
■ thermal currents into internal walls
■ the rest (remaining energy as a result
   of the heating of the room)

5-27 Balance of the sum of thermal currents recorded in the course of a week in summer for a south-facing office (22 m²), comprising internal and external loads, ventilation, conduction and thermal storage.

By the next morning, the room is likely to have cooled down from, say, 27 to 25 °C. In comparison with the external temperature of, say, 28 °C in the evening and 18 °C on the following morning, conditions within the room will be perceived as far too warm. In other words, a night-time cooling of the room in proportion to the cooling of the external air will be unconsciously expected. In such situations, relief can be obtained only through night-time ventilation that permits a natural exchange of air and heat during summer nights through a controlled opening of windows or flaps. Mechanical concepts also exist that exploit parts of existing ventilation installations to achieve an increased airflow through the rooms. The important thing is that air with a lower temperature can enter the rooms and that the soffits, walls and furnishings in particular can cool down again by giving off the energy they have absorbed during the day.

In recent years, the "activation of storage mass" has become a generally recognized theme in professional circles. Storage masses in rooms absorb considerable quantities of heat, which are then no longer available for heating up the air. Heavy building components heat up less and more slowly than light ones. Through a process of radiation exchange, the lower surface temperature of heavier objects has a positive effect on the perceived room temperature. An exposed concrete ceiling could, therefore, be described as a passive cooling soffit. If temperatures remain high for several days, the slab retains its effectiveness only if the thermal storage mass is regularly drained. The provision of storage mass makes sense, therefore, only if there is scope for regular cooling—for example, through natural night-time ventilation.

The effect of night-time ventilation in a room with a double-skin facade is demonstrated by the thermal currents flowing between the room and soffit areas with a storage capacity (50% of the floor area of the room) calculated for a hot week in July. Figure 5-25 shows the range of external and room temperatures in the course of a week, as well as the ceiling and facade temperatures for the same period. The ceiling slab absorbs heat as long as the room temperature exceeds that of the soffit; conversely, when the ceiling is warmer than the air in the room, the storage mass will give off heat. This may be seen in the graph of weekly temperature values (ill. 5-26). Since there is provision for nocturnal ventilation, the ceiling is able to cool down again at night. To provide a comparison, the cooling loads resulting from insolation are also shown. To a large extent, these are stored temporarily in the ceiling and have a delayed effect on the room.

The overall balance of thermal currents for the week in question is shown in diagram 5-27. The internal and solar heat loads are counteracted above all by the heat exchange that occurs via the windows as a result of ventilation and conduction. In the process, heat loads may be caused by the windows as long as the air in the facade intermediate space is warmer than that in the offices. The ventilation of the double-skin facade functions well in this respect, with the result that undesirable heat gains remain within reasonable limits. A third important factor in this context is the thermal storage action of the ceiling slabs, which function like an accumulator.

Conclusion: the effects on cooling loads

By drawing up a thermal balance for a room at the height of summer as in ill. 5-27, one can differentiate between

■ semi-constant loads that are independent of the facade;
■ loads that are only indirectly dependent on the facade; and
■ loads that are caused directly by the facade.

The internal loads caused by people and especially by computers have a major influence on the thermal balance, quite independently of the facade, and it is not possible to control these significantly through the form of construction. It may be in the interest of users, therefore, to reduce this portion of the heat load by optimizing the organization of work; e.g. through earlier working hours in summer or the use of energy-saving computers with low heat emissions (e.g. with flat panel instead of CRT displays). In this way, it may be possible to achieve a greater degree of thermal comfort.

The scope for night-time ventilation is indirectly influenced by the facade construction. With single-skin facades, protection against the ingress of rain is especially important, and the question of security may arise. The type of sunshading and its position will also influence the daylighting. In extreme cases, a situation may occur where users close the sunblinds and then, to compensate for the reduced brightness, turn on the lights internally, thus causing more heat to be released. This phenomenon, which contradicts all rules of common sense, occurs more frequently than one may suspect. In drawing up calculations for cooling loads, therefore, the question arises whether the thermal emissions from the lighting should be added to the other cooling loads that occur when the sunblinds are closed in order to err on the side of safety in dimensioning the requisite mechanical cooling system. An alternative lies in optimizing the lighting when the sunblinds are closed; e.g. by using so-called "daylight blinds" (see the chapter on "Daylight").

The intensity of the insolation, which acts as a heating load in the room, is directly influenced by the facade construction. It depends primarily on the area of glazing in the facade, the quality of the sunshading and the efficiency of the natural room ventilation (if there is no mechanical system). In the case of double-skin facades, additional factors will have to be considered, namely, the heating up of the air in the facade intermediate space and the thermal gains to which this leads. These gains occur both directly, in the form of warm air flowing into the room, and indirectly, in the form of heat entering via closed windows.

In the context of cooling loads, if one studies the differences between double- and single-skin facades resulting from the principles of construction, the following aspects may be described:

■ Given a well-planned ventilation system, sunblinds suspended in the cavity of a double-skin facade have almost the same energy effect in summer as sunshading situated outside a single-skin facade. A lower degree of soiling and the evident reduction in the effect of the wind on the blinds in the protected intermediate space are notable advantages in respect of permanent operations. The sunshading effect of the blinds in the intermediate space is considerably better than that of an internal sunblind, something that is of advantage especially in high-rise buildings.

■ Where the glazing for the inner layer of a double-skin facade is identical to that of a single-skin facade, the total energy-transmission factor (g-value) will be roughly 10% lower for the double-skin construction as a result of the additional outer layer. This additional skin also reduces the level of insolation in summer, even in the case of diffuse loads (overcast sky) and for facades that are not exposed to direct sunlight.

■ The ventilation of the internal rooms requires a smaller airflow volume than the ventilation of the facade intermediate space, as explained in the chapter on "Aerophysics". The internal ventilation will depend largely on an optimum positioning and degree of opening of the casements in the inner facade layer. The opening lights need be no different from those in a single-skin facade. The air flowing into the double-skin facade, however, should enter the interior spaces by as short a route as possible so that the heating up of the facade will cause a minimum of direct thermal gains.

■ As a rule, a double-skin facade presents no security risk in conjunction with night-time ventilation, since even when the inner skin is open, the outer skin still provides protection against unlawful entry. Furthermore, the outer facade will normally provide protection against rain independently of openings in the inner facade.

In principle, therefore, double-skin facades provide virtually the same scope for thermal protection in summer as a single-skin facade—indeed, much greater scope in the case of high-rise buildings. One condition for this, however, is that the ventilation of the intermediate space should be appropriately dimensioned. This is also clearly evident in the calculated energy needs for cooling shown in ill. 5-28. Where identical parameters exist for single-skin and double-skin facades (in respect of the proportion of glass and the type of glazing in the single or inner facade skin and the external sunshading to the single-skin facade), there will be only minor differences in terms of the cooling-energy needs resulting from the facade itself.

These differences are more likely to result from alternative air-conditioning concepts and different standards of comfort in summer.

The fact that in everyday practice, many structures with double-skin facades need extensive mechanical cooling can be explained by the extent of the glazing. The scope for sunshading provided by double-skin facades and the optical properties of the glass in the outer skin have been exploited to create completely transparent facades, especially in high-rise buildings. In many cases, the inner skin is also constructed with only small opaque areas or without any at all, with the result that very large "collector surfaces" are created for solar radiation. Especially in corner rooms, this leads to the dominance of external cooling loads, which can be balanced out only by mechanical cooling systems.

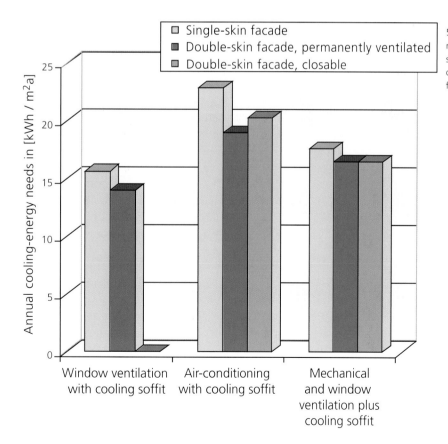

5-28 Annual cooling-energy needs derived from thermal simulation for building; calculated as mean values for a standard story.

Conclusion: the effects on cooling loads

6 | Daylight

Today, daylight is undoubtedly one of the most important requirements for a natural, healthy, productive working environment. Good natural lighting and unimpeded views out of a building belong to the minimum standards required by guidelines for workplaces in many countries. The comprehensive standards drawn up by the European Union for workplaces at electronic screens also stipulate salubrious—above all non-glare—daylight conditions. In all these measures, however, attention is focused not so much on a simple maximization of the light available in a room, as on improving the quality of lighting by ensuring an even but intense standard of illumination in all areas.

In terms of natural lighting needs, double-skin facades are no different from single-skin types. For that reason, the authors will deliberately forgo a detailed description of this extensive subject and restrict themselves here to a treatment of the main differences specific to double-skin facades. These include:
■ the reduction of the quantity of light entering the rooms as a result of the additional external glass skin;
■ the additional effective room depth caused by the facade projection;
■ the compensatory effect of larger areas of glazing; and
■ the scope for installing light-deflecting elements in the facade intermediate space where they are protected against the weather.

The additional outer layer of glazing implied by a double-skin facade automatically means a worsening of natural-lighting conditions. If the additional glazing consists of a single layer of clear glass, the reduction will be at least 10%. If special high-transparency flint glass is used, the reduction will be only 7–8% under favorable conditions. The level of daylight transmitted will also be reduced slightly if the glass thickness is increased for structural reasons.

Since laminated safety glass is in general thicker than single panes of toughened safety glass of the same load-bearing capacity, the choice of safety glass in the outer pane will influence the amount of daylight entering the room. Variations of only a few percent in the degree of transparency, however, will be of relatively minor importance for the natural-lighting quality. An important measure of the quality of natural lighting is the so-called *daylight factor T_Q*, calculated under overcast conditions. The daylight factor describes the relationship between the lighting intensity on a horizontal plane in an internal space and that on a horizontal plane outdoors. The outdoor lighting intensity can vary by day generally between 5,000 lux when the sky is heavily overcast and over 100,000 lux when the sun is shining from a clear sky. For office workplaces, an artificial lighting intensity of 300 to 500 lux is recommended. Where natural lighting is available, lower values are regarded as acceptable, since daylight has a more favorable spectral composition and the room is likely to be more evenly illuminated.

In view of the fact that daylight values fluctuate strongly, the minimum requirements are not defined in the form of an absolute lighting intensity in lux, but as relative values, using the daylight factor at desk height (0.85 m). In this context, the value $T_Q = 0.9\%$ is the lowest admissible level for places of permanent work /D1/. This value must be guaranteed at half the room depth. Since daylight conditions are relevant above all for places of work, it may be adequate under certain circumstances if the value is met at the workplace itself, where this is near a window.

Fine distinctions of this kind may prove to be important, since the daylight factor decreases rapidly with the depth of a room, as is shown in ill. 6-1. It also becomes clear, why differences in the transparency of the facade caused by the outer skin—which affect the lighting conditions in a room only to a certain proportion—are of less importance. With increasing distance from the window, the view of the sky is diminished, and less daylight penetrates into the depths of the

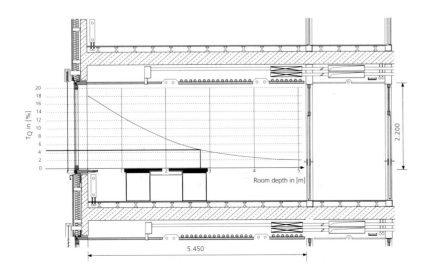

room. A further contributory factor in this respect is the distribution of luminance with an overcast sky, the values of which are three times higher at the zenith than on the horizon. This results in a big increase in the daylight factors immediately next to a window, which can easily be three to five times as high as the values in the middle depth of the room.

The projection of the outer facade beyond the face of the building also effectively increases the room depth in relation to workplaces by the depth of the facade intermediate space when the divisions of the facade cavity between stories are opaque (i.e. not transparent). In this case, the projecting divisions form an extension of the floor slab within the intermediate space. Ill. 6-2 shows the resulting shift of the curve of the daylight factors towards the outside. If the projecting opaque story division is set at a higher level than the soffit of the room, the daylight factor will be reduced primarily in the front area (see ill. 6-3). For the areas toward the back of the room, the edge of the ceiling in the plane of the inner facade will be decisive in determining the view of the sky and thus the daylight factors. It is sensible, therefore, to step the ceiling up towards the window if a suspended soffit is specified (e.g. to accommodate services or other installations).

The wish to improve natural lighting to values around $T_Q = 2–3\%$, as recommended by Bartenbach, for example, in /D2/, raises the whole question of optimization. Increasing the area of the window is the first and most obvious means of achieving this. Widening the dimensions of a rectangular window opening to form a continuous strip produces almost linear increases in lighting values. Eliminating the parapet wall to achieve floor-height glazing improves the lighting values less than proportionally, however, as ill. 6-5 shows. This is explained by the reduced lighting effect of those areas of glazing that lie below desktop level. On the other hand, the external cooling loads, which have to be considered in the context of thermal insulation in summer, increase in linear fashion, regardless in which direction the area of glazing is enlarged. It is important, therefore, to weigh up the pros and cons very carefully.

A second means of optimizing daylight values is by using so-called *optical or light-deflecting systems*. Their effect is based on the redistribution of the daylight—which exists in abundance near the windows—into the depths of the internal spaces. In most cases, systems of this kind consist of light-colored, reflecting or mirror elements in the area of the facade. These deflect the light upwards towards the ceiling and are usually combined with light-colored, reflecting or mirror soffit areas that, in turn, redeflect the light downward onto the working surfaces. One problem in se-

lecting and positioning elements of this kind is the fact that ultimately the amount of light available in the facade plane is merely redistributed and reduced a little with each reflection. Increasing the brightness in the depth of the room, therefore, automatically implies a certain degree of shading in the area near the facade.

Since the daylight factor when the sky is overcast forms the decisive value, a daylight system will have to be capable of reacting to diffuse light; in other words, light entering from all directions. It is not adequate simply to plan for the reflection of parallel rays of direct sunlight with a single angle of incidence. One exception to this are systems that are situated in front of the windows for only part of the time, such as so-called "daylight louver blinds". These are a development of the common louvered sunblind, but with a number of louvers in the upper third of the blind fixed at a flatter angle. Their function is not to improve the lighting when the sky is overcast, though, but to reduce the level of dimming caused when the sunblinds are lowered. Otherwise, there is a danger, as described in the section "Thermal insulation in summer", that the occupants of the rooms will have to turn on the electric lighting while the sun is shining outside.

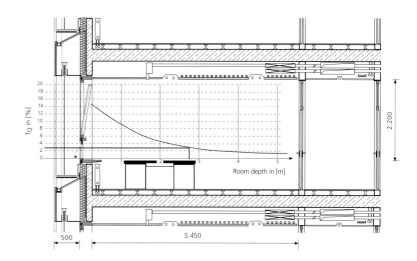

6-2 Daylight-factor curve over the depth of a room with a double-skin facade; projecting top division set flush with soffit.

6-3 Daylight-factor curve over the depth of a room with a double-skin facade; projecting top division stepped up from soffit.

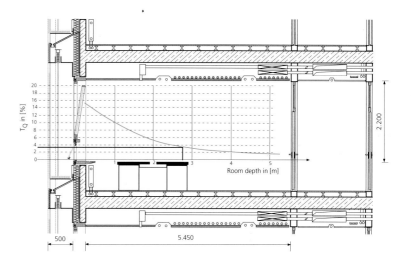

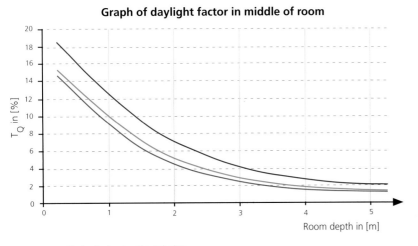

Graph of daylight factor in middle of room

T_Q in [%] — y-axis (0 to 20)

Room depth in [m] — x-axis (0 to 5)

——— Single-skin facade without shading
——— Double-skin facade, corridor depth 0.5 m, horiz. division 30 cm above top edge inner window
——— Double-skin facade, corridor depth 0.5 m, horiz. division flush with top edge inner window

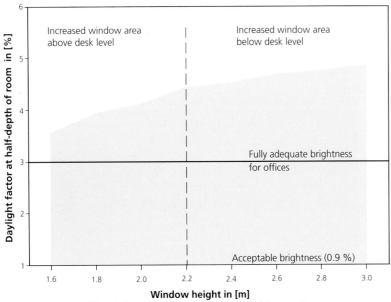

Daylight factor at half-depth of room in [%] — y-axis (1 to 6)

Increased window area above desk level

Increased window area below desk level

Fully adequate brightness for offices

Acceptable brightness (0.9 %)

Window height in [m]
(the window extends ove the fulll width of the room)

☐ Daylight factor for undeveloped situation (light transmittance = 66 %)

All elements of light-deflecting systems in double-skin facades can be protected against the weather and soiling by installing them in the intermediate space between the two skins. Since protection of this kind is crucial to the good functioning of many systems, they have hitherto commonly been incorporated in the cavity between panes of insulating double glazing. This is a technically elaborate procedure, however, since the space available is usually limited; and in most cases, the thermal insulation provided by the double glazing will be impaired if, for example, it is not possible to fill the cavity with an inert gas. The location of light-deflecting elements in the intermediate space of a double-skin facade is a sensible step, therefore, provided a completely dust-free installation is not required.

It remains to be seen what effects this will have in the future on the use of light-deflecting systems or on light deflection in general in conjunction with double-skin facades. Up to now, other aspects have evidently enjoyed a greater priority in the planning of this type of facade. In central Europe, daylight-deflecting systems are found in building only in exceptional cases.

6-4 Comparison of daylight-factor curves in middle of room.

6-5 Changes in daylighting levels with increased height of window.

7 | Fire Protection

Double-skin facade construction is still not covered by statutory building regulations. Virtually no information exists on the behavior of this kind of facade in the case of fire. In other words, there is no general basis for assessing the safety of this form of construction when subject to fire. For that reason, a specific assessment will have to be made for each scheme and approval sought from the appropriate building authorities for each individual case where a double-skin facade is to be used. As a rule, the authorities will require a technical report to be drawn up in respect of fire protection.

A basic treatment of the question of assessing the behavior and protection of these structures in the event of fire is given by Wolfram Klingsch /F1/. Since many German fire authorities make reference to this work, a summary of the contents will be given here.

Building materials and forms of construction

The external and internal layers of the facade consist in part of different materials. Whereas the outer skin will be constructed with non-combustible materials (building materials class A), the framing of the inner facade may sometimes consist of wood, which belongs to building materials class B (essentially combustible materials). The exclusive use of class A materials is prescribed for the horizontal and vertical divisions within the facade cavity. The horizontal divisions will usually consist of steel or aluminium; the vertical divisions may also be in glass.

Regulations relating to the facade construction require the individual glazing elements of the outer skin to be fixed independently of each other. The supporting structure should be dimensioned in such a way that local failure caused by fire does not result in a defect extending over a large area.

Fire protection risks

Klingsch assumes initially that the smoke extract from rooms and the spread of smoke from room to room via the facade is basically no different in the case of double-skin facades from single-skin types. Special attention should be paid, however, to the following aspects of double-skin facade construction with respect to fire protection:

Localization of the fire space:
When the energy released by a fire is low and no thermal destruction of the outer facade occurs, it may be difficult to localize the fire space visually from the outside. It is almost impossible for people in the rooms behind the double-skin facade to break the toughened glass in the outer layer by mechanical means. The use of safety glass (single-layer toughened glass or laminated safety glass) also makes access for the fire department from the outside much more difficult. In addition, sound contact between inside and outside is virtually impossible.

Smoke in the facade intermediate space:
Under certain circumstances, the air-intake and extract openings in the outer facade may not provide an adequate means of removing smoke from the intermediate space. As a result, and depending on the form of construction, smoke escaping through the inner facade into the intermediate space between the two skins may accumulate and spread horizontally and/or vertically. Additional measures may, therefore, be necessary to activate the natural flow of air through the facade space; for example, through the installation of smoke extract units or mechanical fans. In such cases, the air-intake openings in the outer facade skin will have to be appropriately dimensioned: the openings should not be smaller than those for the air-extract. If an installation is necessary to remove smoke from the facade intermediate space, its operation will have to be activated by a smoke-alarm system.

Fire spread:
The risk of fire spread exists where hot gases and flames escape through the inner facade into the intermediate space. The possible spread of fire vertically and horizontally to which this may lead will depend initially on the divisions within this space. If the fire is of longer duration, the risk will cease to be dependent on the type of construction, since the divisions in the intermediate space are, as a rule, not classified according to their fire-resistance.

Assessment of risk

Klingsch suggests classifying the fire risk according to the use and the height of the building as well as to the type of construction of the double-skin facade. In terms of building height, the classification follows that contained in model building regulations (the figures are applicable in Germany, but the principle is the same in other countries, too):

Type I   buildings of low height   H ≤ 7m
Type II   medium-rise buildings   H > 7m
          up to high-rise level   H ≤ 22m
Type III high-rise buildings   H > 22m

This classification is based on the different scope that exists for fire-department operations in rescuing people. In high-rise blocks, for example, the increased problem of locating the fire space from the outside and determining where people are situated within the building is not the main problem, since buildings of this kind will have at least two escape routes, or one fire-escape staircase with a provision for preventing the entry of smoke.

The situation is different with buildings below high-rise height; in other words, where the second escape route is via the fire department's ladders. In such cases, locating people behind the outer facade can be crucial to saving life, and it may be necessary to take certain additional measures in this respect. In terms of actual fire-fighting, though, the risks will generally increase with the height of the building.

The following categories are suggested with respect to building uses:
Type a: office uses and the like
Type b: housing
Type c: special uses with large numbers of people; e.g. places of assembly, hotels, schools, hospitals, old-people's homes, etc.

This classification takes account of the different risks to the people who use the rooms behind the double-skin facade. In office buildings, for example, one may expect the effects of fire in the facade space to be recognized at an early stage by users. This may not be assumed, however, for bedrooms in dwelling blocks, hotels, old-people's homes or hospitals. Similar risk situations may also occur in spaces used by large numbers of people.

In the context of the different forms of double-skin facade construction described at the beginning of this book, the risk categories can be defined as in the box below (7-1).

7-1 Risk factors, according to Prof. Klingsch /F1/.

Parameters		Description		Risk
Type of double-skin facade construction	A₁	Individual room type with peripheral horizontal and vertical divisions	Individual air-supply and extract openings *(box-type window)*	Low
	A₂		Connected to joint ventilation shaft *(shaft-box facade)*	Low
	B	Story type, in which several rooms are linked; horizontal divisions story for story *(corridor facade)*		Medium
	C	Multi-story type, in which different rooms and user areas are linked horizontally and vertically *(multi-story facade)*		High
Height of building (Classification according to model building regulations)	I	Low-rise buildings		Low
	II	Medium-rise buildings (up to boundary of high-rise)		Medium
	III	High-rise buildings (groups 1 and 2)		High
Building use	a	Office use and the like		Low
	b	Housing uses		Medium
	c	Special uses such as places of assembly, hotels, schools, hospitals, old people's homes, etc.		High

Fire-protection measures

If a certain overall risk threshold for buildings with double-skin facades is exceeded, additional technical fire-safety measures will be required. To what extent they will be necessary will depend on the degree of risk. This means that one has a free choice between the various types of double-skin facade construction, since the risks involved in each case can be counteracted with additional technical fire-protection measures.

These additional measures include
■ automatic early fire-warning systems in the rooms and the facade intermediate space;
■ automatic activation of the smoke-extract system for the facade intermediate space; and
■ automatic fire-fighting systems in the rooms and/or the facade intermediate space.

Automatic early fire-warning systems, based on smoke-detector apparatus are of special importance. Only rarely can systems of this kind be omitted. Where the potential risk is high, a sprinkler installation will be necessary for the rooms adjoining the double-skin fa-

cade. As a rule, this will prevent the spread of fire via the facade intermediate space. In certain cases, an installation may be necessary with a greater density of sprinklers in the areas near the facade. Where there is a sprinkler installation in the rooms, the problem of fire protection will be reduced basically to the extraction of smoke from the facade intermediate space.
In special cases, a dry-system sprinkler installation may be necessary in the facade space itself. This is a technically elaborate and expensive measure. Special fire-extinguishing installations of this kind, tailored to cover specific risks, are not always compatible with the requirements of insurance organizations. The table below provides a summary of the fire-protection measures required in conjunction with double-skin facades in relation to the type of construction, the height and the use of the building. Other building-authority requirements have to be taken into account as well, of course. For example, regardless of the contents of the table, a sprinkler installation will have to be provided in high-rise office blocks where this is required by local or regional building regulations.

Height of building	Form of facade construction	Building use		
		Offices	Housing	Special uses*)
I ≤ 7 m	A₁, A₂	1	1	1
	B	1	2	2
	C	2	2 + 4	2 + 4
II > 7 m ≤ 22 m	A₁	1	1	1
	A₂	1	2	2 + 4
	B	2	3	3
	C	3 + 4	3 + 4	3 + 4
III > 22 m	A₁	3	3	3
	A₂	3 + 4	3 + 4	3 + 4
	B	3 + 5	3 + 5	3 + 5
	C	3 + 4 + 5	3 + 4 + 5	3 + 4 + 5

7-2 Fire-protection measures according to /F1/.

Key to facade type
A1 = box window
A2 = shaft-box facade
B = corridor facade
C = multistory facade

Key to measures required
1 No additional measures necessary
2 Automatic early fire-warning system with ventilated facade intermediate space
3 Automatic early fire-warning system in rooms
4 Additional measures for activating ventilation in facade intermediate space
5 Sprinkler installation in rooms

*Special uses such as places of assembly, hotels, schools, hospitals, old-people's homes, etc.

8   Aerophysics

Aerophysics is not a discipline or term with which one is generally familiar in building, although it has played a role in construction for a number of years now. Aerophysics involves all questions relating to the flow of air toward, around and within buildings. It is an omnibus term like constructional physics, since it covers various aspects such as aerodynamics and thermodynamics. In addition, building regulations governing, for example, window ventilation and conditions of internal comfort also have to be taken into account in this context; and in some cases, it also touches on structural aspects: for example, aerophysical investigations in wind tunnels can provide more precise data about the wind loads acting on tall buildings than the relevant standards can.

To provide readers with a quick overview of the subject, the basic aspects are discussed in the first part under the headings, "The causes of airstreams", "The magnitude of airstreams", and "Aerophysical requirements". This is followed in the second part by an examination of the airflow processes that result from thermal buoyancy in double-skin facades, and the interpretation of these processes with the help of nomograms. Finally, the possible optimization of airflow resistances is considered. The third part of the chapter is devoted to the main effects of wind on double-skin facades and the influence it has on the internal spaces. Special phenomena and effects that occur in conjunction with high-rise buildings are described in the following chapter.

Basic principles of aerophysics

The causes of airstreams
The first and central question in this respect is: what causes air to move?

Pressure differences in the broadest sense of the term are always the motive force of air currents. In other words, in order to achieve a state of equilibrium, air flows from a space with high pressure to one with low pressure if the two spaces are linked. In the context of building, there are three main causes for pressure differences:
■ pressure differences caused by mechanical operations;
■ pressure differences caused by thermal buoyancy;
■ pressure differences caused by the action of wind.

a) Pressure differences caused by mechanical operations

Let us begin with the fan as the most common means of propelling air mechanically. Everyone is familiar with the table fan that resembles a small propeller and which is used to set the air in a room in motion in summer. Its effect is described here as an example of a general phenomenon.

The propeller consists of a number of vanes that, in turning, push the air in a certain direction. The word "mechanical" may be taken quite literally in this case; for the moving vane is constantly compressing the air on its front face and thus creating a state of excess pressure. Conversely, on the rear face, space is made free and other air flows into it. A smaller volume of air in a given space signifies negative pressure, which results in an inflow of air from the surrounding space— up to the point where a pressure equilibrium is established.

With this, the main aspects of mechanical operations have been described. Suffice it to say that air is moved in a similar way if one closes a door quickly, although in this case, the process is usually so short that the effects will be perceived only indirectly; e.g. when a tipped window slams shut as a result. A further example may be mentioned in the context of elevators moving in a shaft, where the cars constantly push a body of air in front of them and draw air in their wake. In this case, the process of pressure equalization occurs on the individual floors of the building. Depending on the air speed, it can result in whistling noises around the edges of doors.

b) Pressure differences caused by thermal buoyancy

Mention is often made of thermal buoyancy or uplift as a cause of air currents. All this means is that hot air rises, and cool air sinks.

The reason for this is that air undergoes a change of density with changes in temperature. Warmer air takes up a greater volume than cold air; alternatively, one can say that warm air is lighter than cold air per unit volume. Similarly, a material that is lighter than water, such as wood, will float to the surface. A heavier material, such as iron, will sink to the bottom. The same occurs with warmer and cooler air when it comes into contact with air of an intermediate temperature.

Double-skin facades provide a good example of the occurrence of pressure differences. As a result of insolation, the air in the intermediate space between the two skins becomes warmer than the external air. The air in this space will, therefore, be lighter than that outside. The intermediate space is in contact with the external air via openings at the top and bottom, so that a process of pressure equalization occurs. The cooler external air is heavier and causes a state of excess pressure at the bottom, thereby forcing its way into the intermediate space. The warmer air within this space is lighter and rises upward, thus causing a state of excess pressure at the top, where the heated air is ejected.

If one considers the pressure differences in the context of the warmer facade intermediate space, there will be excess pressure at the top and negative pressure at the bottom. The pressure difference between the two explains the phenomenon of thermal buoyancy. Alternatively, this can be viewed from the perspective of the cooler external air. In this case, there will be excess pressure at the bottom and negative pressure at the top. The difference will be the same, of course, only in the latter case, it will result in a thermal down-current. The magnitude of the thermal uplift or down-current will depend solely on the integral difference of density over the whole height between inside and outside; or, expressed more simply, on the mean temperature difference multiplied by the effective uplift height. In the case of double-skin facades, the uplift height is the difference in height between the air-inlet and air-outlet openings.

The pressure difference of the thermal uplift Δp_{th} is thus:

$$\Delta p_{th} = \Delta \rho' \bullet g \bullet \Delta h \bullet \Delta t_m \quad [Pa] \quad (A1)$$

where
$\Delta \rho'$ is the specific change in air density with temperature change in $[kg/m^3\ K]$
g is the acceleration due to gravity in $[m/s^2]$
Δh is the effective uplift height in $[m]$
Δt_m is the mean excess temperature in $[K]$.

The mean excess temperature Δt_m has to be calculated in relation to the temperature development over the full height. The specific change of density $\Delta \rho'$ is derived from the general law of gases, where $\Delta \rho' = \rho/T_m \approx 0.004\ [kg/m^3 K]$. (The absolute temperature T_m is derived from the equation $T_m = t_{zu} + \Delta t_m + 273.15\ K$)

Mention should also be made of the fact that thermal uplift can occur between different spaces in exactly the same way as between enclosed spaces and the external air. This applies to processes like the air currents in chimneys or other stacks and vertical shafts, as well as to natural window ventilation, which functions for a room in exactly the same way as for the double-skin facade described above. Finally, thermal uplift or down-currents can also have an effect within an enclosed space. For example, in halls with tall glazed facades, a phenomenon known as a "cold-air drop" can occur in winter under unfavorable circumstances. The air that has cooled down near the facade will be heavier and can fall like a torrent of water.

c) Pressure differences caused by the action of wind

Wind can have a major influence on air currents in and around buildings. This is explained by the fact that the building forms an obstacle to the airstream. The wind has to make a detour around the building, resulting in excess pressure on the windward side and negative pressure on the leeward side. The above heading might more correctly read "pressure differences caused by the actions of inertia", since these are really the cause of the obstacle effect.

Wind is generated by thermal buoyancy in the areas of high and low pressure seen on weather charts. The wind is simply the balancing current between areas of different air pressure. Tall buildings in particular stand in its way, and the portion of the airstream that encounters a building will be dammed up in front of it, thereby creating a state of excess pressure. The magnitude of this excess pressure—correctly referred to as "stagnation pressure"—will depend on the wind speed. Pressure of this kind occurs when the wind is completely halted by a wall. The *stagnation pressure q* can be calculated as follows:
$$q = \rho/2 \bullet v^2 \quad [Pa] \quad (A2)$$

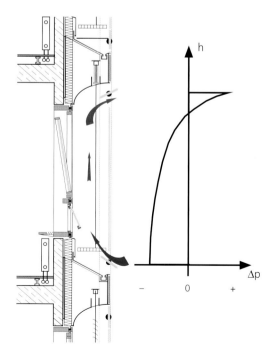

8-1 Typical pressure difference between facade intermediate space and external air as a result of thermal uplift.

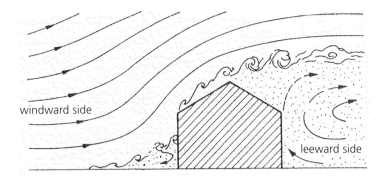

windward side

leeward side

8-2 Airstream flowing round a house.

where ρ in [kg/m³] is the density of the air (Greek rho), and
v in [m/s] is the wind speed.

The stream of air that is just able to swerve past the mass of the building rushes at increased speed round its edges. This is explained by the fact that there is less space available for the volume of air that has been carried up to the building by the wind, and the only way of compensating for this is for the air to pass at a greater velocity round the sides. At the same time, there is a tendency for this air to draw more in its wake, which leads to a state of negative pressure or suction.

At the back of the building, there would theoretically be enough space for all the air to flow on undisturbed again. But here the inertia makes itself felt most strongly. The air accelerated around the sides of the building simply shoots straight on, so that a state of negative pressure occurs behind the building. This, in turn, causes eddies to spin off at the sides of the onrushing air stream. These eddies fill the leeward space with air. For that reason, leeward zones are often extremely turbulent.

8-3 Undimensioned pressure distributions for two main wind directions for the "City Gate" building, Düsseldorf. The mean specific wind-pressure coefficients cp for the facades are given.

In calculating the pressure differences caused by the wind flowing round a building, it is important to define them in a form that applies approximately to all wind speeds. Since the pressure differences are proportional to the square of the wind speed, the stagnation pressure described above is used as a reference value. Local excess pressures or negative pressures can then simply be set in relation to this maximum excess pressure and given as *specific wind-pressure coefficients cp*:

$$p_{wind} = cp \bullet q \quad [Pa] \quad (A3)$$

Their distribution is largely independent of the wind speed, although the shape of the building and the wind direction (the direction of the airstream in relation to the building) can have a major influence on the distribution of the cp-values. For that reason, these values are always measured for all wind directions at certain spacings (e.g. in wind-tunnel tests). On the basis of these values, it will then be possible subsequently to calculate the resultant pressure on the building

for all wind directions and speeds. In the present context of pressure differences, the difference between wind-pressure coefficients Δcp can be used in an analogous form.

Wind and its effects are of great significance for the planning of tall structures. They are, therefore, treated in greater depth in the chapter "High-Rise Buildings".

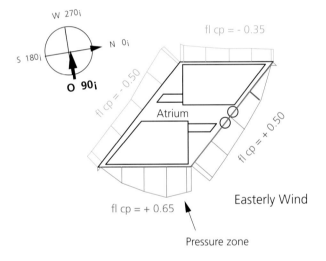

W 270i

fl cp = - 0.35

N 0i

S 180i

O 90i

fl cp = - 0.50

Atrium

fl cp = + 0.50

Easterly Wind

fl cp = + 0.65

Pressure zone

Southwesterly wind

Suction zone

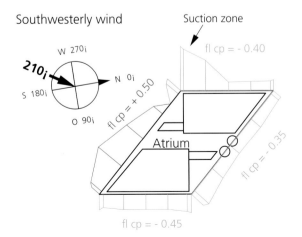

W 270i

fl cp = - 0.40

210i

N 0i

S 180i

fl cp = + 0.50

O 90i

Atrium

fl cp = - 0.35

fl cp = - 0.45

The magnitude of airstreams

Of the many different aspects relating to aerophysics, only the motive forces behind air currents have been discussed so far. The second central question is: what is the magnitude of an airstream?

Generally speaking, this is the product of the motive pressure differences and the resistances encountered, and it will be defined in terms of air speed and air throughput. These aspects can also be illustrated taking a double-skin facade and the ventilation of the intermediate space as an example.

The motive pressure differences responsible for thermal uplift in this form of construction have been discussed above. The pressure differences between the upper and lower openings can be regarded as forces acting on the areas of the openings, whereby the motive force is the product of the pressure difference taken in conjunction with the opening area. This force pushes just enough air through the opening to equalize the resistance caused by the throughflow of this air, so that an equilibrium of forces is attained.

The resistant forces, therefore, are related to the area of the opening and the pressure loss occurring during the throughflow of air. As in the case of wind pressure, this pressure loss can be described as a *specific pressure loss* ζ (Greek zeta), related to the stagnation pressure of the accelerated air:

$$\Delta p_{loss} = \zeta \cdot q \quad [Pa] \quad (A4)$$

In accordance with professional usage, the specific pressure loss ζ will hereafter be referred to in abbreviated form as the *zeta value*.

Zeta values are characteristic of the geometry of a specific opening and thus provide important standard values for the resistance encountered. This will be evident, however, only in conjunction with the appropriate reference speed. In the context of double-skin facades and the air flowing through them, the authors take the speed through the narrowest cross-section of the external openings as their reference value. This has proved its validity, since in almost all cases the air flows considerably more slowly in the facade intermediate space itself, and comparatively small pressure losses occur. The opening sizes in the external skin—not the much greater depth of the facade intermediate space—are of primary importance in dimensioning the flow of air through this space.

As a rough guide to setting out double-skin facades, it is generally adequate to add together the pressure losses resulting from the airflow through the intake and outlet openings, to calculate these with the typical zeta values, and to balance them with the motive pressure differences.

Under normal circumstances, only as much air is admitted at the bottom as flows out at the top. This seemingly banal statement is known in aerophysics as the continuity equation and forms an important basis for the requisite calculations. Basically, this equation says that the air throughput—a product of the air speed in the opening and the opening area—will remain constant within the system if no air is diverted for other purposes. The continuity equation is formulated as:

$$\dot{V}_{in} = \dot{V}_{out} \quad \text{or} \quad A_{in} \cdot v_{in} = A_{out} \cdot v_{out} \quad (A5)$$

whereby

$\dot{V}$ is the local airflow volume in [m³/s]
A is the local opening area in [m²]
v is the local air speed (derived from A) in [m/s].

In terms of ventilating the facade intermediate space, this means that if the air-inlet opening is only half the size of the extract opening, air speeds twice as great as those in the air-extract opening will be necessary to balance out the difference. Since the stagnation pressure increases as the square of the air speed (see equation A2), the pressure losses at the air-inlet opening will be four times as great. Where the overall opening area is limited in size, therefore, it is always of advantage to divide it equally between air-inlet and outlet needs and to locate these openings as far as possible towards the bottom and top respectively.

The concept described above, according to which the airflow through a space is a product of resistances where the additive pressure losses are just balanced by the motive pressure differences, can be seen as analogous to the concept of pressure equilibrium in the field of mechanics and can be formulated as follows:

$$\Delta p_{th} + \Delta p_{wind} = \Delta p_{loss} \quad [Pa] \quad (A6)$$

where

Δp_{th} is the thermal buoyancy pressure in accordance with (A1) in [Pa]
Δp_{wind} is the possible difference in wind pressure in accordance with (A3) in [Pa]
Δp_{loss} is the pressure loss in the airflow in accordance with (A4) in [Pa].

This concept applies generally to the flow of air through any sequence of spaces or buildings; it can be used, for example, in programs for calculating networks of ducts. It does not, however, provide any useful information on airflow conditions within the individual spaces nor in the intermediate space between facade skins, since only the air throughput from one space to another is in a state of equilibrium at the intermediate openings.

Air currents within spaces or even details of the airflow through air-inlet and extract openings have a perceptible influence on the overall airflow pattern and its assessment. Aspects of the airstream passing through an opening, for example, are ultimately responsible for the typical pressure-loss coefficients (zeta values).

The local air speed and temperature are decisive for any assessment of thermal comfort at the workplace. If questions of this kind cannot be determined in an approximate form by using standard values, airflow trials or simulations—computational fluid dynamics (CFD)—will have to be carried out to clarify them.

Case study: resistances in laminar and turbulent airflow

In most cases, the definition of the zeta value given above is quite adequate in practice for describing the effects of resistance, although one should be aware that effects which deviate from the norm may occur in the case of low airflow speeds. For an understanding of this chapter, it is not necessary to go into the deeper relationships that exist in fluid dynamics. They are, therefore, summarized in the following section.

A distinction is made between two basic kinds of airflow:

- turbulent airflow and
- laminar airflow.

The air currents occuring in our surroundings are mainly turbulent ones. *Turbulent* means that the forces of inertia dominate in such an airstream and result in all kinds of eddies and a mixing of the air. The forces of inertia depend on the local air speed in relation to the magnitude of its local change of direction. One might compare this with a journey by car. With increasing speed, the radii of the curves will have to be greater so that the vehicle is not thrown out on one side. The same applies to air currents. If the curve into which the airstream is forced is too tight, eddies will be caused comparable to a car skidding. In fluid mechanics, index values are used to define phenomena of this kind in air currents. In the present case, it is the so-called *Reynolds number Re*.

The Reynolds number describes the relationship between the air speed v, a typical length L, and the kinematic viscosity of a fluid or air ν (Greek nu). At room temperature, the kinematic viscosity of the air is roughly $\nu = 15.5 \cdot 10^{-6}$ m²/s:

$Re = v \cdot L/\nu$ [-]   (A7)

The typical length L is a quite abstract dimension within the universal concept of the Reynolds number. It can be the depth of an airplane wing, the diameter of a tube, the thickness of a boundary layer, or the running length of a sheet or panel. In the present case, it is the dimension of the change of direction of the airstream.

Applied to the example of the car, one could interpret the Reynolds number as the speed of travel (v) times the dimension of the lateral change of direction (L) in the curve, divided by the road adhesion of the vehicle. The Reynolds number thus describes the relationship between the centrifugal force (in this case, the force of inertia) and adhesion (here, frictional force). If the ratio exceeds a critical value, the vehicle will start to skid. In exactly the same way, there is a critical Reynolds value above which turbulence occurs in a free airflow around an object or through a space.

8-4 Calculation of airflow through internal space by means of CFD simulation. Representation of temperatures (top) and local air speeds (bottom) in winter, with heating provided solely by a heating soffit. Critical airflow speeds can occur beneath desktop level when the temperatures sink too low.

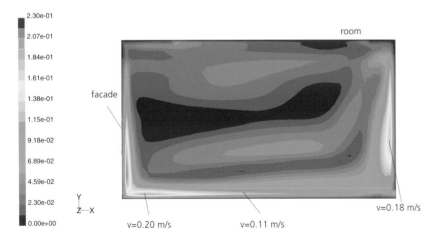

In the case of double-skin facades, this is around Re$_{crit}$ = 10,000 to 20,000. If an airstream passes a critical point and becomes turbulent, it takes a long time before the eddies and turbulences calm down again, even if the air speed is considerably reduced. Remaining with the analogy of the car, this means that it will continue to skid from side to side for a long time. That explains why most air currents in our surroundings are turbulent.

Initially, the basic condition of any airstream is laminar. The definition of the word *laminar* is the opposite of turbulent. In laminar air currents, the friction forces prevail over the forces of inertia. In other words, returning to the image of the automobile, all vehicles would be driving smoothly next to each other in their own lanes along a highway, with none veering to and fro. A similar situation can occur in double-skin facades where the airflow speed through the openings is low (less than v ≈ 10 cm/s).

In such situations, the zeta value will no longer be constant, for it is based on a predominance of forces of inertia and their relation to the square of the airflow speed. The forces of friction, however, are only proportionally dependent on the airflow speed. Since they determine the resistances in the laminar range, the relationship of the hitherto constant zeta value to the square of the speed will lead to rapidly increasing resistance/drag coefficients with a decrease in speed. It is important to be aware of this if one wishes to assess the flow of air in these areas. It may even be necessary to do without general methods such as those based on the use of the zeta value and to determine the actual resistances in trials or with the help of simulations.

8-5 Airflow round a sharp bend in a conduit; the current is unable to follow the line of the corner and breaks away from the sides.

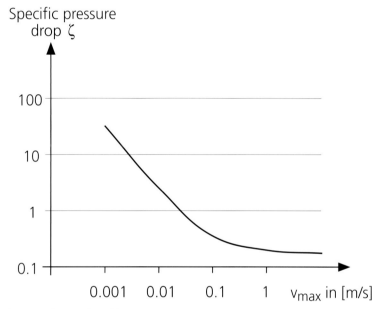

8-6 Increase in zeta value with low airflow speeds, caused by the dominant influence of friction in relation to the forces of inertia.

Aerophysical requirements

The relevant airflow patterns for double-skin facades can be largely determined on the basis of the information contained in the previous chapters of this book. A third and final crucial question remains to be discussed, however: how strong should or may the airflow be?

This aspect touches on statutory regulations relating to natural ventilation and comfort requirements at the workplace. In the case of double-skin facades, a further question arises, concerning the requisite ventilation of the facade intermediate space. The "strength" of the airflow is described in terms of the volume of air needed for ventilation, and the speed of the airstream—for example, around people, where it may cause a sensation of drafts.

Regulations and requirements affecting room ventilation

Guidelines for workplaces are usually based on certain parameters, and boundary values exist for the provision of adequate natural ventilation. For example, in offices where the ventilation is effected from one side, the minimum opening area in the facade should be 2% of the floor area. The maximum room depth can also be set at two and a half times the clear room height. Where cross-ventilation is foreseen via windows in opposite faces of a building, a fivefold room depth can be permitted.

In the experience of the authors, the 2% opening area required by guidelines for workplaces in standard offices should be available for both the air intake and the air extract; and to improve the thermal uplift in the intermediate space, the vertical distance between the respective openings should be as great as possible. In the case of double-skin facades, this value provides a useful point of reference, below which one should not go unless absolutely necessary.

Compliance with the two-percent rule, however, does not mean that the openings will automatically gain statutory planning permission, since one might rightly observe that a double-skin facade offers a greater resistance to air currents than a single-skin facade (for which the guidelines were drawn up). In case of doubt, it will be necessary to prove that adequate room ventilation is guaranteed; for example, by means of airflow trials. In early projects in which a double-skin facade construction was used, this was generally done to furnish the client with proof. These trials demonstrated that where a double-skin facade was used, ensuring a flow of air in the depth of the rooms and providing an adequate supply of external air were generally less critical factors than the regulations suggested.

On the other hand, simulation calculations carried out parallel to these trials showed that a reliable extraction of heat from the rooms and from the facade intermediate space can be a much more critical aspect, and that this should not be neglected in dimensioning the openings. In this context, compare the remarks at the end of this section with the general approach to their application contained in the second part of this chapter.

As far as internal room conditions are concerned, regulations governing mechanical ventilation plant state that such plant is adequate if it guarantees 30-70 m^3 of external air per person per hour. Assuming an area of 10 m^2 per workplace and a room height of 3 m, this would amount to 1 to 2 air changes per hour. In practice, for economic reasons, modern air-conditioning plant for offices generally provides a maximum of 2 to 3 air changes per hour. The hourly *air-change rate* (ACR) is defined as the relationship between the volume of air supplied per hour and the volume of the relevant space.

Where natural window ventilation is required to function as intermittent ventilation for a large part of the year, a much higher air-change rate should be possible when the inner facade is open. This will help to meet user expectations that, on opening the windows, they will perceive a noticeable draft of air as confirmation that the ventilation process has started. With a twofold air change per hour, this would not be the case. Psychologically, this then results in a sense of uncertainty and discomfort, which has become known as the *"aquarium effect"*.

In tests to determine the airflow through rooms and in measuring the reduction of pollutants, a decrease in the concentration of a tracer gas is frequently cited as a representative figure for the air change. A common definition is: "When the concentration has decreased by 95%, one air change has occurred in the room." But this is, in fact, a correct physical definition of the *air exchange rate (AXR)*. It is also what is meant when people talk of hygienic "air exchange" in the context of safeguarding health.

Air exchange differs from the above definition of air change not only in the method of measurement. Given a well-mixed airflow in a room, a 95% reduction in the concentration of the indicator substance amounts to a calculated air change rate three times as great as the air exchange rate! Only where the air in the room is completely displaced by the incoming airstream without diffusion, will the air change and the air exchange have the same value—something that never occurs with free ventilation. In applying specified and measured values, therefore, a clear definition is required; i.e. whether an hourly air change or an hourly air exchange is meant.

Among other things, the purpose of the investigation of the air exchange in airflow trials for enclosed spaces is to determine the relationship between a motive temperature difference and the resultant air exchange or air change. The relationship between the two can be regarded as a standard value for the quality of the ventilation, taking into consideration all influences such as resistances and the available opening sizes. The magnitude of the resultant air change is a function of the square root of the temperature difference between inside and outside, as laboratory trials have demonstrated. To facilitate a simple conversion of the measured results for various situations, it has proved sound practice to give the specific air-exchange rate (AXR') in relation to a motive temperature difference of 1 kelvin. Air-exchange rates for other temperature differences can be obtained by

$$AXR = AXR' \cdot \sqrt{\Delta t} \quad [1/h] \quad (A8)$$

where
AXR is the desired air-exchange rate in [1/h]
Δt is the relevant temperature difference in [K], and
AXR' is the measured specific air-exchange rate in [1/h $\sqrt{K}$].

How much intermittent ventilation does a person need?

Many people avail themselves of what is known as "intermittent ventilation". They ventilate a room for a certain period by opening the window and then closing it again as soon as the space becomes too cool or when the noise from outside is too loud. After a while, the window is reopened to ventilate the room again. In this way, the air change process takes place in smaller doses distributed over the entire day. The method prevents excessive heat losses and limits the periods of high noise disturbance caused by open windows.

In the section "Sound insulation against external noise," the question of the permissible opening time for windows was discussed in the context of statutory guidelines for workplaces and an admissible assessment level for mental work. In accordance with the guidelines, the minimum required ventilation with external air is 35 m³ per hour per person. It may be necessary, therefore, to calculate whether it is possible to provide an adequate supply of external air during the periods of intermittent ventilation, which are limited by acoustic factors.

In order to assess this, it is necessary to know the volume of air passing through a window during the period of intermittent ventilation. This depends on the temperature difference between the inside and outside as well as on the size of the opening and the kind of window. The calculation is the same as that used in the following passages for the summer months. In the case of short-period intermittent ventilation, one can assume a constant excess temperature in the room.

Calculations indicate that in this way, very high values can be achieved in terms of a spontaneous air change during the short ventilation periods, especially in winter. Experience shows, however, that a maximum of 4 to 6 spontaneous air changes per hour occur, since in order to avoid drafts, most users do not open the windows too wide. For a room with three window bays (and a spatial volume of 60 m³), this means a momentary airflow volume of roughly 4-6 m³/min. From this, it is possible to define the necessary ventilation period per hour in relation to the number of persons occupying the room. For one person in the room, 6-9 minutes per hour will be sufficient. For two persons, 12-18 minutes will be necessary.

Comfort requirements

A whole series of investigations has been made and regulations drawn up relating to comfort in rooms served by mechanical ventilation. The air temperature and the perceived temperature, the humidity and the air movement in the room all play an important role in this respect. The way these parameters are perceived depends on the individual attire and physical activity of the persons in the room /A1,A2,A3/. A further interesting aspect is that requirements and expectations vary from country to country, depending on climatic, cultural and historical factors. Conditions provided by a typical air-conditioning plant in the U.S., for example, would be perceived in Europe as providing only a limited degree of comfort.

Concrete values applicable to free ventilation may be defined as (a) adequate temperatures within a room (i.e. perceived temperatures) where a sedentary activity is carried out (at least 21 °C); (b) the avoidance of air movements (i.e. greater than 0.13–0.2 m/s) where people are sitting, and especially around their ankles; and (c) the avoidance of temperature differences between ankle and head level (i.e. not greater than 2.5 kelvin).

A simplified method is often used for assessing perceived temperatures /A1/—for which the term *operative room temperature* is used—in which the mean values of the air temperatures in the room and the surface temperatures of the space-enclosing elements are taken into account. This allows the heat exchange—caused by convection as well as by radiation—between a person and his or her room surroundings to be defined in a single figure.

Moreover, a person perceives cold walls and warm ceilings as far more unpleasant than warm walls and cold ceilings. If cold wall surfaces occur only on one side of a room, a draft-like sensation may also be felt. This is referred to in /A1/ as *radiation temperature asymmetry*.

Standard values for the ventilation of facade intermediate spaces

The removal of heat from a room or from the facade intermediate space can be a major criterion in dimensioning openings in double skin facades. The temperatures reached on hot days—a reflection of the building physics—are an important factor in this respect. If possible, room temperatures should remain below the peak external temperatures; and the temperatures in the facade space should not be much above this level if they are likely to be felt by users.

Since, on the one hand, the difference between room and external temperatures is a motive force for the ventilation, yet on the other hand, excessive heat gains have to be avoided, the maximum excess temperature of the exhaust air (in relation to the external air) is often defined as a criterion. This provides a direct measure of the extracted amount of heat. It is the decisive factor for the approach described in the following section for conditions of full insolation.

In determining the maximum excess temperature, the temperature of the exhaust air is not as important as the temperature measured at head level within an accessible facade space and that at roughly half the height of the windows, or more precisely, above the height of the air-intake openings in the inner facade. For example, since the temperature in the facade corridor increases with height, it will be necessary in calculations at the planning stage to reduce the extract-air temperatures to the temperature at head level and vice versa.

In this respect, one method has proved useful for obtaining an initial approximation value, whereby the temperature increases as the square of the height. This method gives a mean value for the conditions prevailing in a building when the sun is shining; it also provides a reliable assessment of the warm-air buffer beneath the ceiling. The temperature at head level can be expressed as the square of the relationship between head level and the overall height of the facade multiplied by the extract-air temperature. Alternatively, this can be expressed in the formula:

$$\Delta t_{head} = \left(\frac{h_{head}}{h_{out}} \right) \bullet \Delta t_{out} \quad [K] \quad (A9)$$

where

Δt_{head} is the difference between the temperature at head height and the external temperature in [K]

Δt_{out} is the difference between the exhaust-air temperature and the external temperature in [K]

h_{head} is the head height (above the air-intake opening) in [m]

h_{out} is the height of the air-extract opening (above the air-intake opening) in [m].

A second way of expressing these requirements is by directly specifying the necessary opening sizes in the outer skin. This approach, adopted from experience gained with hall structures, requires a prior calculation of the ventilation needs of the facade intermediate space. Care must be taken, however, in specifying and especially in implementing the superficial dimensions. Depending on the method used to calculate these areas, a distinction can be made between:

- aerodynamically effective areas
- aerodynamically free areas and
- geometric or elevational areas.

Aerodynamically effective areas are the simplest to calculate, since they are theoretical areas where no further pressure losses occur. These areas are calculated when the nature of the opening on the outer skin, and thus the specific zeta values, are still unknown. The problem is that these areas do not actually occur in the building. At the outset, the planner has to calculate the losses resulting from greater or smaller flow resistances in order to obtain the cross-sectional dimensions of the openings in a building. As a result, the construction will, in part, be emburdened with aerodynamic considerations.

Aerodynamically free areas are increasingly specified, therefore. These areas already contain an allowance for normal airstream resistances. For common opening types such as top-hung, bottom-hung, or pivoting casements, the aerodynamically effective area may often be 10-20 percent less than the area of the smallest aperture in an open state. In the case of a bottom-hung (tipping) casement, this represents the sum of the triangular areas at the sides plus the rectangular opening at the top between the opening light and the frame (cf. illustrations below, where the opening angle may be up to 30°).

This presupposes, though, that the space between the top of the tipped window and the ceiling is at least as great as the width of the opening. If this is not the case, the space between the top of the window and the ceiling should be taken as the dimension for the smaller cross-sectional area. A similar assumption is that there is not a further bottom-hung casement immediately adjoining the tipped window; for in that case, the inflow and outflow of air through the triangular areas at the sides is likely to be restricted.

It should be noted that this method cannot be applied unconditionally to openings with inbuilt elements and complex airflow routes; in other words, to areas through which the air cannot flow unimpeded. This aspect is described in greater detail in the section "Aerodynamic optimization".

Geometric areas are the areas of openings seen in elevation in the facades or the roof. Architecturally, these areas are the easiest to define; but in order to determine their effect as opening areas, it is necessary to specify the kind of opening and the opening width as well. It will then be possible to calculate the aerodynamically free areas.

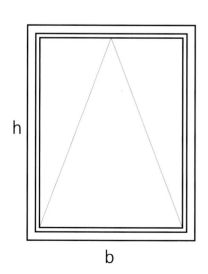
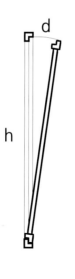
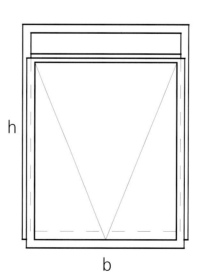

8-7 Left: diagram of bottom-hung casement.
The geometric area is
$A_{geo} = b \bullet h$
The aerodynamic free area is
$A_{aero} \approx (b \bullet d) + 2 (h \bullet d/2)$

8-8 Diagram of slide-down/push-out casement.
The geometric area is
$A_{geo} \approx b \bullet h$
The aerodynamic free area is
$A_{aero} \approx (b \bullet d_1) + (b \bullet d_2) + 2 (h \bullet d_1/2)$

Thermal uplift in double-skin facades

In this section, the balance between the warm-air extract and the motive forces will be examined in greater detail. The following section focuses on the optimization of the resistance factors that restrict the removal of warm air.

Attainable air change with free ventilation

In the principles outlined above, the main forces activating free ventilation were defined as wind and thermal uplift. Mention has also been made of the requisite air change. In the context of double-skin facades, an adequate removal of warm air at the height of summer plays a decisive role.

On the one hand, this function reflects the relatively frequent calm, windless conditions that exist, particularly on hot days, in most regions with a moderate climate. To some extent, coastal areas are an exception in this respect. On the other hand, the airflow volume necessary for the removal of hot air from a facade space exposed to insolation is considerably greater than that required for room ventilation.

This is easily demonstrated. In windless conditions at the height of summer, a natural exchange of air in the rooms and in the facade intermediate space can be effected only by means of thermal buoyancy. The motive force for the thermal buoyancy is the outcome of temperature differences between inside and outside caused by heat loads. The air, which is heated by people, by computers and by the surfaces on which the sun shines, rises to the ceiling and flows along the soffit out of the room. At the same time, cooler air streams in at the bottom of the windows to replace it. A similar process occurs in the facade intermediate space: the sunlight, shining on an apron wall perhaps or on an area of sunshading, is converted into heat.

In a typical three-bay room occupied by two people, it would be necessary for reasons of hygiene to ensure a supply of 70–100 m³ of external air per hour. Assuming a floor area of 20 m² and a room height of 3 m, this would mean a 1.67-fold air change per hour. Where a PC is installed at every workplace, internal loads of roughly 450 W will accrue for the people and computers alone. To remove this heat by means of the airflow volume mentioned above, the exhaust air would be heated to 13.5 K (at 100 m³/h) over the fresh-air intake temperature. Temperature differences of this magnitude are fortunately rare in offices. What is more likely to occur in reality is a larger airstream volume in the range between 250 and 300 m³/h as a result of the internal loads, even when a window is open only in a tipped position. The temperature differences will sink to around 5 kelvin. The specific air change for the room size described above is:
$ACR' \approx 2 \ [1/h\sqrt{K}\,]$.

The precise volume of the air change depends largely on the opening areas and the resistances in the facade. If the heat load to be extracted increases, the temperature difference will also increase, and with it the airstream volume between inside and outside—until a state of equilibrium is reached again. Rooms with cooling soffits have a smaller excess of heat and thus a lower degree of thermal buoyancy and a smaller natural air change.

The same balance will now be drawn up for the facade intermediate space, and the calculating process will be described in greater detail. This presents no real problem, since only the size and the resistance effect of the opening in the outer skin have to be considered, and these can be simply described using the specific pressure loss coefficients ζ (zeta values) mentioned at the beginning of this chapter.

If one assumes a fully glazed outer skin with an elevational area of 12 m², the maximum insolation value in the facade intermediate space will be roughly 6.5 kW in front of the sunshading. Even if the sunshading is completely white, experience shows that at least 30% of the heat radiated into this space will be absorbed and will have to be extracted mainly by means of the air-change process. This heat, which has to be removed by convection, can be calculated as follows:
$$\dot{Q}_{conv} = \rho \bullet c \bullet \dot{V} \bullet \Delta t \ \ [kW] \quad (A10)$$

where

$\dot{Q}_{conv}$ is the heat to be removed by convection in [kW]
ρ is the density of the air in [kg/m³]
($\rho \approx 1.2$ kg/m³ at 20 °C)
c is the thermal capacity of the air in [kJ/kg K]
($c \approx 1$ kJ/kg K at 20 °C)
$\dot{V}$ is the resultant airstream volume in [m³/s]
Δt is the temperature difference between the air supply and the extracted air in [K].

According to the equation (A10), if one limits the admissible heating-up of the exhaust air compared with the fresh-air supply to $\Delta t = 5$K, an airflow volume of $\dot{V} = 1,170$ m³/h would be needed to remove the heat released by the sunblinds.

Calculation of requisite opening sizes for air-intake and extract

The question now arises: what opening areas would be necessary in our facade example to achieve this airflow volume? For this purpose, it will be necessary to establish the pressure equilibrium between thermal uplift and pressure losses mentioned in the general principles. In order to determine the amount of thermal uplift, the relationship between the mean temperature difference Δt_m and the temperature difference between air intake and extract Δt has to be clarified. This can be done by integrating the function that describes the rise in temperature with increasing height. Using the approach to air temperature stratification described in the basic principles (A9) (in which the temperature increases as the square of the height), this integration produces the simple relationship:

$$\Delta t_m = \Delta t/3 \quad [K] \quad (A11)$$

The available thermal uplift pressure, derived from (A1) is thus:

$$\Delta p_{th} = \Delta \rho' \bullet g \bullet h \bullet (\Delta t/3) \quad [Pa] \quad (A1a)$$

where
$\Delta \rho'$ is the specific change in density in [kg/m³K]
($\Delta \rho' \approx 0.004$ kg/m³K)
g is the acceleration caused by gravity in [m/s²]
($g \approx 9.81$ m/s²)
h is the effective uplift height in [m]
(in this case, h = 3 m).

The result is a motive pressure difference in the thermal uplift amounting to $\Delta p_{th} \approx 0.2$ Pa at 5 kelvin excess temperature. In accordance with the pressure equilibrium formula (A6), the pressure losses have to just reach this value. The method described under (A4) can be expressed in the equation:

$$\Delta p_{loss} = \rho/2 \bullet v^2 \bullet \Sigma\zeta \quad [Pa] \quad (A4a)$$

where
v is the resultant air speed in the areas of the openings in [m/s]
$\Sigma\zeta$ is the non-dimensional sum of the pressure loss coefficients.

Where the openings have the appropriate form and the airflow route is subject to low losses, it is possible to achieve values of $\Sigma\zeta = 3$ to 4 where the cross-sections of the air-intake and extract openings have equal dimensions.

The air speed in the openings is $v \approx 0.33$ m/s, and the requisite opening size for the air throughput already calculated (V = 1,170 m³/h) is $A \geq 1$ m² for the air intake and extract respectively.

According to the procedure described here, the resultant air speed v will in general be the mean speed through the smallest opening or the smallest cross-section through which the airflow passes. To calculate the total pressure losses, these have to be related to the same speed. This can be done using (A5) and will provide the following formula, for example, for two openings:

$$\Sigma\zeta = \zeta_1 + \left(\frac{A_1}{A_2}\right)^2 \bullet \zeta_2$$

Calculation of excess temperatures in the facade intermediate space

An excessive increase in temperature in the space between the facade skins in summer has a number of disadvantages. The decisive factor, as in the previous example, is usually the heat liberated as a result of absorption by areas of sunshading. Often, however, the dimensions will be determined before the geometry has been worked out in detail. In many cases, the openings will have to be kept as small as possible; e.g. for acoustic reasons. In situations of this kind, a cautious approach is necessary in determining what zeta values can realistically be achieved and in ensuring that these factors are observed in the course of the planning.

It will then be possible to estimate in advance the maximum resultant excess temperatures and airflow volumes in the ventilation of the intermediate space. To avoid boring readers with a long-winded development of formulae, we shall depict these relationships for the calculation in the form of nomograms, from which the data for the individual stages can be derived. The general principle of the basic formulae has already been given.

The first nomogram shows the relationship between the height of the facade and the maximum amount of heat from the sunshading that has to be extracted for various degrees of thermal absorption.

The second nomogram shows the thermal uplift available as a function of the excess temperature for various uplift heights, i.e. the differences in level between air-intake and air-extract openings.

The third nomogram shows the pressure losses in an optimized double-skin facade for various opening sizes in relation to the respective airflow volume.

The fourth nomogram shows the resultant excess temperatures for different opening sizes, again assuming an optimized airflow; i.e. favorable resistance coefficients ζ.

Nomogram 5 shows the opposite case: where the resultant airflow volume and the related excess temperature are given for predetermined opening sizes for various overall resistance coefficients. This raises the question of the size of the specific pressure loss ζ and the scope for optimizing these values. Where such values and the related minimum cross-sections are the dominant factors determining the specific pressure losses, the details can be decisive.

8-9 Nomogram 1
Heat to be extracted from a double-skin facade with sunshading in the intermediate space in relation to the height of the glazing and the color of the sunshading:
30% = brilliant white
50% = bright color
70% = dark colors

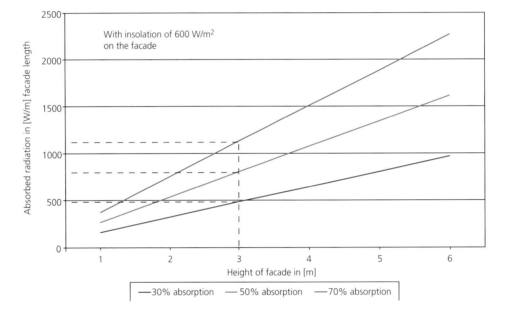

8-10 Nomogram 2
Thermal uplift in double-skin facades in relation to excess temperature of exhaust air and uplift height.

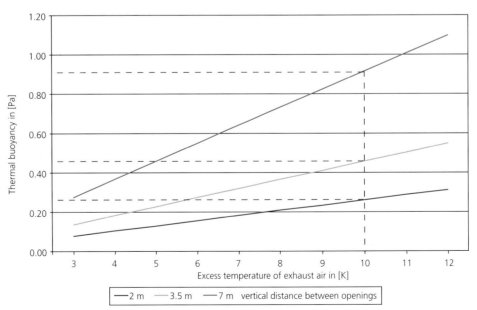

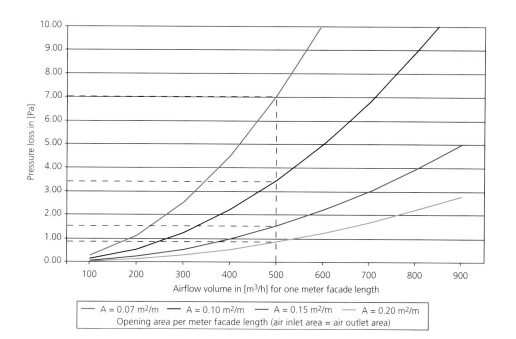

8-11 Nomogram 3
Pressure loss in airflow through
a double-skin facade in relation
to the openings and requisite
airflow volumes.
Without fan support, the pressure loss cannot exceed the
thermal uplift.
Favorable airflow resistances
were assumed: $\Sigma\zeta = 3$.

A = 0.07 m²/m   A = 0.10 m²/m   A = 0.15 m²/m   A = 0.20 m²/m
Opening area per meter facade length (air inlet area = air outlet area)

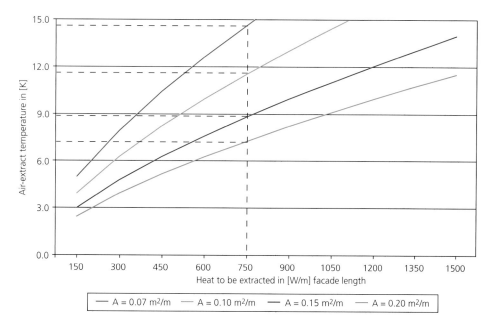

8-12 Nomogram 4
Development of excess temperature in the exhaust air of a
double-skin facade in relation
to the existing openings and
the insolation.
Favorable airflow resistances
were assumed: $\Sigma\zeta = 3$.

A = 0.07 m²/m   A = 0.10 m²/m   A = 0.15 m²/m   A = 0.20 m²/m

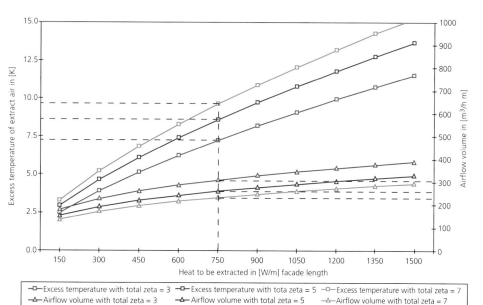

8-13 Nomogram 5
Development of excess temperatures and airflow volumes in a
double-skin facade in relation
to the airflow resistances ζ and
the insolation.
Based on openings for air intake and extract each amounting to 0.15 m² per meter length
of facade per story.

Excess temperature with total zeta = 3   Excess temperature with tota zeta = 5   Excess temperature with total zeta = 7
Airflow volume with total zeta = 3   Airflow volume with total zeta = 5   Airflow volume with total zeta = 7

Aerodynamic adjustment in shaft-box facades

A special aspect of shaft-box facades is the way the extract airstreams from a number of facade intermediate spaces can be grouped together into a single shaft. If the individual box windows adjoin the shaft at different levels, various thermal pressure differences will exist to activate the ventilation system. If the openings were all identical, the lowest box windows would be better ventilated, the upper ones less well ventilated. Since the maximum volume of air to be extracted is also limited by the cross-section of the shaft, some form of adjustment has to be made where there are a large number of adjacent box windows. This is referred to as an "aerodynamic adjustment": balancing the resistances in the individual box windows with the available uplift forces in each case achieves a state of equilibrium between the various airstreams.

The volume of air flowing through the individual box windows is dependent on the heat liberated in each case and the resultant excess temperature within the box window. In this respect, the quantity of air is self-regulatory. Moreover, there will also be a certain airflow from the thermal uplift in the shaft, which in some cases may be the dominant element. This additional source of buoyancy may mean that smaller air-intake openings will be possible.

In balancing out the airflow losses, the bypass opening into the shaft should also be taken into account. On the other hand, the air-extract opening at the end of the shaft represents a major source of resistance for the entire system. It has an influence on all the box windows, and the utmost care should be devoted to optimizing it if the attainable volume of extract air is relevant.

In the past, laboratory trials were carried out for the purpose of aerodynamic adjustment. The thermal uplift was simulated, using large-scale models (typically 1:5 to 1:10), and an adjustment of the resistances was sought by a process of trial and error.

In principle, the conditions can be determined just as well by calculation, although in view of the large numbers of interacting resistances, they can be quantified only with complex computer programs or CFD simulations. Even then, the aerodynamic adjustment will have to be determined as a rule through a series of trials, since no analytical solution is known at present.

8-15 Far right: model (scale 1:7) of shaft-box facade for the ARAG 2000 project in Düsseldorf.
Using a special gas, the thermal uplift can be simulated under trial conditions; the air supply for all areas can be optimized and confirmed.
Trials carried out by RWTH Aachen, Prof. Ruscheweyh.

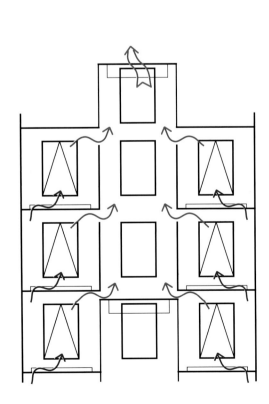

8-14 Principle of a shaft-box facade. To ensure the same air change on all floors, the openings and resistances have to be coordinated with the different uplift heights on each story.

Aerodynamic optimization of resistances

In this section, various design aspects of double-skin facades are considered that determine whether the airflow will be efficient or inefficient. Questions relating to openings in the inner skin also apply analogously to single-skin facades. At the outset, a summary is given of the routes by which air flows through double-skin facades and the resistances or pressure losses to which it may be subject.

■ External air enters the intermediate space of the facade via air-intake openings in the outer skin. Usually, the height of the air-intake openings will be smaller than the depth of the intermediate space, so that an initial peak velocity will occur in these openings, together with a corresponding loss of pressure.

■ When the sunshading is lowered in the facade intermediate space, the airstream may be divided into two parts. A major portion of the air is likely to be heated up by the sunshading and rise directly to the air-extract opening at the top. The remainder of the air, at a greater distance to the sunshading, will not be heated to the same extent and will ascend more slowly. If the sunshading is situated in the front third of the intermediate space, as recommended in the chapter "Thermal Insulation", this residual volume of air will largely determine the conditions existing in front of the inner facade layer. Only where the cavity between the facade skins is relatively shallow (less than about 40 cm) are significant pressure losses likely to occur. Otherwise, the intermediate space offers no major resistance to the airflow.

■ When the windows in the inner facade skin are open, part of the air will also enter the room if a motive force exists such as internal heat loads. Depending on the form and size of the window openings, the air will possibly have to pass through further constrictions, which again result in increased local speeds and pressure losses. These, in turn, function as additional forms of resistance that restrict the potential degree of room ventilation. Depending on the form of the opening, losses can also occur as a result of air flowing out from the rooms into the facade intermediate space.

■ In most double-skin facades, the greatest pressure losses occur when the air passes through the extract opening. The acceleration of the air through this comparatively small aperture is not basically different from that occurring at the air-intake opening at the base; but at the air-extract opening, the airstream will be subject to greater deflections in passing round obstacles such as sunshading or rainwater traps.

Air-intake openings

In designing the air-intake openings, the first question to be considered is the need to provide some form of protection against the weather. Protection against birds or insects may also be necessary. In this respect, there is broad scope for optimization. If the openings and built-in elements have an inappropriate aerodynamic form, for example, airflow resistance can reduce the air throughput to a fraction of its optimum value.

Simple slits in the external glazing ensure a virtually undisturbed flow of air. If a weatherproof grating is inserted in the opening, however—consisting of common Z-section louvers, for example—the obstruction to the geometric surface area will already amount to roughly 50%. The choice of more streamlined louvers can play a major role in reducing constrictions in the openings in the outer facade.

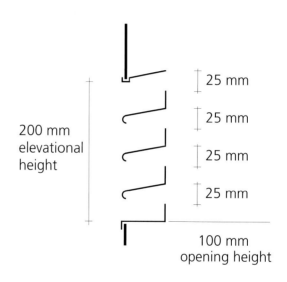

8-16 Example of a standard weather-protection grille consisting of so-called "Z-section louvers".
In this case, the open cross-section is only 50% of the elevational area. Further reductions are caused by the breakaway of flow.

The problem of pigeons around buildings raises the question of protection against birds in general. If protection of this kind is required, it will mean fitting wires or nets over openings in the outer skin to prevent birds entering the building. Certain species seem to be magically drawn to cavernous openings. The planning team will then be confronted with questions that can rarely be answered: which kinds of birds have to be considered on a particular site; and what is the maximum size of openings that can be left uncovered? One is familiar with the argument that some small birds can slip through holes only 1–2 cm in diameter. That would justify the installation of an anti-bird grating or net with a small mesh size (5–10 mm).

The effect this will have on the airflow depends on the diameter of the wires used. In order to ensure greater durability, these are often specified a gauge or two thicker than necessary. Depending on the diameter of the wires, they can cumulatively cause a considerable degree of obstruction, as the table below illustrates.

Wire thickness	0.3 mm	0.5 mm	1.0 mm
Mesh spacing	Geometric degree of obstruction		
5 mm	12%	19%	36%
8 mm	8%	12%	24%
10 mm	6%	10%	19%
20 mm	3%	5%	10%

As described in the basic principles, air is forced to flow through the constricted area of the openings at a greater speed in order to achieve the same throughput. This means that pressure losses increase quadratically. Obstructions of up to 10% of the area result in an increased pressure loss (up to about 20%) and may be regarded as acceptable. In planning the facade, this represents a compromise between choosing extremely fine wires or a mesh with larger spacings. The situation is somewhat better if, instead of using a mesh, wires are spanned in only one direction to prevent the ingress of birds.

In projects that have been executed to date, protection against birds has been omitted altogether in many cases, although allowance was made for its subsequent installation. As it transpired, a genuine need arose only in isolated cases; and in most instances, the birds were much larger than initially assumed.

Providing protection against the ingress of insects is even more critical than bird-exclusion measures. Not only is the geometric obstruction caused by insect screens considerably greater; air can no longer flow normally through the fine mesh, so that an even

greater resistance is caused. With mesh spacings of 2 mm and a wire diameter of 0.5 mm, the obstructed area amounts to 50%; the effectiveness of the ventilation, however, is reduced by about 85%. If one wishes to compensate for this by increasing the overall opening area, it would have to be at least seven times as large as a similarly functioning opening with no inbuilt elements; and that is without taking account of the further problem of soiling, as a result of pollen in the air, for example.

Inner facade
The effectiveness of the inner facade in terms of its ventilating function will depend on the opening movement of the windows—the actual free cross-section in an open position—and the distribution of the opening areas over the height. A bottom-hung tipped casement, for example, will have a different aerodynamic effect from a slide-down/push-out casement.
■ At the base of a bottom-hung casement, the resistance to the airflow is relatively great, since the tips of the triangular openings at the sides are of only minimal area. The inflow of external air is thus restricted and the potential rate of air change in the room reduced. In contrast, the outflow of air at the top is much stronger as a result of the wider opening between the casement and the frame.
■ In the case of slide-down/push-out casements, the projection of the casement at the bottom creates a relatively large opening that functions well aerodynamically and facilitates a plentiful ingress of air. At the same time, when the casement is lowered, air can flow out unimpeded through the opening at the top. Laboratory tests carried out for an actual building revealed an air change in the room roughly three times greater than that with a bottom-hung tipped casement.

8-17 Comparison between various casement opening types in the inner facade skin and their relative ventilating effectiveness in relation to the elevational area of the opening light.

up to 25 %	up to 70 %	up to 80 %	up to 90 %	up to 100 %	up to 100 %	up to 100 %
bottom hung tipped casement	horizontally sliding casement	slide down, top hung casement	vertically sliding casement	side-hung casement	vertically pivoting casement	horizontally pivoting casement

The situation changes when a bottom-hung casement is supplemented by a top-hung flap at the bottom of the window. In this case, the flap functions wholly as an air-intake opening and the bottom-hung tipped light mainly as an escape route for exhaust air. The airflow through the triangular openings at the sides and the resistance at these points is not so important.

A comparison of the relative ventilating effectiveness of different kinds of opening is shown in ill. 8-17 on the opposite page. Casement forms with ample openings at the top and bottom are very efficient. A vertically pivoting casement in alternate bays can be just as effective as a means of ventilation as twice as many bottom-hung tipped lights. Other aspects, of course, also play an important role in the choice of window types, including the price, ease of cleaning, appearance, availability of ironmongery, and the facility for regulating the ventilation in small doses.

Air-extract openings

The principles applying to inbuilt elements in air-intake openings, as described above, also apply to air-extract openings. An additional factor has to be considered in this context, however, namely the deflections to which the airstream is subject. These will result in further resistances, the magnitude of which depends largely on the routing of the airstream and the extent to which it is free of turbulence.

As described in the basic principles, vortices may occur along the path of the airstream, with eddies spinning off along the edges and at tight curves. Once these turbulences have formed, they can considerably reduce the effective area of an opening. The cross-section available for the airflow will then be the residual area free of turbulence, the dimensions of which are the only ones that should be used in calculations. To illustrate this, a situation will be considered that commonly occurs in the detailed planning of double-skin facades.

Outer facade

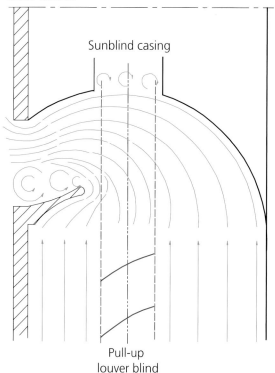

Sunblind casing

Pull-up
louver blind

8-18 Airflow around a rain-deflecting fin, made visible in a water-tank test. Large eddies spin off at the sides and reduce the effective cross-section of the opening for the outflow of air.

Example of optimization in practice

To minimize cleaning costs, it may be desirable to protect the air-extract opening against the ingress of rainwater and prevent water from running down the inside face of the glazing and leaving marks. If a weather-shield grating is not installed, a metal strip is usually fixed internally as a rain baffle and drip. This projects at least 5–10 cm into the intermediate space between the facade skins and thus into the airflow between the outer facade and the sunshading. In order to escape from the intermediate space, therefore, the warm air in front of the sunshading has to be deflected at an angle of 90° toward the rear and then 180° toward the outer face. This results in turbulences that again hinder the flow of air out of the intermediate space.

This effect may be counteracted by drawing deflector plates over the projecting edge. For the total deflection of 270° required in this case, the procedure would be relatively elaborate and would also interfere with the sunshading.

A compromise solution consists of fitting a metal deflector strip into the opening to divide the duct through which the extract air flows and to prevent the spread of turbulence. This can be supplemented by additional baffle plates as necessary.

If the effectiveness of the air-extract opening is not to be impaired—which would lead to higher temperatures in the intermediate space—the obstruction caused by the independent eddies of air should be offset by a geometrically larger extract opening, possibly

8-19 Airflow around a rain-deflecting fin, made visible in a water-tank test. Optimized state achieved by additional deflector plates.
Eddies still spin off at the side, but these are restricted in size and in the degree of obstruction they cause in the effective cross-section of the opening for the outflow of air.

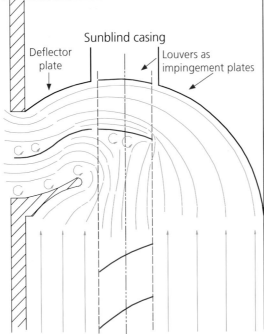

with additional elements to channel the airflow. An optimum positioning and detailing of such elements (e.g. deflection or baffle plates) requires the collaboration of aerodynamics experts. They conduct computer-aided airflow simulations (CFD) and/or trials on models under laboratory conditions, using air or water to obtain a precise analysis of the situation.

Early consultation with such specialists can help at the beginning of the detailed planning to identify most of the potential problems and to minimize supplementary measures. It also means a reduction of adjustments and optimization processes in the planning at a later stage or even after completion of the project.

The reduction of excess temperatures through the optimization of resistances is important, and not just in terms of the absolute temperatures in the intermediate space. The process is also related to a further problem indicated by laboratory tests: the greater the excess temperature in the facade intermediate space, the greater the thermal buoyancy. This may lead to the creation of an unintended bypass, which can result in a reduction of the supply of external air to the rooms. To ensure a proper ventilation of the rooms, therefore, the effective aerodynamic area of the air-intake and extract openings should be adequately dimensioned.

Return flow in upper stories of a building
Normally, no one considers where exhaust air goes after it has been extracted from the rooms of a building. After all, it is not highly contaminated with pollutants. The air may be somewhat heated and possibly humid, but these properties are quickly dissipated in the outside air. In principle, this lack of concern for what happens to the air extracted from a building is not unjustified, particularly when the wind is blowing. A special situation arises, however, when there is no wind. In such cases, there is a danger of *recontamination*—even in harmless situations—where natural window ventilation is provided.

This specialist expression describes the effect of exhaust air flowing back into the building as part of the fresh-air intake. This can occur to a serious extent when the exhaust air flows out of the building vertically below an air-intake opening. In such cases, thermal buoyancy may bear it up directly into the air-intake opening. This phenomenon was demonstrated years ago in the context of single-skin facade construction with conventional rectangular openings. When there

8-20 Airflow simulation (CFD) to analyze conditions for an even flow of air in a high-rise development at the Olympic Park, Munich.
Client: REMU, Munich.
The illustration shows directional airflow arrows. If they rotate in a circle, this indicates a stationary vortex that will potentially allow only a small degree of ventilation. The color range indicates the air temperatures in °C.

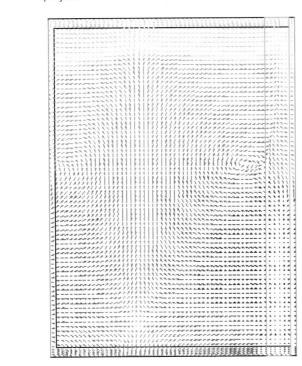

30.0
29.0
28.0
27.0
26.0
25.0
24.0
23.0
22.0
21.0
20.0

was no wind movement externally, and where the windows were set vertically above each other, it was shown that the air-intake contained a 20–25% proportion of exhaust air from the floor below. This can lead to a transmission of smells and germs.

In double-skin facades, therefore, the air-intake and extract openings in the facade should be staggered if possible. This prevents exhaust air flowing upward and directly entering an air-intake opening. Since the openings in any given story should be vertically as far apart as possible to exploit the effect of thermal uplift, it would seem only logical to plan the horizontally staggered openings all at one level. The height of the staggered openings should be doubled to compensate for the loss of width.

With a staggered layout of the openings, the amount of recontamination will be considerably reduced. In trials, values of between 5 and 10% were achieved under windless conditions. This can be regarded as a very good result for a multistory building. Measures of this kind also prevent the rapid spread of smoke in the event of fire. In terms of fire protection, therefore, a staggered layout is also favored in many cases. This, of course, presupposes an airtight division between stories.

Example of recontamination in a building

The negative thermal influence of a high level of recontamination can be seen in the example of a trial structure erected to test the effects of double-skin facades. A glazed skin was erected over three consecutive stories of an existing building. The openings in the glazed skin were situated above each other. Illustration 8-21 shows the temperature curves on a sunny Saturday afternoon—in other words, without the effects of users. There was an evident rise in temperature from floor to floor caused by the process of recontamination.

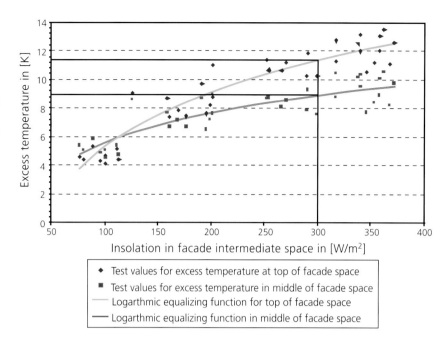

8-21 Plotting temperatures in a mock-up double-skin facade. As a result of recontamination through the re-entry of warm extract air, much higher temperatures were recorded at fourth floor level (shown in the graph above) than at second floor level (below).
The temperatures on an intermediate floor lie somewhere between the two. Recontamination of this kind, with excess temperatures pushing each other up from floor to floor, can be significantly reduced by staggering the air-inlet and outlet openings.

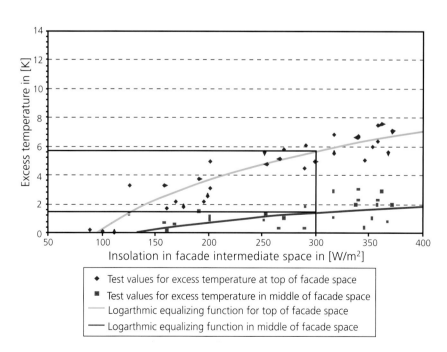

The effects of wind on double-skin facades

Does a double-skin facade reduce wind pressure?

The opinion is often expressed that double-skin facades reduce the effects of wind pressure. In this context, it is necessary at the outset to define what is meant by "wind pressure". Wind pressure always comprises static and dynamic elements. The dynamic element results from the gustiness of the wind; in other words, short-term changes of wind speed and direction caused by eddies in the airstream as it flows past a building. The static element, which is the outcome of large-scale air movements, is subject to only gradual changes of pressure. Static pressure leads to pressure differences between the windward and leeward sides of a building.

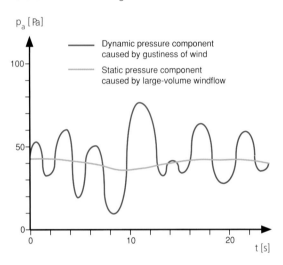

8-22 Example of wind-pressure curve, made up of dynamic and static elements. The mean static pressure corresponds to a wind speed of about 8 m/s or almost 30 km/h.

The effect of sudden changes of wind pressure is dampened in double-skin facades by the combined effect of openings in the inner and outer skins in conjunction with the intermediate space, which acts as a buffer. This characteristic is particularly important in high-rise buildings, where peak wind pressures caused by gusts can be many times greater than the static pressure. A similar principle is used in hydraulic engineering with the construction of moles or breakwaters. Only a fraction of the short-term surge of water can flow through the openings in the outer barrier. The main volume is repelled by the breakwater. The broader cross-section of the space in front of the second layer then absorbs the force from the inflowing stream of water or air (cf. ill. 9-1 on page 113). In practice, this may be demonstrated by the fact that the sunshading suspended in the intermediate space between the facade skins will be subject to reduced wind effects.

On the other hand, a more or less constant wind pressure will spread through the rooms. The airflow volumes necessary to achieve this effect (pressure increase and reduction during the requisite period in which an equilibrium between inside and outside is attained) are so small that the openings in the facade represent no real resistance to them. It is all the more important, therefore, to ensure an effective windward/leeward division in the plan layout. The aim of this should be to ensure that, as a rule, at least two closed doors separate the rooms on the windward side of the building from those on the leeward side. If zones of different pressure were linked with each other—by opening doors, for example—an airstream of varying strength would be set in motion, the tendency of which is to establish a state of equilibrium. In an extreme case, if the two realms were separated by only one closed door, the entire pressure difference that has built up around the building acts upon this door.

Quite apart from the unacceptable extreme situation where doors can no longer be opened or where they slam in the faces of users, the forces acting on a door handle should not exceed 40–50 N for reasons of comfort. An upper limit for ease of handling is given as 120 N in the German standard for fire-resistant doors and escape doors. That is equivalent to a weight force of 12 kg.

Effects of wind on rooms adjoining double-skin facades

If a state of pressure equalization is achieved throughout the building, one talks of "cross-ventilation". The strength of the cross-ventilation will depend on the airflow resistances within the facade and inside the building, and on the pressure difference that has been brought into a state of equilibrium. The magnitude of the cross-current of air will depend mainly on the sum of the airflow resistances. These, in turn, are largely determined by the smallest cross-section through which the airstream has to pass on its route through a building. If the doors are closed, the smallest opening will usually be formed by the slits around their edges. If the doors are open, however, the open area of the facade will usually be the decisive factor in terms of resistances. As a rule, this area is likely to be smaller in the outer layer of double-skin facades than in a single-skin facade.

If the openings in the inner skin are also of similar size, the doubling of the resistance resulting from the two layers will have a better braking effect against too strong an airflow through the facade. The cross-currents, which initially increase exponentially with the wind pressure, will be subject to an upper limit. This limit will be much lower than in the case of single-skin facades. Even so, the potential supply of fresh external air by means of cross-ventilation will be greater than the actual volume required. In practice, therefore, it is usually necessary to throttle the cross-ventilation by partly closing the openings in the inner facade skin.

Effects of wind on the ventilation of double-skin facades

Earlier sections describing the approximate dimensions of the requisite openings were deliberately based on a state of windlessness. The proportion of the time when windless conditions prevail ($v_{wind} \leq 0.5$ m/s) measured at a height of 10 m, is on average only roughly 1–5% annually, with regional variations. What influence, then, does the wind have on the ventilation of double-skin facades? The additional motive force resulting from pressure differences around buildings caused by wind has already been discussed in the section on basic principles. The cross-ventilation to which this leads was also described in the previous section. In view of its potentially undesirable force, this phenomenon should be prevented as a rule. In addition to this, though, a further form of cross-ventilation can occur within the facade if the external wind pressures at the openings in the outer skin vary.

Depending on the type of double-skin facade construction, the openings in the outer layer may be close together or far apart. In the case of box windows, the openings will be only a few meters apart, whereas in a corridor facade, the distance between two openings may easily be half the side length of the building. Especially at the corners, however, there will be great differences of wind pressure—as a result of the flow of air around the building—so that significant pressure differences may be expected at these points.

Across the width of a box window, there will be only relatively small pressure differences, amounting to roughly 0–5% of the stagnation pressure of the undisturbed wind stream. For a corridor facade extending from the middle to the corner of the building, the differences can easily have an effective value of 20–40% of the wind pressure.

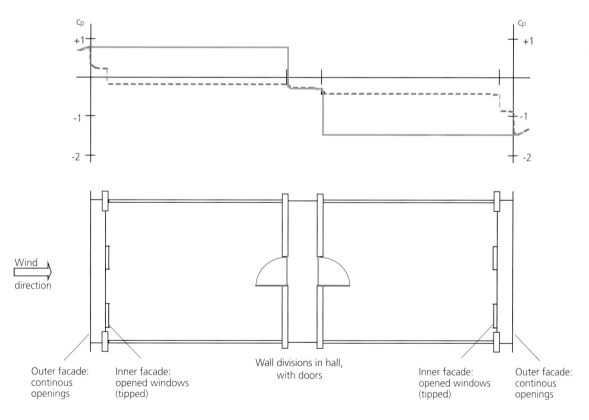

8-23 Wind-pressure curve across the width of an entire story with open windows; the doors were alternately open and closed.

Outer facade: continous openings

Inner facade: opened windows (tipped)

Wall divisions in hall, with doors

Inner facade: opened windows (tipped)

Outer facade: continous openings

Wind direction

Built example: effect of wind in the facade corridor of the "City Gate", Düsseldorf

In the "City Gate" development in Düsseldorf, the facade corridors are divided at the corners and in the middle of the building into roughly 20-meter-lengths. These divisions were created in the first instance by the location of the escape staircases; but they are also desirable in terms of the aerophysics of the building to avoid greater pressure differences along the lengths of the facade corridors.

In view of the external pressure distribution, the horizontal airflow along the corridors was investigated at the planning stage by means of airflow simulations. It was shown that with an external wind speed of 9 m/s (roughly force 7 on the Beaufort scale), velocities of around 5 m/s could occur through certain openings and would remain perceptible in the corridors at a speed of about 2–3 m/s. It was also shown that in its path along the corridor, the airstream would make a number of lateral movements, so that the corridor space would be well ventilated across its full width.

Measurements taken in the facade as executed confirm this data. Although the wind had no determinable effect on the ventilation in the three-bay mock-up facade, in the full facade corridor as executed, it had an appreciable influence. On calm, windless days, the thermal ventilation dominates, as predicted, resulting in excess temperatures of up to about 9 kelvin in the exhaust air. The horizontal air speeds along the length of the corridors remained low. If sun and wind occur in conjunction with each other, however, the wind plays a major role in reducing temperatures, and the excess temperatures sink to about 3–4 kelvin. The speed of the horizontal airflow then exceeds that of the vertical airstream—caused by thermal uplift—by a factor of 2 to 5.

A major effect of this "cross-ventilation" along the corridor is that the wind is perceptible to users within this space—an experience they described as very positive: they enjoyed protected surroundings, while remaining in contact with the natural environment.

The speed of the airstream along the corridor can be set in relationship to external wind speeds. This effect is known as the *wind penetration* into the corridor. The maximum dimension of this phenomenon will depend on the direction of the wind, since this determines the external pressure distribution. An analysis carried out over a period of several months during the process of measurement on the "City Gate" shows that the mean wind penetration was around 20% and that the peak value for a specific wind direction can reach up to 50%. This confirms the values calculated from airflow simulations carried out at the planning stage. The amount of wind penetration is also important in determining the wind speeds at which damage is likely to be caused to the sunshading system in the facade intermediate space.

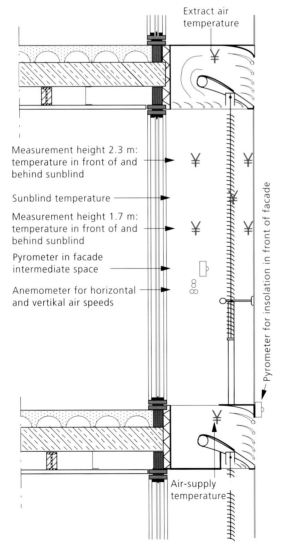

Extract air temperature

Measurement height 2.3 m: temperature in front of and behind sunblind

Sunblind temperature

Measurement height 1.7 m: temperature in front of and behind sunblind

Pyrometer in facade intermediate space

Anemometer for horizontal and vertikal air speeds

Pyrometer for insolation in front of facade

Air-supply temperature

8-24 Position of sensors in the facade of the "City Gate", Düsseldorf.
The measurements shown here were carried out in the summer of 1998 at 16th-floor level in the finished building.

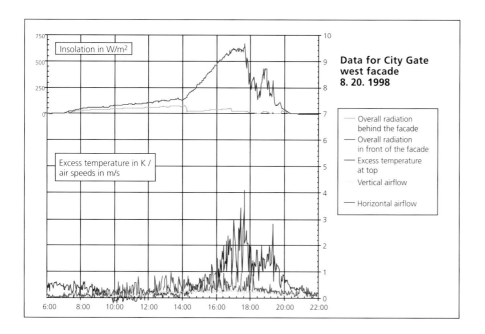

8-25 Excess temperatures and air speeds measured in a facade corridor of the "City Gate", Düsseldorf, on a sunny, windless day.

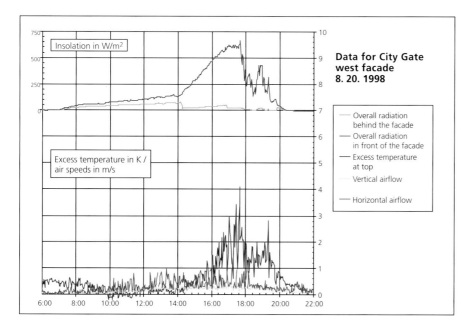

8-26 Excess temperatures and air speeds measured in a facade corridor of the "City Gate", Düsseldorf, on a sunny but windy day.

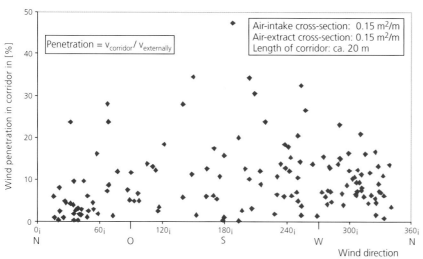

8-27 Degree of wind penetration in the facade corridor in relation to the wind direction.

The effects of wind on double-skin facades

9   High-Rise Buildings

In high-rise buildings, two additional aerophysical phenomena manifest themselves which need to be examined separately. The first of these, directly related to the height of the building, is the strong thermal uplift that occurs in continuous, vertical, shaft-like spaces (elevator and other service shafts, staircases, etc.) especially in winter. The second is that the effects of wind greatly increase with height.

To be able to react to these phenomena in an appropriate manner, a precise survey of the wind loads acting on the building will generally be necessary. This can be obtained by measurements in a wind tunnel. In buildings with double-skin facades, natural window ventilation will be possible even at greater heights, though this also poses certain questions: for example, what effect does the wind have within the rooms on each story; and what measures will have to be taken to avoid undesirable effects? These considerations can impose major constraints on the layout of the floors.

Vertical airstreams in buildings

The basic principles of thermal buoyancy were described at the beginning of the chapter on "Aerophysics" and subsequently applied to various situations in double-skin facades. The uplift effect in shafts can also be calculated, using formula A1, which was introduced in that chapter:

$$\Delta p_{th} = \Delta \rho' \bullet g \bullet \Delta h \bullet \Delta t_m \ [Pa] \quad (A1)$$

where
Δp_{th} is the thermal uplift pressure in [Pa]
$\Delta \rho'$ is the specific change in density of the air in relation to the temperature, $\Delta \rho' \approx 0.004$ [kg/m³ K]
$g \approx 9.81$ [m/s²] is the acceleration due to gravity
Δh is the effective uplift height in [m]
Δt_m is the mean excess temperature in [K].

In shafts situated in the interior of a building, the temperature will be more or less constant over the entire height, since a heat exchange will usually occur with the evenly heated adjoining spaces on each floor. In this case, $\Delta t_m = t_i - t_a$ and is likely to result in high values particularly in winter, as described above. In this form, the equation corresponds with the classical stack formula.

If one substitutes numerical values for a high-rise building in winter, at an internal temperature of 20 °C in a continuous shaft extending over the full height (e.g. an elevator shaft), the uplift pressures shown in the table will be valid. It is worth noting that the value for the thermal uplift pressure Δp_{th} in [Pa] where $\Delta t_m = 25$ K will be roughly equal to the value for the effective uplift height Δh in [m]. These uplift pressures can result in two undesirable effects.

■ If the shaft is linked with the outside air at one end only, which is often the case where ventilation is required, the uplift pressure will function with full force at the other end. Where the ventilation occurs above roof level, this will cause great suction forces on inspection doors at the foot of the shaft. In winter, these forces can assume a critical value if the building is more than 100 m in height. Since the elevator doors are not airtight, the negative pressure resulting from thermal uplift can also affect airtight doors such as those in an elevator lobby.

■ If the shaft is linked with the outside air at both ends, the uplift pressure will possibly suck large quantities of air into the shaft and transport it upward. This can result in local sensations of drafts and the sound of wind whistling around the edges of doors. The entrance halls of buildings are often affected by these phenomena if no separate lobby to the elevators is created. Where a canteen is situated on one of the lower floors adjoining an elevator lobby, the air currents sucked into the elevator shaft will possibly distribute cooking smells throughout the building.

Height of building	20 m	60 m	100 m	150 m
External temperature	Thermal uplift pressure			
0 °C	≈ 16 Pa	≈ 50 Pa	≈ 80 Pa	≈ 120 Pa
-5 °C	≈ 20 Pa	≈ 60 Pa	≈ 100 Pa	≈ 150 Pa
-10 °C	≈ 24 Pa	≈ 70 Pa	≈ 120 Pa	≈ 180 Pa

These problems occur more frequently in high-rise buildings than one might imagine. Since the question of free airstreams caused by thermal uplift does not fall within the responsibility of any planning discipline, these phenomena may often be overlooked where there is a lack of experience in planning tall buildings. In many cases, the cause of these phenomena will not be evident to the layman.

The following example sounds rather like an anecdote. While acting as consultants for the provision of free ventilation in an extension to a building, the authors were approached by the client in respect of the existing structure, which consisted of a roughly 60-meter-high tower dating from the 1960s. In the winter soon after it had been taken into occupation, complaints were made about drafts in the entrance hall. The doorman's area had thereupon been enclosed within glass walls and provided with a separate heating system. When external temperatures fell below 0 °C, one could repeatedly observe how the glazed entrance doors would swing open as if by magic and remain in this position, even though the entrance area was protected from the wind. Conditions in the entrance hall were correspondingly bleak, and the client had abandoned the idea of installing the proposed customer terminals which were to have been accessible round the clock.

An analysis of the situation revealed the causes, which corresponded to those described above. The elevator shafts were linked with the external air via the machine rooms at the top. In order to avoid overheating in summer, the large openings there were protected against the weather only by gratings. Access to the elevator lobby on the ground floor was via an open corridor linked with the entrance hall. When the external temperatures sank, ever greater quantities of air were propelled up the elevator shafts as a result of the thermal uplift. Below a certain external temperature, the suction effect was so great that the air streaming in through joints and gaps was no longer adequate, and the entrance hall doors were forced open by the pressure of air from outside.

Quite apart from the spectacular effect of doors opening as if moved by an invisible hand, airstreams of this kind cause considerable energy losses, so that one is faced with the question of appropriate countermeasures.

Measures to restrict vertical airstreams

Under certain circumstances, it is possible to limit the effective thermal uplift in staircases and service shafts by dividing them in their height. This is likely to be a suitable option in very tall buildings where the spaces for mechanical service are distributed over the height anyway.

For service shafts that extend over great heights, it is important to control the air-intake and outlet conditions at the ends. If one end of the shaft is virtually sealed off from the external air, thermal pressure will build up there, while the "open" end will be subject neither to great pressure nor to strong air currents.

If there are openings on several or all stories of the building, as is the case with elevator shafts or shafts for sanitary installations, it will be necessary to ensure a tight seal against external air at each of these levels. In buildings with facades that cannot be opened, this will present no problem. Where the facade is used for window ventilation, however, it will generally be necessary to create an air lock with at least two airtight doors between the shaft and the office or dwelling areas. This may also be necessary for fire-protection purposes; and even if it is not a statutory requirement, it will at least improve safety conditions.

It can be a very elaborate process (and architecturally obtrusive) if the access zone to the elevators in the entrance hall or adjoining a canteen has to be separated from the adjoining areas. But this is a common and logical requirement where large numbers of people use these areas at peak periods. In such cases, it is advisable to make a precise analysis of all contingent conditions for each specific scheme to prevent undesirable drafts.

In many cases, attempts are made to separate the various functional areas in canteens—kitchens, smoking and non-smoking sections, or a cafeteria—solely by a mechanical air-extract installation. That will function only if the free ventilation caused by the shafts does not result in similar or even greater volumes of air being channelled through these areas. Otherwise, the only remedy is to construct a series of firm divisions, and these can take up a lot of space. The situation resembles that at the entrances to department stores, which has given rise to a great deal of discussion. Air-curtain installations are often provided to ease the problem, but this solution will be successful only where the appropriate ancillary conditions exist.

One alternative, though not always feasible, is to create a further link between the air-bearing shaft and the external air, via which air can be sucked in. This will mean not only that the shaft will be freely ventilated; technically speaking, it will possibly become an external space that will then require the appropriate thermal insulation to those areas adjoining heated sections of the building.

Wind characteristics

Since wind movement is usually a phenomenon extending over a larger space, in the lower strata of the atmosphere (up to 400 meters in altitude) a so-called "boundary-layer profile" will develop. Obstacles on the surface of the earth, together with the topography of the ground, will exert a local influence on the wind. Above all, they will have a braking effect, so that the wind will attain its full speed and a stable direction only with increasing altitude. Over flat areas where the vegetation or building development is of even height, plotting the gradually increasing windspeeds at greater altitudes will produce typical curves. As a reference value, meteorologists take the *mean wind speed at a height of 10 m, v_{10}.* This is usually given as a mean value over a period of 10 minutes. The equation (H1) can be applied in converted form for other altitudes, as long as the effect of local obstacles and the microclimate as influenced by the topography are not dominant factors.

$$v_n = \left(\frac{h_n}{10} \right)^{\alpha} \bullet v_{10} \ \ [\text{m/s}] \quad \text{(H1)}$$

where
v_n is the wind speed at altitude n, in [m/s]
h_n is the height n, in [m]
α is the roughness factor [-].

The *roughness factor* α is the standard value derived from the typical curve. It will be roughly 0.16 for extensive areas of water, roughly 0.20 for forest areas, and roughly 0.22–0.24 for evenly developed urban fabric. (H1) is especially valid for strong wind conditions where a building is not situated in a valley or hollow or set among a group of structures of similar height.

The annual range of mean wind speeds can be obtained with a fair degree of accuracy from wind statistics (at v_{10}) provided by the nearest larger meteorological station. These values can be extrapolated for other altitudes using equation (H1). Data of this kind is contained, for example, in /H1/ and /H2/ and can normally be obtained from regional or state weather services. Organizations of this kind usually offer additional services such as climatic surveys. It will then be possible, for example, to design and orient a building to take account of peak gale forces over a statistical period of 50 years.

A constant airstream, as defined by the mean wind speed v_{10} and equation (H1), will always be accompanied by a certain turbulence, sometimes stronger, sometimes weaker. Airflow patterns near cold fronts also result in a number of larger or smaller turbulences in the air—rather like the eddies that spin off an airstream as a result of obstacles. These turbulences are felt as wind gusts around buildings. By a "gust" one understands an increase of wind speed that is limited in place and time. It will usually occur in conjunction with a slight change of wind direction as well. Since a gust is caused by turbulence, there will always be a brief reduction of the wind speed immediately before or after the gust. Overall, therefore, an even flow of wind will be accompanied by a constant fluctuation of wind speeds and directions measured at any one location. The most common frequencies of wind gusts range from one second to several minutes. As a rule, therefore, wind gusts will not have any effect on the building as a whole, but they do have a major influence on the dimensions of individual sections of the facade that are smaller than or similar in size to the diameter of the eddy.

Stationary and instationary wind loads

The loads exerted by wind on a building play an important role in the structural engineering of high-rise developments. A distinction should be made between stationary loads that act on the entire building and instationary loads resulting from gusts. Instationary loads are of significance only in dimensioning the facade, and they exhibit a number of special characteristics in the context of double-skin facades. Furthermore, the influences of the surroundings manifest themselves through instationary loads. This applies especially to other tall buildings within a radius of up to several miles.

The magnitude of both instationary and stationary loads can be determined in wind-tunnel tests, since the primary difference between the two lies in the evaluation of short-term fluctuation ranges as a result of wind gusts. In depicting the findings for stationary loads, a form of representation has also been developed for instationary loads known as the *peak-factor method*, according to Davenport /H3/. This describes instationary loads with the factor k as a multiple of the stationary loads. Where the layout of a building is relatively straightforward and there are no other tall buildings in the vicinity, the typical values will be in the range k = 3–7. For more complex layouts, especially where the building has acute-angled corners, and where tall neighboring structures exert a negative influence, values of over 10 have been measured on occasion.

With a permanently ventilated double-skin facade construction, the question arises how these loads are distributed between the two facade layers—and how they continue into the internal spaces when the windows are open. Observing similar aerodynamic conditions in wind-tunnel tests, it was possible to demonstrate that these loads are distributed over both facade planes, so that neither of the skins has to bear the full load as long as the rear venting system is maintained. The effect might be compared with that of a "breakwater" and could be described as a wave-breaking effect. The outer facade layer is affected mainly by the short-term wind forces from gusts, while the steady components of the wind penetrate into the intermediate space. This means that the outer skin is largely relieved of constant wind loads, whereas the inner skin is screened from the effects of short-term elements. This principle is illustrated in the diagram below, which shows the pressure curves outside the facade, within the facade space and in the rooms themselves (when the windows are open).

Wind-load distribution for typical plan forms

The main distribution of wind pressures in and around high-rise buildings has been established through research and is by no means an unknown quantity. The actual size of the loads, however, can be strongly influenced by surrounding conditions and especially by other tall buildings; and it will be necessary to quantify these effects in wind-tunnel tests for each specific case. The airflow around high-rise buildings consists of the following elements:

- the so-called *horseshoe vortex* at the base of a building;
- the *airflow around the plan form*—which will be more or less constant over the entire height of the building; and
- the so-called *topflow* at the top of the building

The *horseshoe vortex* derives its name from its form, since the wind on the windward face exerts a downward pressure and curls round the foot of the building on both sides. In the process, the wind energy from the upper air strata is drawn down to ground level, where it results in a noticeable increase in the wind speed. In extreme cases, it can lead to serious impairment of the ambient comfort in these areas, even for passersby. When very tall buildings are erected in the U.S., the actual high-rise tower will usually be surrounded at the base by a lower plinth structure, which ensures wind-protected access to the building. In densely developed European and Asian cities, how-

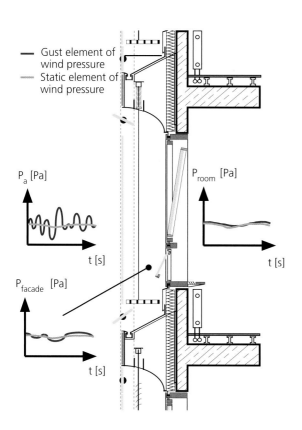

— Gust element of wind pressure
— Static element of wind pressure

P_a [Pa]

t [s]

P_{room} [Pa]

t [s]

P_{facade} [Pa]

t [s]

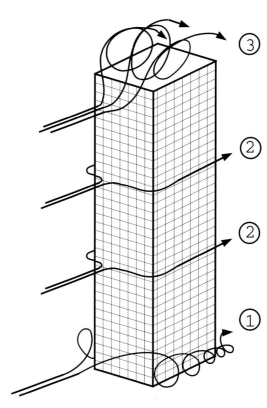

9-1 Far left: reduction of fluctuations in wind pressure by equalizing effects in the double-skin facade ("wave-breaking effect").

9-2 Diagram of airflow around high-rise buildings:
1 horseshoe vortex round the base of the building
2 airflow around cross-section of building
3 topflow over the roof of the building

ever, tower blocks often rise directly from the street, so that it is possible for the wind to descend to the entrance area at ground floor level.

The *airflow around the plan form* or horizontal section of a high-rise building may be compared with the airstream around an airplane wing. In view of the great elongation of tall buildings (i.e. the relation of the height to the cross-section), the airstream around them will be virtually two-dimensional over the middle section. In other words, the wind will flow more or less in the plane of the plan layout. This airflow pattern results in a typical pressure distribution, which is dependent on the plan form of the building and the direction of the wind. The pressure distribution will be virtually constant over the height of the building. Where the plan form is angular, there will usually be a breakaway of the airstream behind the corners that are set at right angles to the wind. As a result of this, suction peaks with very high negative cp-values will occur behind these corners.

Where the building has a circular plan form with no pronounced angles, the points of separation will depend above all on the airflow speed and the radius of the curve. With a cylindrical tower, the suction peaks will occur at an angle of about 70° to 100° on both sides of the airflow direction, depending on the wind speed.

At the top of a high-rise structure, where a large part of the wind flows upward over the roof, a three-dimensional airstream will develop—comparable to the situation at the foot of the building. The breakoff of the airstream here is referred to as the *topflow*. Again, its form will depend on the shape of the building on plan and the outline of the roof. Over flat roofs, the topflow will result in large-scale turbulence, which may be referred to as a separation bubble. One positive aspect is that the wind forces have little effect on the flat roof itself. As a result of the back-current within the separation bubble, the air usually flows over the roof surface in the opposite direction to the prevailing wind. The form of topflow, therefore, will have a major influence on the erection of a weather station or a wind gauge, as well as on the layout of the necessary chimney stacks and air-extract heads, which require steady airflow conditions.

9-3 Far right: qualitative pressure distribution around a high-rise building with a square plan, where the wind direction is at right angles to one side.

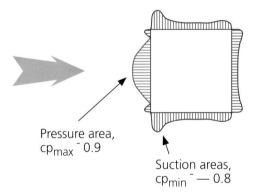

Pressure area, cp_{max} ⁻ 0.9

Suction areas, cp_{min} ⁻ — 0.8

9-4 Far right: qualitative pressure distribution around a high-rise building with a square plan, where the wind direction is on the diagonal.

9-5 Right: qualitative pressure distribution around a cylindrical high-rise building.

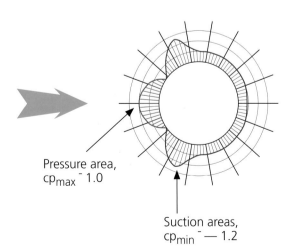

Pressure area, cp_{max} ⁻ 1.0

Suction areas, cp_{min} ⁻ — 1.2

Pressure area, cp_{max} ⁻ 0.8

Suction areas, cp_{min} ⁻ — 1.2

Measures to achieve a windward/leeward separation

Two strategies exist to prevent the wind pressures around tall buildings resulting in unwanted drafts internally when the windows are open.

■ The layout can be divided in such a way that the sequences of rooms are clearly oriented to either the windward or the leeward side of the building. In this case, the two sides should be separated from each other by self-closing, tightly sealing doors or, even better, by air locks with two sets of doors. The system will have to function for wind from all directions.

■ A facade with an intermediate buffer space can be erected around the entire building. By creating a by-pass airstream through the intermediate space, a state of pressure equilibrium can be achieved on the different sides of the building, thereby eliminating pressure differences (to a large extent), so that they will have no effect in the internal spaces.

The first strategy has serious implications for the planning of the layout and the desired use of a building. As a rule, this approach functions well where the access cores are situated at the centre of the layout, in which case only the corridor around these cores will have to be divided into separate sections. Group or open-plan offices where openable windows are required will have to be clearly assigned to a particular zone (windward or leeward) and cannot be ventilated from two sides as a rule. In individual unit offices at the corners of a building, one of the two faces will have to remain closed for most of the time. The intermediate space of the double-skin facade should be closed off with cross-divisions at the corners of the building.

Good conditions for an effective windward/leeward separation can be created in housing developments as well, provided the dwellings are not laid out around corners. Two-bay strip developments, on the other hand, can be problematic when the wind acts on one of the long faces of the building, since one can hardly expect all room doors to remain permanently closed. Moreover, in such cases, the sealing quality of all door surrounds will have to be optimized to allow a controlled reduction of pressure and to prevent the wind whistling round the edges of the doors.

The second strategy can be implemented only in conjunction with double-skin facades where the intermediate space is in a corridor or multistory form. This method is suitable for all areas where local pressure or suction peaks have to be reduced. The greater the external pressure difference that has to be reduced, however, the greater the depth of the facade intermediate space will have to be in relation to the size of the openings in the external skin. Otherwise only a partial reduction of these effects will be achieved; since

where there is a strong flow of air through the intermediate space, the space itself will become a source of great resistance. In view of the larger apertures that will be required for the air-intake in summer, these constraints usually require the provision of openings that can be partly or completely closed. On the other hand, the pressure equalization in the facade intermediate space increases the wind loads acting on the outer surface of the facade, sometimes appreciably, and especially at the corners.

The implementation of both these strategies parallel to each other is not only possible; in some cases, it is the only way to limit undesirable effects of wind within the rooms. At all events, a detailed investigation of the situation on the basis of pressure coefficients obtained in wind-tunnel tests is recommended, because a good windward/leeward separation can considerably reduce wind-induced drafts where natural window ventilation is foreseen. It will also increase the period in which window ventilation is possible during the course of the year. This may amount to a gain of as much as 20 to 30 percent of the operating time of the building.

9-6 Example of measures to achieve a windward/leeward separation by closing off compartments in the layout and in the facade: Business Tower, Nuremberg.

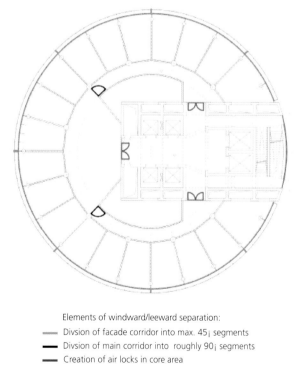

Elements of windward/leeward separation:
— Divsion of facade corridor into max. 45¡ segments
— Divsion of main corridor into roughly 90¡ segments
— Creation of air locks in core area

Protection against driving rain

A secondary aspect of the process of windward/leeward separation is the protection of the external facade against driving rain. Water penetration is possible wherever wind flows through an opening or through cracks and joints where pressure differences exist. If a successful windward/leeward separation is achieved in the layout, no pressure differences will occur at the facade openings that could drive water into the intermediate space, let alone into the rooms. Apart from the effects of splashing, the water can run off entirely down the outer facade.

If the facade corridor is used to equalize major pressure differences, though, the airflow through the openings on the windward side will be from outside to inside, so that water running down the outside of the facade can be drawn into the intermediate space. In such cases, the geometry of the openings will have to be optimized to prevent greater quantities of water penetrating the outer skin and causing serious soiling.

9-7 Ensemble of high-rise towers at Potsdamer Platz, Berlin;
left: Potsdamer Platz 11 by Renzo Piano and Christoph Kohlbecker;
center: Potsdamer Platz 1 by Prof. Hans Kollhoff;
right: Sony Tower by Helmut Jahn.

The close proximity of a number of high-rise buildings, as here at Potsdamer Platz or in the city center of Frankfurt, results in local areas of shading and complex interactions with the prevailing wind stream, which in turn can also cause a local boosting of wind speed.

Control concepts for closable facades

In seeking to adapt the building physics of a facade to weather conditions, the question of finding an economical solution arises. Generally speaking, electrically operated sunshading systems are uncontroversial today; whereas the purpose and cost of motor-operated flaps in double-skin facades are rightly subject to debate in some cases. Once one has decided in favor of motor-operated flaps, however (e.g. to reduce the effects of wind), an appropriate control concept has to be developed.

Flaps are usually incorporated in the external skin where individual control of the inner facade is to be left to the users. The main purpose of the flaps is to close the intermediate space within the facade to save heating energy and to reduce the effects of heavy wind loads. Reference values for the operation of the flaps are usually the external temperature and the local wind pressure. Since the wind pressure cannot be measured at all points, the facade will have to be divided into zones subject to similar pressure. It will then be sufficient to take measurements at reference points in a limited number of zones. The wind-pressure distribution for various wind directions, as measured in wind-tunnel tests, can provide valuable help in determining the division of the facade into zones and the location of the measurement points. The fact that the airflow around the cross-section of a high-rise building is constant over most of its height allows the number of zones to be kept to a minimum: it will usually be adequate to divide the height of the building into between one and three zones, whereas five to ten zones may easily be necessary around the perimeter.

The pressure difference across an entire story will have to be calculated for the control system in order to ensure that the facade will be closed at least on one side before the wind force reaches unacceptable levels in door openings. At the same time, the air-conditioning system will require a signal to show when external air has to be supplied mechanically.

An overall check of the system in operation and the regulation of each flap should not be overlooked during the phase when the building is taken into operation. Checks of this kind occur automatically in the case of other mechanical services: in the process of accepting the work, the various installations are tested for completeness and defects. The same thoroughness is rarely applied to facade controls, however. In the brief time available at the completion of construction, and in view of the newness of the technology, the mere existence of measured values and control elements for the operation of the facade will often pass as proof of the fulfilment of contractual obligations. The function and suitability of the control software are usually not tested—or only inadequately—because of a lack of criteria. In view of the central role played by the weather in this technology, almost any combination or sequence of operating modes is conceivable, and it is impossible to consider them in their entirety, even for specialists in this field.

It is advisable, therefore, to include in the planning concept for the various programs a system that will facilitate an undisputed localization and elimination of any undesirable control phenomena that may occur. This should ensure that any additional needs and expectations—which often arise only when the systems are in use—can be quickly accommodated and that omissions of this kind will not be teething problems that detract from the full use of the building over a longer period of time. The spectrum of causes ranges from changes in the periods of use by different tenants to inaccurate measurement values.

Diverse user needs, extremely variable parameters—especially the weather—and the many possible permutations of operating conditions make the planning of facade controls an area subject to a large number of imponderables. Furthermore, the response to the controls is usually directly visible or perceptible to users. As a result, faults, or phenomena that are perceived as such, can lead to a sense of dissatisfaction or even insecurity.

An active supervision of the regulation of the facade controls and the process of taking them into operation, as well as adequate provision for this in the time schedule, is strongly recommended. Future operating staff should be drawn into this process wherever possible to acquaint them with the control system at an early stage.

10 Special Characteristics of Facade Construction

This chapter describes how the planning of a double-skin facade is implemented at the construction stage, with reference to the main contingent conditions that play a role in the execution of the work. The description begins, therefore, with general notes on important constraints affecting the planning, the tendering and the award of contracts, the release of details for construction, and the execution of the work. This is followed by a description of various facade types and forms of construction, their respective characteristics, and the conditions governing their use. The following chapter is devoted to a discussion of supplementary aspects of facade construction, including the question of fixings and adjustments in relation to the load-bearing structure.

Double-skin facade construction: an individual prototype

The planning of a facade, like that of any form of construction, implies the development of an individual prototype. This guiding principle should always be borne in mind when the pros and cons of various systems are discussed. The choice of a particular facade system can be made only after a close analysis of the constraints to which each individual scheme is subject. The choice should not be made on the basis of a discussion of general advantages and disadvantages.

Thanks to the work of large system-construction firms over the past few years, it is now possible to use serial components from various standard systems on a large scale in the execution of constructionally and formally simple single-skin facades. As an outcome of intensive developments, the major companies marketing these systems are expanding their catalogues of products at a great pace. The times when one could obtain little more than a range of aluminum sections with simple corner details are past.

In the context of global economic developments, more and more high-quality construction products are being generated and produced in extensive ranges—not only by systems manufacturers, but also by the glass industry in collaboration with partners from the supply sector. For example, since the winter of 1998/1999, the glass industry (in this case, the Saint Gobain company) has been marketing a complete all-glass casement construction system with aluminum supporting sections, a full range of ancillary fittings and ironmongery, as well as finished glass elements. Similarly, system-product firms now offer complete solar and photovoltaic panels in combination with fully glazed units. Where required, facade supporting sections are available almost automatically with all fittings for abutments to other parts of the structure.

Some architects who work in the field of design see this as a development in the wrong direction, fearing that it will restrict their freedom of design and that new facade types will come to have an increasingly "uniform" appearance.

Architects who are more concerned with construction and site management, as well as general contractors and the clients themselves, are usually happy with the development of complete facade products. They see the application of a system that has been coordinated and tested down to the finest aspects of building technology as a means of reducing the risk of damage to the outer skin of a building.

Most system manufacturers in the field of facade construction have become extremely flexible in terms of technical prefabrication, and especially in their readiness to adapt system products to specific requirements. These manufacturers are thus helping to avoid the development feared by planning architects and facade designers, particularly in individual facade projects and large-scale schemes.

Complete product ranges of this kind—in the form of a series of individual components—can be used to advantage in the constructional development of double-skin facades. Compared to single-skin types, these require a relatively high degree of individual development, both constructionally and formally, since the double-skin form has to comply with more extensive planning constraints. These include
■ additional requirements for fire-protection between the inner and outer facade skins;
■ aerophysically effective components to optimize the airflow through the facade;
■ drainage of the facade intermediate space; and
■ providing scope for access to the intermediate space.

Additional formal aspects that may have to be considered include

■ the visual effect of two layers of materials set in front of each other, with twice the number of elements and the twofold dimensions this implies;
■ air-intake and extract openings; and
■ the visual effect of depth.

    Elements of the facade that possibly reduce the degree of transparency include
■ vertical divisions in the facade cavity; and
■ horizontal elements to make the facade intermediate space accessible.

    Further general aspects that have to be taken into account in the overall planning of double-skin facades include
■ mechanical services
■ energy optimization
■ building physics
■ aerophysics, and
■ cost limits.

Ultimately, of course, the above-mentioned constraints inevitably lead to the design of an individual facade prototype. The aim of this complex planning program is to create a high-quality end product for client and users alike. Its scientific, technical and constructional implementation can be achieved only with the help of a team of specialist engineers or, better still, a specialist engineering office where a collective body of knowledge exists. Additional experience gained from projects that have already been realized is another key factor in terms of technical development and especially in meeting economic targets.

    In recent years, attempts have been made to develop a universal double-skin facade type that can be manufactured in serial form. The aim was to provide a complete facade system that could be ordered from a catalog, with virtually constant dimensions and materials. With this in mind, the ALCO company developed its so-called Twin-Face Facade; and some time afterwards, the SCHÜCO company developed a double-skin system facade that was presented as a prototype at the BAU-Messe building fair in Munich in 1997.

    Some facade manufacturers and developers have come to recognize, however, that a complete package in the true sense of the term is very difficult to sell and that it has to be adaptable to the specific needs of every building, as described above. These companies are, therefore, pursuing developments aimed at achieving adaptability to individual situations.

A well-tried approach to implementing planning measures

The mock-up facade: of advantage to all concerned

In view of the different forms of construction developed for double-skin facades, it has now become indispensable to erect a mock-up of the facade—a procedure with which one is familiar from the construction of single-skin types. In the course of the facade planning, and at the latest when the tender documents for the facade are prepared, agreement should be reached with the client whether a full-size mock-up section of the facade should be constructed, and if so, to what degree of detail it should be executed.

    During this decision-making process, certain recurring practical questions and counterarguments will be presented for discussion; for example:
■ What benefits will the construction of a mock-up facade bring?
■ Whom does the mock-up help?
■ Why does the mock-up have to be built wholly with original components?
■ Is a real mock-up not far too expensive in the context of a cost-benefit analysis?
■ Is one not wasting valuable construction time by building a mock-up—time that is not really available?
■ We can imagine how the finished facade will look, without a mock-up.

Depending on the brief, the dimensions and the type of construction, a complete mock-up facade section is indeed a major cost factor, especially when it is to be manufactured and erected by the nominated facade construction firm strictly in accordance with the original design. To cover the cost of facade mock-ups in single-skin construction to the dimensions given below, a sum of roughly € 20,000–40,000 should be included in the cost estimate; for double-skin facades a sum of € 25,000–50,000 will be necessary.

A reasonable size for the mock-up of an office facade, for example, would be as follows:
■ height: one full story, plus abutments with the story above and below
H = ca. 3.5–4.0 m
■ width: two-facade bays
W = 2 x ca. 1.2–1.4 m
■ overall size of mock-up:
$A_{mock-up}$ = ca. 8.0–12.0 m²

The mock-up of the double-skin facade shown in ill. 10-1 was erected for the "Business Tower" project in Nuremberg, a high-rise office block roughly 134 meters in height. A relatively large mock-up was built that included the typical office spaces to the rear. In relation to the size and significance of the development itself, however, this facade mock-up was wholly appropriate and a necessary preliminary measure that was certainly justified by the cost-benefit ratio.

Advantages for those involved in the project

A mock-up of a facade is of advantage not only to those involved in the planning. It should not be seen, therefore, as an object that merely satisfies the egoistic needs of certain parties. A full-size mock-up true to the original design offers major advantages to everyone concerned.

■ Clients
The clients, or their representative committees, who are normally not involved in day-to-day building matters, will be able to view the actual outer skin of their proposed development in its true colors and dimensions. The clients thus see a segment of what they will actually get.

One should imagine the board or management of a company having to determine or consent to the coloration of the entire facade of a major new building development purely on the basis of a small hand-held color sample. Then, when the building is completed, it transpires that this was not the right decision. Suddenly, the cost-benefit approach towards the mock-up facade is relativized in the light of events and appears to be reasonable in comparison with the overall cost of the facade construction.

■ Architect
The architect can check his provisional choice of colors again and possibly change certain aspects, provided this does not affect details for the production of which special tools have already been manufactured. (In this context, see also section "Choosing the right moment for giving the go-ahead for large-scale production").

■ Facade construction firm
The mock-up facade will provide the company executing the work with an opportunity to make a final check on the technical aspects. In this way, any construction defects that have gone unnoticed in the CAD planning up to that point can be rectified before starting on the bulk production. One may also recognize further scope for optimizing the assembly process, which may be of economic benefit for the facade construction firm.

■ Facade consultant
The facade consultant will be better able to undertake a realistic investigation of all constructional and formal details. The materials and the quality of the processing they undergo can be subjected to a preliminary quality control on the basis of the specification and bills of quantities prior to giving the go-ahead for large-scale production. Compliance with the conditions of the contract can thus be checked for the last time.

10-1 Mock-up facade for Business Tower, Nuremberg

What about loss of time?

The alleged loss of time caused by the erection of a mock-up facade can be counteracted or at least minimized by foresight in the scheduling. In the case of well-organized and fast-moving projects run by a general contractor, there need be no loss of time at all if the contractor uses the carcass construction period to prepare for the facade assembly work and creates scope for a mock-up without impinging on the time schedule.

Conclusions

In the light of the above remarks, where larger facade projects are planned—especially in double-skin construction—the following conclusions can be drawn:

A mock-up facade offers significant and quite evident advantages for all parties involved in a project. The cost-benefit analysis is clearly in favor of the user. A decision to do without a mock-up facade may lead to subsequent problems that can no longer be remedied.

Choosing the right moment for giving the go-ahead for large-scale production

As described above, a mock-up facade has advantages for all involved in a project, provided the entire components are approved prior to manufacture on the basis of a mutual assessment of this construction. From this point in time, all decisions relating to formal and technical aspects, coloration and materials will be settled, so that the facade construction firm will be able to order the entire range of elements required for the facade from its supplier.

Unless it is unavoidable, exceptions should not be made by giving premature clearance for individual facade components, since almost without exception this will affect other units that have not been approved.

Example 1: premature clearance of facade sections can create problems

Very often, the facade construction firm or the general contractor will want the facade supporting sections to be approved in advance; for example, before the fixings for the external sunblinds have been resolved in detail. Delivery dates may be cited as a reason for this. In the transmission of tensile stresses from the sunshading stays, however, the interdependence of the two systems is a crucial structural factor—a factor that often goes unrecognized or is underestimated. The outcome can be a compromise solution for the bracket fixings for the sunshading system, which may ultimately have to be executed in a different form from that initially envisaged. Formal and visual "disappointments" are, therefore, inevitable if clearance is given to certain elements in advance of the construction as a whole.

10-2 Photo of model of Business Tower, Nuremberg, and surrounding complex. Architects: Dürschinger + Biefang in collaboration with Jörg Spengler.

A well-tried approach to implementing planning measures

On the other hand, the mock-up facade should not be seen as an excuse for experimentation on the part of the client and his architects. Valuable planning and construction time can indeed be lost if a series of modifications are made at the mock-up stage. Facade components for which special tools have to be manufactured should not be changed unless absolutely necessary.

Example 2: changes in the construction at the mock-up stage are expensive

The planner, the client or the developer would like to modify the form of the special facade sections. In the authors' opinion, however, far-reaching changes of this kind should not be ordered by a responsible planning team at the stage when the mock-up facade is assessed: in other words, shortly before clearance is given for large-scale production of the components. If there are nevertheless good reasons for making major changes of this kind, it is only fair to reimburse the facade construction firm for the costs already incurred for making special tools. Furthermore, the unavoidable delays this will cause in the scheduling of the project will have to be taken into account.

Since facades, and especially double-skin types, are individual composite products with a large number of interdependent aspects, involving structural engineering, sound insulation, statutory building permission, etc., the facade construction firm should present all relevant certificates of approval before the go-ahead is given for large-scale production.

The presentation of relevant proof documents at a later date involves a great risk for the client, the architects and the facade construction firm itself, since a "modification" of individual facade elements after orders have been placed is rarely possible. In such cases, which are unfortunately not uncommon in practice, all the client can usually expect is a reduction in value. For the user, this represents an undesirable and often unacceptable compromise.

Test certificates and evidence of compliance with the conditions of construction, which will be required prior to granting clearance for large-scale production, include (without any claim to comprehensiveness):

■ proof that all necessary sound insulation tests have been carried out by an independent, recognized testing institute;

■ proof that all requisite structural tests and analyses have been made, with a written certificate of approval by the controlling structural engineers;

■ official planning approval for the specific elements of the project, if necessary with a test certificate and with written confirmation of clearance for production by the relevant local building authority;

■ all testing certificates issued by independent, recognized testing institutions in respect of the

 • U-values of the various facade elements;

 • impermeability of the facade construction against driving rain; and general impermeability of joints, especially around opening elements.

10-3 Mock-up facade for Valentinskamp 1, office and commercial development, Caffamacherreihe, Hamburg.

In the construction of double-skin facades, it will usually not be possible to do without a test analysis of the aerophysical functions; for example, in the form of

- tests on models or
- airflow simulations.

Since these tests will usually have been carried out during the planning phase prior to awarding the contract to the facade construction firm, it will not be necessary for this firm to repeat them.

At the point where the construction is approved and the go-ahead is given for large-scale unit production, it is important to check whether the basic aerophysical parameters have been precisely implemented. This will ensure that the underlying principles for the tests carried out during the planning stage are still valid. Furnishing proof that these basic parameters have been observed should be a condition of the aerophysical planning and should be specified in the contract documents, so that the facade contractor will also have an agreed basis on which to check and confirm the values.

If these aerophysical tests are not conducted or commissioned by the planning team at the planning stage, but form part of the overall responsibilities of the facade contractor, the required proof must have been presented by the time clearance is given for large-scale production of the constructional elements.

10-4 Office and commercial development Valentinskamp 1, Caffamacherreihe, Hamburg: CAD representation during planning phase.
Client: Deutsche Immobilien Fonds AG.
Architects: Reimer und Partner, Elmshorn.

A well-tried approach to implementing planning measures

Facade types

Determining the architectural form of the windows and facade will have an effect on the construction down to the very details. In this section, different facade types will be discussed as the basis for the facade design. In the following sections, the types of construction (post-and-rail or framed) and the form of erection (assembly of prefabricated elements or conventional construction) will be considered, together with the implications of opting for a particular type. After a brief description of the origins of the various facade types, modern built examples will be given in which double-skin forms of construction have been employed.

Solid facades with conventional openings

Looking back over the history of building, the traditional form of facade and window construction may be seen as a closed external wall punctured by rectangular openings. In southern regions, depending on local weather conditions, larger or smaller openings were formed in the carcass structure to provide protection against strong insolation and long periods of heat. Similarly, in the northern regions of Europe and in the Alps, individual openings were created in the structure to protect the internal spaces against long periods of cold weather. Windows, usually of wood, were inserted in these openings and sealed around the edges.

In classical forms of construction, the carcass structure in southern countries was built of locally available materials—often stone. In northern regions, the structure was usually of timber or masonry; and in the Alps mainly of timber.

In traditional forms of architecture, the non-transparent areas of the outer skin were clad either with materials locally available in a particular region or with other weatherproof materials; or they were rendered. With solid forms of construction—in brickwork or stone, for example—it was often not necessary to clad the structure. In modern architecture, the conventional facade with discrete punched openings has undoubtedly lost ground, but it retains its significance both from an aesthetic, formal point of view and because of the good energy balance it provides.

The non-transparent area of the facade will be thermally insulated and then rendered, or finished with modern cladding systems. The cladding, with a ventilated cavity to the rear, is fixed to the carcass structure by means of a weather-resistant supporting construction. Adequate ventilation—i.e. an air layer of sufficient depth between the thermal insulation and the rear face of the cladding—ensures the removal of all moisture that may penetrate the outer skin as a result of weather conditions. In the detailed planning, structural tolerances will have to be taken into account in determining the depth of the air cavity. Practical experience shows that the admissible tolerances specified in the relevant standards are often exceeded. No air cavity should be planned with a depth of less than 30 mm, therefore. Proper ventilation is the only means of ensuring that any moisture that penetrates the construction is removed without causing damage.

10-5 L-Bank, Stuttgart.
Architects: Müller, Djordevic, Krehl, Stuttgart.
Completed in 1993.
Modern solid facade construction with stone cladding and traditional incised openings.

Cladding materials

Today, the range of materials available for cladding purposes far exceeds those traditionally used. Traditional types of cladding that are still in use (or are being applied again) in modern architecture include:
■ rendering
■ wood—especially boarding or shingles
■ stone
■ ceramic tiles.

A brief but representative selection from the wide range of modern materials used for cladding would include
■ composite systems with thermal-insulation
■ fibre-cement slabs
■ large-size, thin ceramic slabs
■ various smooth and textured metal sheets such as aluminum and stainless steel
■ printed glass in many different designs
■ stainless-steel woven mesh
■ reconstructed stone
■ terracotta, etc.

The new lightweight cladding materials that are available are especially suited to rehabilitation schemes where the limited load-bearing capacity of the existing structure means that it cannot support large additional loads.

Traditional box-window construction

Double-skin facades also have their basis in traditional forms of construction: they are related to the principles of the rectangular punched opening in a solid facade. The box window, for example, which was commonly used at higher altitudes in the Alps, was built into the thick, well-insulated external walls of solid timber buildings as a means of protection against very low temperatures in winter.

Example: box window in a house in Mürren

The box window consists of an inner and outer casement, each with single glazing. The space between the two layers is about 20 to 40 cm. The cushion of air (thermal buffer) between these two skins provides additional insulation and also ensures that the inner casement has a higher surface temperature. At the same time, a natural means of air-intake and extract for the rooms in winter is provided by additional small ventilation flaps built into the opening casements. In the present example, a house in the Alpine town of Mürren, Switzerland, the winter ventilation flaps are even of different sizes.

10-6 Far left: traditional house in Mürren in the Swiss Alps.

10-7 Close-up of a box window; the ventilation flap for use in winter is clearly visible.

10-8 Extension for
Energie-Versorgung Schwaben,
Stuttgart.
Completed in 1998.
Box windows with flaps
externally.
Architects: Lederer,
Ragnarsdottir, Oei, Stuttgart.

Modern forms of box-window construction

The following two examples show forms of box-window construction that were planned and implemented
for modern office block facades with different user
requirements.

Built example 1: extension of building for
Energie-Versorgung Schwaben AG
(an energy-supply organization) in Stuttgart

Architects:
Lederer, Ragnarsdottir, Oei
Freie Architekten Dipl.Ing. BDA AI

Box-window construction
Inner facade: wood casements in laminated construction board with bottom- and side-hung opening lights
in aluminum
Facade intermediate space: depth approx. 45 cm
Sunshading: aluminum louver blinds
(louver width: 80 mm)
Outer facade: slide-down/push-out casement construction, operated by electric motors

Date of completion: 1998

10-9 Detail of box window
construction with external
window flaps.

10-10 Far right: functional
diagram of box window.

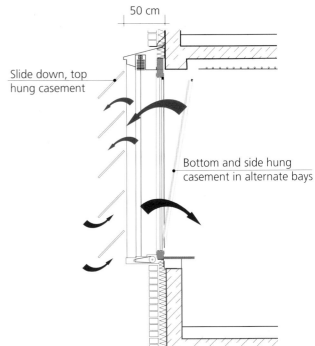

50 cm

Slide down, top
hung casement

Bottom and side hung
casement in alternate bays

Built example 2: rehabilitation planning of the high-rise block of the Federal German Ministry for Food, Agriculture and Foresty (BML headquarters building), Bonn

Client: Federal Republic of Germany
Project management: Federal German Office for Building and Regional Planning
General planners and architects:
Ingenhoven Overdiek Kahlen und Partner
Facade planning for general planner:
DS-Plan GmbH, Stuttgart

Box-window construction
Inner facade: wood casement construction with side- and bottom-hung opening lights
Facade intermediate space: depth approx. 75 cm
Sunshading: aluminum louver blinds
(louver width: 100 mm)
Outer facade: all-glass pivoting lights, operated by electric motors

Date of completion: 2000

Division of trades

In everyday practice, the rear-ventilated cladding described in the above examples forms an important distinction in terms of the division of trades.

■ In conjunction with the box-window construction to the offices of the energy-supply company, the architects specified a dark engineering-brick outer skin of facings with a ventilated cavity to the rear.

■ In the box-window construction for the ministry building, the architects proposed a rear-vented outer skin, with perforated sheet aluminum over the areas of the columns, and wood or screen-printed glass to the apron-wall areas.

For economic reasons, the engineering-brick facings to the energy-supply building were not executed by the facade construction firm, but by the general contractor responsible for the carcass structure. In this way, it was possible to avoid additional costs, such as surcharges for subcontractor's work and excessive safety margins (usually charged by the main contractor as a percentage added to the subcontractor's sum) that would have been incurred if the contract for the facing skin had been awarded to the facade construction firm. For the latter, having to execute an engineering-brick facade would have been completely alien to the firm's trade skills. Here, too, the inevitable outcome would have been additional costs.

In contrast, the glass and wood or sheet aluminum used for the rear-ventilated cladding to the BML building are materials that facade construction firms have

10-11 Photo of model of refurbished facade to Federal German Ministry for Food, Agriculture and Forestry (BML), Bonn.

experience in handling and calculating. The entire facade construction work was, therefore, specified as part of that trade, which in this case also made sense economically.

Where it is sensible to divide the execution of the facade work between different trade contractors, as in the case of the energy-supply headquarters, a certain mutual hindrance of the work will be virtually unavoidable. To minimize the interference, or rather to ensure a maximum of harmony between trades in the execution of the scheme, a detailed schedule of work should be drawn up.

As early as the planning stage for the facade construction, all details of abutments between the work of different trades or contractors should be coordinated, especially where the permissible constructional tolerances differ.

10-12 Tower block: part of BML complex, Bonn. Architects: Ingenhoven Overdiek Kahlen und Partner, Düsseldorf.
Photo of model of building.

Strip-window facades

In many ways, strip-window facades and traditional solid facades with punched openings are closely related. The similarities between the two extend from the form of construction and the cladding materials to the division of work according to trades. Instead of the individual, incised openings that characterize the latter, the strip-window facade is distinguished by continuous horizontal ribbon openings in the structure. This form of construction articulates a building with a floor-by-floor banding, consisting of continous window strips alternating with continuous solid parapet walls and floor slabs. The vertical loads are usually borne by columns set back slightly from the facade. The strip-like openings are filled with window elements in one of a number of materials that are available for this purpose. The joints between the windows and the structure are then sealed.

10-13 Glazed veranda to house in Mürren in the Swiss Alps.

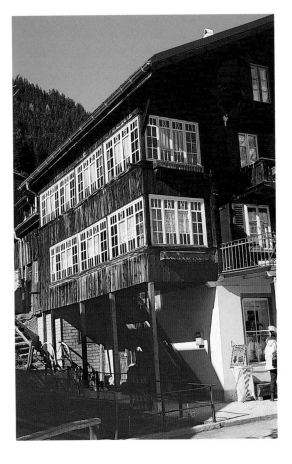

Traditional double-skin construction

As one has seen with incised rectangular openings in the form of box windows in solid facades, the double-skin form of construction is not an entirely new invention. The same might be said of its use in conjunction with strip-window facades. Here, too, it is based on traditional and essentially simple forms of construction, as is reflected in the period required for its erection. The double-skin strip-window facade can be found in Alpine regions in the form of the glazed veranda, for example; but it was also very popular around the turn of the 19th and 20th centuries in urban villas.

The veranda glazing was set at a certain distance from the inner facade with its incised openings—in much the same form as in corridor facade construction today. The intermediate space between the two facade layers can serve as an access corridor and as a veranda area for various uses. With a depth of one to two meters, this veranda space acts as a thermal buffer and ensures that the inner facade has an agreeable surface temperature in winter. In Alpine houses, the inner skin assumes the functions of the external wall - with the exception that it does not provide protection against the elements. During the cold season, the windows and doors in the inner facade layer can be opened for longer periods only on sunny days; and they are kept closed at night. Small window flaps are provided for ventilation during the night or when the weather is bad. The ventilation of the rooms for permanent occupation is effected by the natural permeability of the outer veranda facade or via small elements that can be opened to form narrow slit-like apertures.

Modern double-skin, strip-window facades

The roughly 220-meter-long, four-story facade to the administration building completed in 1998 for DB Cargo, a German railways organization in Mainz, may serve as an example of a double-skin strip-window facade. The construction is a combination of box-window and corridor-facade types: there are no vertical divisions on the structural axes, yet the shallow depth of the cavity between the facade layers means that this space is not a corridor in the true sense.

This facade reflects both the requirements of the investors (who wanted an extremely low-budget design for the entire project) and the formal goals of the architects, who proposed an all-glass outer skin. In a very short period of planning, a permanently rearvented, double-skin, strip-window facade was developed in collaboration with the architects. The aim of reducing the sound-level by at least 5 dB, while at the same time ensuring natural ventilation of the offices for as much of the year as possible, was achieved by designing continuous air-intake and extract slits with the appropriate dimensions. These are laid out horizontally on every floor.

Vertical dividing elements were not inserted in the intermediate space in view of the use of the building. The shallow depth of the cavity and the high level of traffic noise externally made a division of this kind unnecessary. It was not even required to prevent potential sound transmission from room to room.

Built example: new administration building for DB Cargo, Mainz

General planners:
Architectural collaborative INFRA, Mainz, and RKW, Frankfurt am Main
Facade planners for general planners:
DS-Plan GmbH, Stuttgart

Double-skin strip-window facade
Inner facade: aluminum window construction with side/bottom-hung casements
Facade intermediate space: depth approx. 23 cm
Sunshading: aluminum louvered blinds
(louver width: 80 mm)
Outer facade: aluminum load-bearing sections; point-fixed toughened safety glass

10-14 Part of strip-window facade to DB Cargo building, Mainz.

10-15 Far left: functional diagram of strip-window facade.

10-16 DB Cargo building, Mainz.
Architects: INFRA in collaboration with Rhode, Kellermann, Wawrowsky, Mainz, Düsseldorf. Completed in 1998.

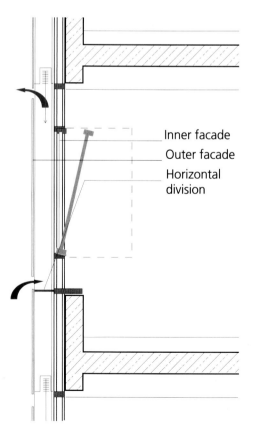

Inner facade
Outer facade
Horizontal division

Curtain-wall facades

The curtain-wall facade can be defined as a story-height form of construction suspended between the floors of a building. The continuous outer skin is point-fixed to the structure only at the front edges of the floors.

It was this form of construction that first allowed a clear separation of the facade from the structure. The need for tightly sealed joints between sections of the work executed by different trades (for example, between facade elements and the load-bearing structure, as in the case of solid outer skins with individual rectangular or strip-window openings) was thus completely obviated. The process of sealing the outer skin occurs within the facade construction itself at the abutments between the various elements.

The facade elements can be largely prefabricated, which allows a high degree of manufacturing precision. In some cases, complete prefabrication at works is possible, with story-height elements delivered to the site. Structural tolerances are accommodated by precise, adjustable, point-fixing brackets. (In this context, see also the section describing "Forms of fixing and anchoring" in the following chapter.) The sealing of the joints between facade elements is executed with individually developed elastic sealing gaskets. Depending on the type of construction—post-and-rail or framed members—expansion and contraction within the facade can be absorbed by elastic sealing gaskets or by flexible bolted connections.

Historical development

The first attempts to "dissolve" the solid outer envelope of a building can be traced back to the beginning of the 20th century. Examples of this include
- the Hermann Tietz ("Hertie") department store in Berlin by Sehring und Lachenmann (1898)
- the AEG Turbine Hall in Berlin by Peter Behrens (1908–09)
- the Fagus Works in Alfeld, Leine, by Gropius and Feyer (1911–16).

The distinction of being the first building with a curtain-wall facade has been accorded by architectural historians to the
- Hallidie Building in San Francisco by W. I. Polk (1918).

Developments of this kind in the direction of dissolving the external wall of a building and erecting story-height glazed elements were pursued by Le Corbusier, Mies van der Rohe and Walter Gropius in the course of the following years. The constructional principle of the curtain wall was also applied to high-rise buildings, as one may see in the example of the

10-17 Lever House, New York: regarded as one of the earliest examples of the use of a curtain-wall facade with an all-glass appearance.
Architects: Skidmore, Owings and Merrill.
Completed in 1952.

- Lever House in New York by Skidmore, Owings and Merrill (1952).

The facade of this tower block was constructed as a glazed curtain wall. The formal appearance was achieved by using modern metal sections and advanced glazing techniques, a system that is still commonly found in modern architecture in both single- and double-skin forms of facade construction.

Modern double-skin curtain-wall facades

The curtain-wall system is the usual form of construction for double-skin facades, especially where a slenderly dimensioned supporting structure is specified. The economic advantages, the possibility of a shorter assembly time, and the clear divisions between the various trades involved are some of the indisputable benefits of this application of modern technology. These advantages apply in particular to large-scale developments and to facades where the components are mainly of identical size and composition.

Project example: high-rise block, Olympic Park, Munich

Client: REMU, Munich

Architects and general planners:
Ingenhoven, Overdiek und Partner
Facade system development:
DS-Plan GmbH, Stuttgart

Double-skin curtain-wall facade in
prefabricated unit-construction system
Inner facade: aluminum window construction with
side- and bottom-hung casement doors
Facade intermediate space: depth approx. 55 cm
Sunshading: aluminum louvered blinds
(louver width: 80 mm)
Outer facade: aluminum supporting sections; linear
bedding of glass

10-18 Photo of model of tower
development at the Olympic
Park, Munich.

Client: REMU, Munich.
Architects: Ingenhoven,
Overdiek und Partner, Düssel-
dorf.

10-19 Far left: elevation of
double-skin curtain-wall facade.

10-20 Section through corridor
in double-skin facade.

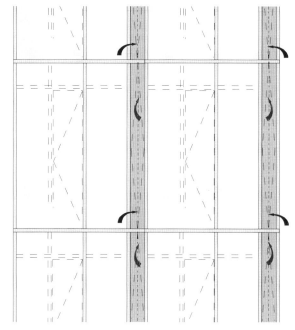

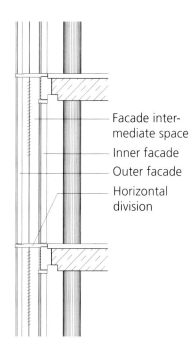

Facade inter-
mediate space

Inner facade

Outer facade

Horizontal
division

10-21 Left: plan of double-skin
facade in tower block at
Olympic Park, Munich.

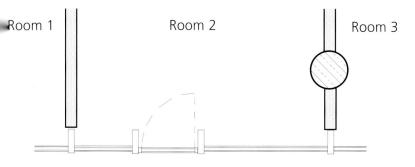

Room 1   Room 2   Room 3

Types of construction

Post-and-rail construction

Post-and-rail construction consists of vertical posts and horizontal members of the requisite dimensions set out in linear form. The materials commonly used for these supporting sections are aluminum, steel and, in recent years, wood as well.

Post-and-rail facades differ from classical framed forms in the way they are glazed. In post-and-rail construction, the glazing is fixed in a separate operation *from the outside*. The glass and the glazing elements are clamped in position by fixing strips—sometimes with additional cover strips—with the specified rebate depth for the glazing.

Both the fixing and the cover strips, like the supporting posts and rails, can be designed and finished to reflect the nature of the material used and in accordance with the wishes of the architects. The depth and elevational width of the supporting members will depend on structural requirements.

The joints between the supporting members are usually formed by connecting pieces, which allow for expansion and contraction by means of a sliding movement. Connections between members in aluminum, for example, are often executed with sliding-bolt or pin joints. The sockets for the connecting pieces are formed by the normal extruded walls of the members. Steel sections often have screwed connections; for example, via lugs or brackets welded on. In the case of U-shaped members, screwed connections with head plates are a common solution.

Wood or wood-and-aluminum sections in post-and-rail construction are usually screw-fixed to elements inserted at the corners. All kinds of elements can be used for this purpose. One common type is a modified form of furniture fitting.

Opinions vary on the technical application of sealing gaskets, especially to glass roofs, but also in the case of vertical glazing in post-and-rail construction. The many different kinds of sealing systems available from specialist manufacturers are often regarded by facade construction firms as based on proven, functional, technical principles; and in many cases, systems of this kind offer cost benefits. For that reason, they are increasingly used without any adequate investigation of the contingent conditions. The application of these mostly two- or three-part sealing systems where they are not appropriate to a specific situation can result in a faulty seal and consequent damage. This can also occur where sealing systems of this kind are executed under bad weather conditions or not in accordance with the system specifications.

In the authors' opinion, the various product ranges that have come onto the market in the past few years in the form of lapped joint seals are a positive development in the field of continuous sealing systems. They can be used unmodified, or in an analogous form, adapted to the specific requirements of a project. This applies in particular to the second sealing plane, which has to ensure safe drainage of the facade.

So-called "lapped joint seals" can be reliably and safely executed and thus guarantee a high level of quality. This is important in facade construction, since it is necessary today to be able to work under almost any weather conditions. The advantages of this sealing strip construction have not been acknowledged by all system manufacturers so far; but the first solutions are already on the market, and others are being developed "behind the scenes" in the labs of leading system suppliers.

In the authors' opinion, the cross-sections of any high-quality post-and-rail system should contain a continuous insulated came—in glass-fibre-reinforced polyamid, for example—regardless of the material used for the glazing sections. The insulating strip is applied in a separate working process.

Key to drawings
1 Fixing strip
2 Cover strip
3 External seal
4 Insulated came
5 Insulating double glazing
6 Internal seal
7 Post
8 Rail
9 Threaded sleeve

10-22 Left: post-and-rail construction in aluminum. Diagrammatic section.

10-23 Center: post-and-rail construction in wood. Diagrammatic section.

10-24 Right: post-and-rail construction in steel. Diagrammatic section.

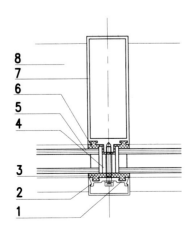
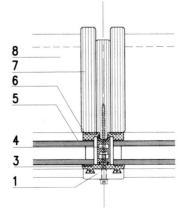
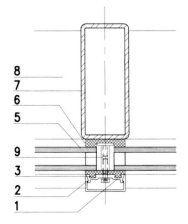

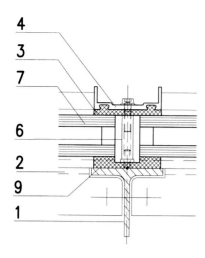

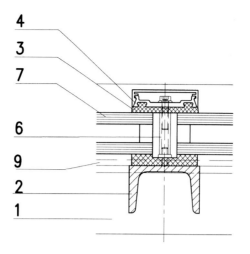

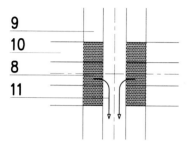

The assembly of a post-and-rail facade is a relatively elaborate procedure. The infill elements—in other words, all panes of glass, panels, and built-in units—are delivered separately to the site and fixed in their respective positions in the facade. In view of the in-situ assembly of this kind of construction, which has to take place under almost any weather conditions, there is great scope for errors. Where the post-and-rail facade does not come in the form of a series of prefabricated elements, scaffolding will be required for its erection.

The infill elements for post-and-rail facades should be built in with an adequate spacing to the peripheral insulating strips. This open rebate is designed to accommodate any expansion and contraction as well as the constructional tolerances of the infill elements.

Framed construction

Facades with a framed supporting structure differ significantly from post-and-rail forms of construction. The cross-sections of the framed members will be prefabricated on an industrial basis with a continuous insulation zone pressed in, so that this otherwise manual process is obviated.

With this type of construction, the glazing is executed *from the inside*. The glass and the infill elements are fixed in the framing members by means of beads or glazing strips. The same range of standard materials is used for the frame members as in post-and-rail construction: aluminum, wood, steel, and plastic. Exotic materials such as bronze or stainless steel are used only in exceptional cases.

With this type of construction, the joints between the framing members are usually in the form of 45° mitered angles, with concealed internal angle connectors at the corners.

The correct choice of seal for a specific system is not as important in framed facades as in post-and-rail construction. The most common type of sealing is with EPDM strips with vulcanized corners. (EPDM is an acronym for ethylene-propylene diene monomer.) Together with silicone, which is normally used for injection seals, EPDM is the most commonly used sealing material in building today.

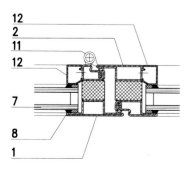

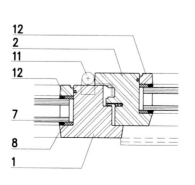

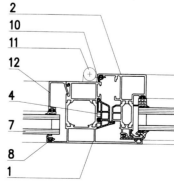

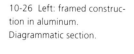

Forms of construction

Prefabricated construction

General description

In principle, prefabrication is possible with both forms of facade construction:

- post-and-rail construction and
- framed construction.

The term "prefabricated construction" implies a strict division (and separation) of the facade horizontally and vertically into large-area elements. The facade supporting members will normally be divided in the middle and inserted in each other in an interlocking form. Prefabricated double-skin facades are usually executed in a framed form of construction.

10-29 Position of abutments between elements in facade of Business Tower, Nuremberg.

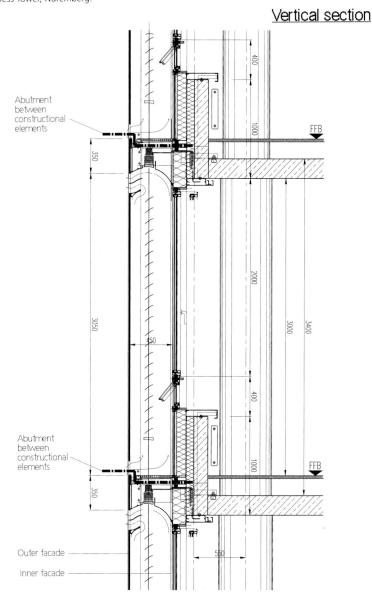

Vertical section

Abutment between constructional elements

Abutment between constructional elements

Outer facade

Inner facade

Aluminum is the most commonly used material for the divided facade sections for both the inner and outer skins, although prefabricated divided sections in wood have also been available for some years now.

These elaborately articulated interlocking sections form the subsequent assembly joint between adjacent elements. In the case of double-skin facades, the abutment between elements will generally be individually designed and developed for each project, a process that presupposes special constructional knowledge. An extremely careful approach to the development of these details is necessary, since the abutment between elements has to meet various technical requirements without any flaws.

The junction between supporting members has to absorb movement within the facade elements; it has to function as a watertight expansion joint; and it has to meet all the technical requirements made of a horizontal and vertical assembly joint.

To ensure absolute watertightness and to comply with stringent windproofing requirements, specially developed integrated EPDM or silicone sealing strips in a number of layers are inserted in the abutments between the supporting members.

Prefabrication means that the facade elements, made up at works and including all glass, panels and other infill components, can be delivered to the site as complete units.

Planning of assembly / lifting equipment

Prefabricated construction offers a number of important advantages for the planning of the assembly work. The greatest advantage is certainly the scope this provides of carrying out the entire assembly work without expensive external scaffolding.

The facade elements are manufactured completely at works and delivered to the site as large-scale units shortly before they are needed. The story-height elements, usually two facade bays in width, will be hoisted into the carcass structure by the general contractor's rotating-mast cranes, which are already on site, or by mobile cranes specially hired by the facade construction firm.

The precise assembly procedure will be determined for each individual site by experienced and specialized fitters working for the facade contractor, taking into account the site layout and the position of the building. The work should be optimized to take advantage of the scope for savings that exists. In many cases, the ingenuity of the assembly people in developing ideal solutions for specific projects should earn the unreserved respect of architects and facade consultants.

There is no generally valid procedure, therefore, and it would be impossible to illustrate the many different conceivable solutions. A high-rise building, for example, will require a different approach from a low-rise structure that covers a large area of the site.

A commonly applied assembly technique for high-rise buildings is to move the units on rails. The facade elements will be hoisted by a rotating-mast crane or a special crane to the respective story, where they will be transported by a fork-lift truck to a stacking platform specially installed for temporary storage.

The facade elements will then be taken to their place of assembly by means of a trolley hoist attached to a peripheral assembly rail, a "monorail", fixed to the underside of the floor slab.

Where double-skin facade elements have to be distributed before fixing in position, the assembly specialist will seek to avoid an intermediate storage phase on each floor, since the relatively great depth of these units—in contrast to single-skin elements—means that they take up a lot of space. In addition, they are much more awkward to handle. Where access to the building permits, double-skin facade elements will be removed from the trucks by means of the monorail and transported via a pre-planned vertical transport route directly to their place of assembly, where they will be provisionally hung in position. While the monorail is transporting the next element, the unit that has just been placed in position will be precisely adjusted and firmly fixed.

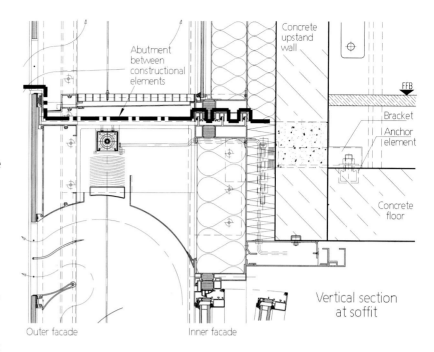

Vertical section at soffit

Outer facade   Inner facade

Depending on the size of the double-skin facade elements, a truck can transport between 8 and 12 units at a time to the site.

Where the monorail system is used without an intermediate storage phase, as described above, it will be possible to assemble one story of the facade of a circular tower block in roughly one to one and a half weeks, providing adverse weather conditions do not impede the progress of the work.

10-30 Detail showing horizontal line of abutment between elements at outer edge of floor slab in Business Tower, Nuremberg.

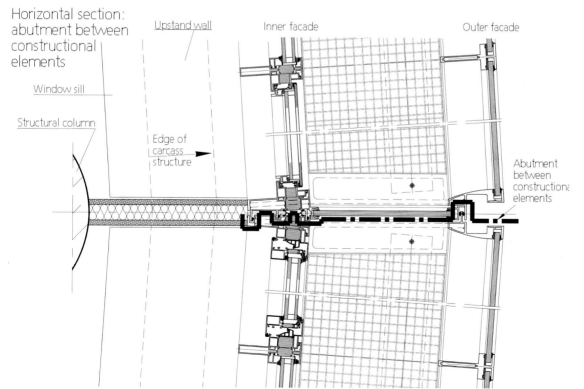

Horizontal section: abutment between constructional elements

Upstand wall   Inner facade   Outer facade

Window sill

Structural column

Edge of carcass structure

Abutment between constructional elements

10-31 Detail showing vertical line of abutment between elements on facade axis of Business Tower, Nuremberg.

A high degree of prefabrication and
short assembly times

Over the past few years, the facade construction industry, like the building sector as a whole, has been
confronted with great challenges in terms of reducing
assembly and construction times. In the context of
scheduling and the punctual completion of works,
facade construction now plays a major role. Delays in
the assembly of a facade can have a disastrous effect
on subsequent phases of the work. If the facade
construction has not been effectively sealed by the
appointed date, or if important components still have
to be fitted, it will not be possible to proceed with the
internal finishings according to schedule. A chain
reaction is thus set in motion, and a series of delays
occurs that can scarcely be made good again. In some
cases, expensive provisional sealing measures may
even be necessary.

The importance of keeping to schedule, especially
in larger schemes, has caused facade technology to
develop in the direction of
- a high degree of prefabrication and
- shorter assembly times,
and these developments will probably continue in the
future.

A further major advantage of extensive prefabrication
and a unit construction system is the "controlled" assembly of the facade elements at works. As a result, a
large part of the assembly process, which hitherto
took place on site in almost any weather conditions, is
now carried out "in the dry". Factory assembly, therefore, greatly improves the quality of the product. An
extensive use of state-of-the-art manufacturing equipment at works also circumvents potentially faulty manual labor on site and results in much greater precision
in the assembly process. The scope for quality control
under factory conditions thus ensures a minimization
of damage in the facade construction.

The prefabrication of double-skin facades has sensi-
bly advanced so far now that transportable facade elements are produced at works as complete preassem-
bled units, comprising the inner and outer facade
skins, plus any horizontal divisions or ventilation boxes
that may be required, and an integrated sunshading
system.

10-32 Far right: principle of
lifting equipment with which
the prefabricated elements are
hoisted into position for assembly. Example: Business Tower,
Nuremberg.

10-33 Site photo during
assembly of the prefabricated
facade elements.

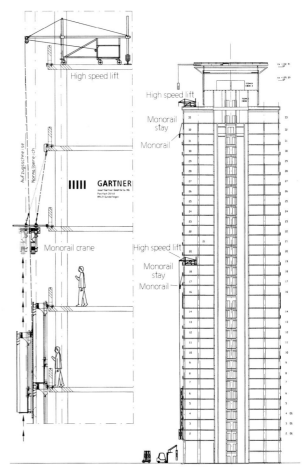

In view of the two-layer construction, these relatively large units are vulnerable to twisting. To ensure that no damage or torsion occurs during transport, special mountings and fixings will have to be developed for this purpose. If the complete double-skin element were to twist in any way during its transport by truck from the works to the site, this is likely to result in damage that would be difficult—if at all possible—to repair.

The precise degree of prefabrication will, of course, vary from project to project and will depend on a number of factors related to the facade technology. It will be influenced, for example, by the nature of the load-bearing structure and by the space available on site.

One should be aware, however, that this form of construction, especially where a high degree of pre-fabrication is involved, will require much greater planning. Not only the intensity of the planning is important in this respect; the professional qualifications of the construction team play a crucial role.

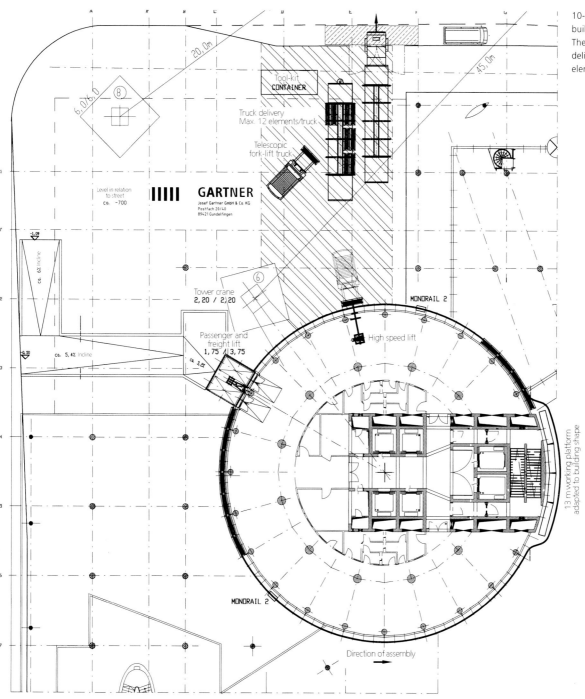

10-34 Plan of Business Tower building site, Nuremberg. The hatched area indicates the delivery zone for the facade elements.

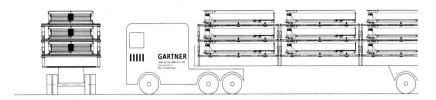

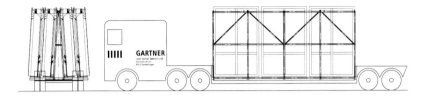

Economies through large-scale production

10-35 Above: alternative forms of loading facade elements on truck for transport.

10-36 Below: vertical section through prefabricated curtain-wall elements at floor level; Business Tower, Nuremberg.

The numbers refer to new members, for which special tools were required.

Planning costs are considerably higher for prefabricated forms of construction. This applies to both the facade planning carried out by the architects and facade consultants, and to the planning of the assembly process by the facade construction firm. The overall planning costs, together with the somewhat higher costs for materials, may be more than balanced out, however, if the project is large enough. For the client and the facade contractor, prefabricated construction undoubtedly represents the most economical solution today where sufficiently large numbers of elements are involved.

Site assembly costs, taken as a whole, will be reduced to a minimum. There will be fewer interruptions to work on site caused by inclement weather; and the higher labor costs for site assembly in the form of

traveling expenses, board and lodging, and absence money can also be saved by the facade construction firm.

Furthermore, it may be possible to assemble the facade without external scaffolding, so that the costs of its erection and long-term hire can be avoided. The rational use of automatic manufacturing plant operated by qualified and experienced staff at the facade construction works will contribute significantly to the process of economic optimization—not to mention the improvement in quality.

The sum of all these factors makes the economic advantages of prefabricated forms of construction plausible for large and very large schemes.

It also becomes apparent that attempts by many clients and project managers to achieve economies by cutting the planning costs of architects and facade consultants are quite certainly misplaced. Measures of this kind will result in an evident loss of quality and functional efficiency. They will also create a great potential for the facade construction firm to claim extras, which can never be made good.

Built example:
Business Tower, Nuremberg

Client:
Business Tower Nürnberg GmbH & Co. KG

Architects:
Architects Working Group
Dürschinger + Biefang / Jörg Spengler
Facade planning:
DS-Plan GmbH, Stuttgart

Facade contractor:
Josef Gartner & Co., Gundelfingen

Height of tower: approx. 134 m
Double-skin facade with permanently ventilated cavity
Unit construction system with extremely high level of prefabrication

Inner facade: prefabricated aluminum special frame construction with side- and bottom-hung casements, and opening flaps, each in every second bay
Facade intermediate space: depth approx. 45 cm
Sunshading: aluminum louvered blinds
(width of louvers: 100 mm)
Outer facade: prefabricated aluminum special frame construction with screen-printed glass panes over edges of floor slabs.

Completion date: 2000

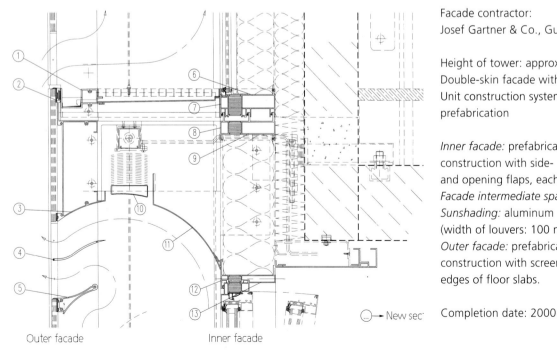

Outer facade   Inner facade   New sec

Special tools for new facade sections

As already described, in schemes that have an individual form of facade construction, and especially in the case of large-scale projects, the standard catalog sections produced by well-known system manufacturers are used less and less. Increasingly, the cross-sections of the supporting members are planned and developed to meet the specific needs of a project.

For double-skin facades in particular, as well as the usual posts and rails, numerous additional elements and sections are developed and manufactured—often in aluminum. Examples of such elements include
■ aerodynamically optimized louvers and deflector plates
■ drainage sections
■ window sills
■ sections for internal sunblinds
■ channel sections for fixing traveling cradles, etc.

In the design and erection of double-skin facades, it is not uncommon for 20 to 30 or even more new cross-sectional forms to be developed in 5 to 10 different component groups, all of which will have to be specially press-moulded for the prefabricated construction.

Not many facade construction companies have their own press-moulding works. As a result, these new sections will often have to be manufactured by other firms on behalf of the facade contractor. Facade manufacturers who have their own press-moulding works have the advantage of being able to control the development and production of the cross-sections themselves, of course.

Nevertheless, the vast majority of facade construction firms that do not have their own press-moulding facilities suffer no great disadvantage, since there is adequate external production capacity to manufacture the requisite members. The new pressings are undertaken by specialist works or increasingly, as already described, by system manufacturers who have an extremely flexible mode of operation. In the past, it was often claimed that the manufacture of new cross-sections was uneconomical on account of the new tools and press forms this necessitated. New facilities in technical tool-making and processing technology have provided scope for economic optimization on a significant scale, especially in larger projects. In the meantime, the one-off additional costs involved have been considerably reduced—in some cases by as much as half.

It is not possible to state the precise additional costs for the development of a new cross-section, since these will depend largely on the size, the form, and the mass of the members. In view of the cost-optimization factors for prefabricated forms of construction described above, the additional costs for developing and producing new sections should certainly not be ignored. But they do not preclude individual solutions for this form of construction.

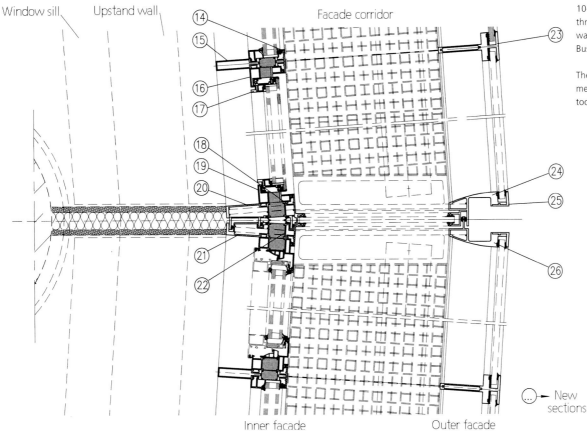

10-37 Horizontal section through abutment of curtain-wall elements on facade axis; Business Tower, Nuremberg.

The numbers refer to new members, for which special tools were required.

Where new sections are to be used, it is essential to take account of this in drawing up planning schedules for the period up to the commencement of the assembly work. The additional time required for the development and production of tools should not be overlooked either.

It is impossible to say exactly how much time will be required for this process, since it will depend on whether the press-moulding plant is working to full capacity or not; i.e. on the state of the building economy in general and ultimately on the overall economic conditions at any given time. The following delivery times may be taken as a rough guide for planning and scheduling at the moment:
- Delivery time for standard catalog sections: 4 to 6 weeks.
- Delivery time for newly developed sections: 5 to 8 weeks.

Competence of the facade construction firm

In building developments where the double-skin facade is to be executed in a prefabricated form of construction, clients, investors and architects alike are advised to take great care to check the professional qualifications of the facade construction firm before awarding the contract. Important in this context is not only the obvious information one requires about a company—basic data such as its size, annual turnover, liquidity, size of staff, etc.; other significant aspects that will help one to make a sound choice include the specialist technical qualifications of the firm and the degree of experience it possesses in the field of technical processing.

Where a contract is to be awarded to a facade construction company whose capability is not precisely known, it is incumbent on the planning team to make a thorough investigation of the background of the firm, including addressing enquiries to the users of reference objects and inspecting the relevant departments and the production plant of the company in question. Legally watertight contracts, a detailed schedule of work and penalty clauses for non-compliance with the terms of the contract are important aspects. They are, in fact, essential conditions for the smooth-running and the optimum execution of the work. On the other hand, if a contractor—in this case, the facade construction firm—is not in a position to manufacture a technically demanding product of this kind to the specified quality and with the requisite engineering know-how, and to assemble it according to schedule, "legal steps" are not likely to help one to obtain the desired product—or only with unwanted compromises.

Clients are not looking for a reduction in quality, for unacceptable compromises and the like. They want a properly functioning, high-quality double-skin facade. Demanding contracts of this kind should, therefore, be awarded only to highly qualified facade construction concerns.

One recommendation the authors can make based on many years of experience in the field of individual facade construction concerns the size of the firm in relation to the volume of the contract to be awarded. It can be stated as follows:

The contract sum should not be more than about a third of the facade construction company's turnover in the previous year.

Experience gained over a period of many years shows that where this rule of thumb is ignored, the facade construction firm will not possess the necessary qualifications, especially in the field of technical processing.

Conventional form of construction

General description

Facades built in a conventional form of construction—like those assembled from prefabricated units—are based on two main forms:

- post-and-rail construction and
- framed construction.

By "conventional construction" one means the assembly of the facade *from individual components* on site. Sections or frames, panes of glass, panels, infill elements and other facade units are delivered separately to the site and assembled in-situ.

Compared with prefabricated forms of construction, conventional systems require smaller quantities of materials and less elaborate constructional and engineering processing.

An experienced facade construction firm interested in economical solutions will use conventional forms of construction only for facades of smaller area. Where only small quantities of the components are required, catalog products will inevitably be used to a large extent. Where larger quantities are involved, a unit construction system will usually be preferred on account of the high degree of prefabrication and the economic advantages it allows.

The use of conventional forms of construction will also be justified where large projections and set-backs occur in the outer plane of the carcass structure (cf. the ministry building in Bonn in the drawing below).

If the facade supporting members are in different materials—for example, the inner facade skin is in wood and the outer skin is in aluminum—one should consider whether it would not be more economical to plan the facade in a conventional form of construction. Again, considerations of this kind will depend on the size of the project and the nature of the carcass structure.

Provision of scaffolding / Lifting equipment

In almost all buildings in conventional forms of construction, it will be necessary to erect scaffolding over the outer face of the structure. The scaffolding must comply with the relevant regulations and codes of practice.

The individual facade components will have to be hoisted into the carcass structure or, depending on the load-bearing capacity of the scaffolding (usually 300 kg/m²), up to the respective scaffolding stages. This will be done either by the pivoting tower crane installed by the general contractor or by a mobile crane hired by the facade construction company itself.

Together with the scaffolding platforms, the available floor area within the carcass structure forms an intermediate storage space from where the facade can be assembled. Special lifting equipment (e.g. glass suction pads) will be necessary to move heavy components such as large panes of glass and to fit them into the facade framework.

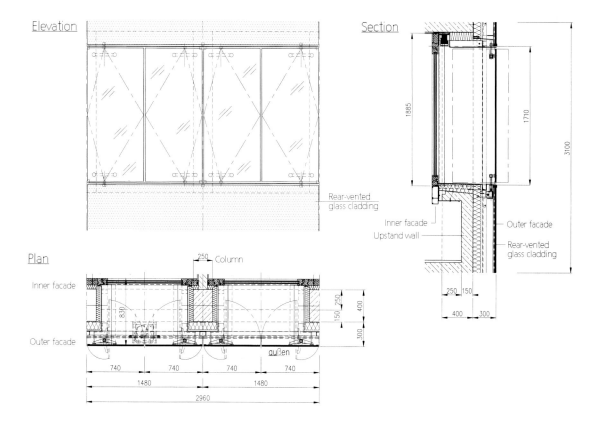

10-38 Elevation, plan and section: box window for the refurbishment of the Federal German Ministry for Food, Agriculture and Forestry (BML) in Bonn.

Architects: Ingenhoven Overdiek Kahlen und Partner, Düsseldorf.

The solid upstand walls, which formed part of the existing structure, were responsible for the bold changes of plane in the facade.

Since the main contractor's pivoting tower crane will probably be in use for most of the time, it is unlikely that it will be available for this time-consuming work. The facade construction firm will, therefore, have to hire a mobile crane for the duration of the glazing work or similar assembly processes where heavy loads have to be hoisted.

A crucial task for the architects is to coordinate the availability of the scaffolding with other trades that work in the area of the facade, such as stonemasons, facing bricklayers, etc. Not only the load-bearing capacity of the scaffolding has to be taken into account, especially where heavy types of cladding are used; the distance of the scaffolding from the face of the carcass structure will also have to be coordinated so that no on-site trade is impeded in the execution of its work.

Under which trade should the scaffolding be included when drawing up the tender documents? Although there is probably no clear answer to this question, one thing is certain: if the scaffolding is the responsibility of the facade contractor, that company will certainly endeavor to complete its work as quickly as possible in order not to prolong the scaffolding standing time unnecessarily. In larger contracts, non-compliance with the facade sealing deadline normally incurs a penalty; and practical experience shows that the facade contractor will usually meet this deadline as a result. The large amount of work that still remains to be executed will often not be completed for months afterwards, much to the annoyance of the contract managers.

The extra costs incurred for unnecessary scaffolding standing time, on the other hand, motivate the facade firm to complete its work and to press for its acceptance. If the scaffolding is written out as a separate trade and is not the responsibility of the facade contractor, the motivation of cost pressures will not be felt.

A lower degree of prefabrication and longer assembly times

Conventional construction, in the context of double-skin facades, should not be understood simply as the supply of the whole facade reduced to its individual components, which then have to be put together on site. Even with traditional kinds of construction, there may be a certain degree of prefabrication, and this should be optimized in the interests of achieving an economic solution. The inner facade skin, for example, may be planned as a unit construction system that is largely prefabricated at works.

In developing a double-skin facade in a conventional form of construction, a farsighted facade engineer will attempt to create a continuous horizontal joint in an open manner and to design the lower abutments (including the adjoining components that close the intermediate space horizontally) as vertically adjustable facade planes separated on each story. A constructional approach of this kind, where the continuous horizontal dividing elements are designed as an adjustable "saddle frame" construction, means that the facade, supplied as a series of individual components, will simply have to be inserted between the horizontal abutment planes. These horizontal abutment elements are assembled in advance in the first stage of construction and are precisely adjusted to the given dimensions. In this way, it will be possible partly to offset the costs resulting from the relatively low degree of prefabrication and the greater amount of assembly work.

The saddle frame construction, together with the higher level of prefabrication of the inner facade, allows the facade sealing deadline to be attained at a much earlier date than would be the case otherwise. This, in turn, will be conducive to an early completion of the building as a whole, since the sealed state of the facade is a crucial deadline for many trades in starting work on the fitting out and internal finishings.

With this form of construction, the external components of a double-skin facade can be assembled after the facade has been sealed and independently of the schedule for the fitting out work. In other words, the erection of the outer skin will not interfere with the execution of the internal finishings, since the external facade components can be assembled from the outside scaffolding.

Built example: Office and commercial building, Valentinskamp / Caffamacherreihe, Hamburg

Client:
DIFA, Deutsche Immobilien Fonds AG, Hamburg

Architects:
Reimer und Partner, Elmshorn
Facade planners:
DS-Plan GmbH, Stuttgart

Facade construction company:
Rupert App GmbH + Co., Leutkirch

Double-skin facade in conventional form of construction with permanently ventilated intermediate space.
Inner facade: aluminum prefabricated post-and-rail construction, with side- and bottom-hung casements in alternate facade bays.
Facade intermediate space: approx. 50 cm deep
Sunshading: aluminum louvered blinds;
louver width: 80 mm
Outer facade: steel supporting sections with point-fixed toughened safety glass

Completion date: 2000

Areas of application; award of contracts

As already indicated in the general description on this subject, a conventional form of construction is relevant primarily for
■ projects with a small facade area
■ facades where there are large jumps in the outer plane of the carcass structure and
■ facades where different materials are used for the supporting members.

The components used in conventional forms of facade construction are normally readily available, mass-produced articles, or individual products that lend themselves to manufacture in larger series. This results in a considerable reduction in the amount of planning work that has to be undertaken by the facade construction firm, for it obviates the development of new glazing and supporting members—an elaborate and technically highly specialized process. The costs involved in this process are usually not justifiable for small series, in contrast to the mass production that is feasible in large projects. The planning work on the part of architects and facade consultants will also be greatly reduced, whereas the demands made on the professional ability of the facade contractor who executes the work will scarcely be any smaller. Having said all this, one should not conclude that the recommendations made here concerning the choice of the right facade firm for prefabricated forms of building no longer apply to conventional construction. The selection should still be made with the utmost care.

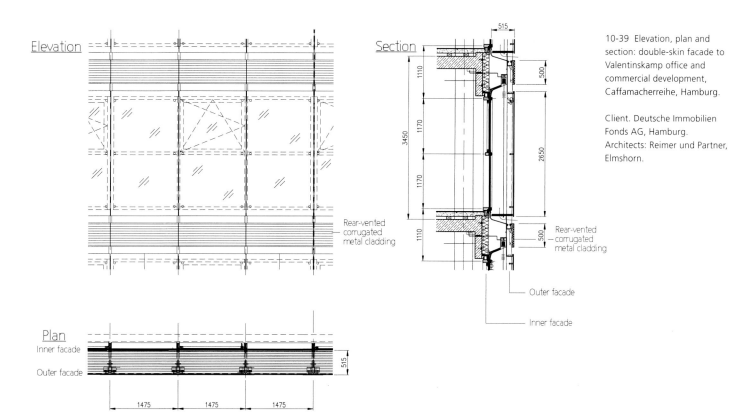

Elevation

Section

Rear-vented corrugated metal cladding

Rear-vented corrugated metal cladding

Outer facade

Inner facade

Plan
Inner facade
Outer facade

515

1475 1475 1475

515
1110
1170
3450
1170
1110
500
2650
500

10-39 Elevation, plan and section: double-skin facade to Valentinskamp office and commercial development, Caffamacherreihe, Hamburg.

Client. Deutsche Immobilien Fonds AG, Hamburg. Architects: Reimer und Partner, Elmshorn.

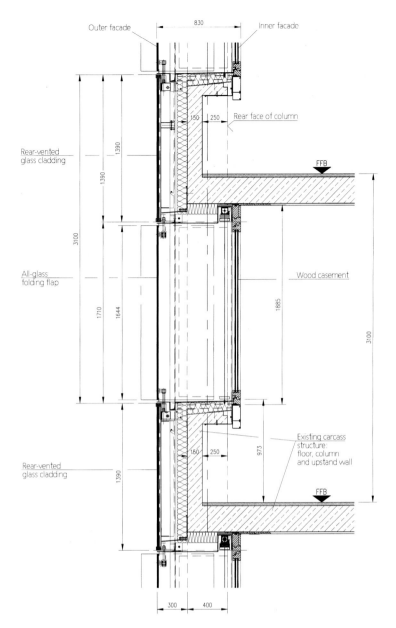

Outer facade   830   Inner facade

Rear face of column

150 250

1390

FFB

Rear-vented
glass cladding

1390

3100

All-glass
folding flap

Wood casement

1710

1644

1885

3100

Rear-vented
glass cladding

Existing carcass
structure:
floor, column
and upstand wall

150 250

973

1390

FFB

300   400

10-40 Sectional detail through box window for refurbishment of BML, Bonn. The inner facade skin was designed in wood; the outer facade with all-glass pivoting casements. Compare with photo on page 33.

The range of suitable facade construction firms will certainly be much greater; for where conventional forms of construction are involved, qualified medium-sized companies do offer serious competition to the big, well-known contractors.

Double-skin facades provide an opportunity to use different materials for the supporting members, with, for example,

■ outer-facade sections in steel or aluminum and
■ inner-facade sections in wood, or aluminum and wood.

Not many facade contractors, of course, can cover the entire range of materials in their own work. Collaborative ventures between companies specializing in certain materials are a good option in ensuring a competitive range of choices for clients. The company with greater experience in double-skin facade construction should assume the technical leadership in such working groups.

In many cases, the range and scope of the different double-skin facade sections on the market are underestimated by clients and investors, and in part by project management offices as well. Arguments in favor of specifying work on a joint-venture basis are often dismissed as a result of all-too pragmatic thinking. One opinion commonly heard is that the facade construction company will have no difficulty in finding a subcontractor to execute the work in the second material.

Depending on the size of the project, however, this is often not the case. If the segment of the work to be executed by the principal facade construction firm is not the main part, that company will rarely be interested in this form of contract, especially where it has an option of other work at the same time. In many schemes with a tendering concept of this kind, a situation arises where the client receives either too few offers for the facade construction or none at all.

Every facade construction firm will be primarily interested in using its own production facilities to full capacity, which means not just the technical processing side; i.e. the engineers and technicians. If a competent facade consultant or an architect with experience in this field is involved in a project where different materials are used for the facade sections, the issue of awarding the contract can usually be resolved by forming a joint-venture team or a consortium of subcontractors. This, in turn, will be based on the trust the individual companies place in the quality of the planning they have to implement.

The rehabilitation project for the Federal Ministry of Food, Agriculture and Forestry (BML) in Bonn provides an easily comprehensible example of a situation where it was logical to use a conventional form of construction because of the extreme differences in the plane of the carcass structure. Here, the deeply recessed inner wood casement construction and the rectangular punched openings in the internal facade skin—dictated by the carcass structure—meant that a prefabrication of the facade was not economically viable. In view of the combination of different materials used in this project:

■ wood for the inner skin,
■ aluminum and glass for the outer skin,

the facade was ultimately executed by a joint-venture group of contractors. A conventional, non-prefabricated form of construction was also chosen because an early facade sealing deadline was essential for the fitting-out work. The constraints of the time schedule were taken into account by using a saddle-frame assembly system and identical wood casement sizes throughout the scheme.

Workmanship and visual quality

The level of workmanship in double-skin facades in conventional forms of construction will clearly be lower than that in prefabricated systems. The much larger amount of assembly work that has to be carried out under all weather conditions, the time pressures and the greater proportion of less precise on-site assembly techniques all take their toll in terms of appearance and workmanship.

To rule out any misunderstandings: this does not mean that a serious, unacceptable loss of quality is the logical outcome of this form of construction. Nevertheless, as in other sectors of industry, a higher working quality can obviously be expected from the use of precision equipment under factory conditions than from on-site assembly. Nor can one overlook the fact that fewer and fewer facade construction firms work with their own, practiced and properly trained assembly gangs. The fall in facade construction prices, which has continued for some time now, has led to economies being made in this area. Less qualified personnel is increasingly being employed for the assembly teams and, unfortunately, even gangs from subcontractors that belong to other branches of industry.

If clients or investors wish to avoid the resulting loss of quality—usually irreparable subsequently—their only hope is to implement a process of specialist quality control. Controls of this kind, which should go beyond normal site management, do not have to be carried out every day; and it is not necessary for someone to be on site for this purpose all the time. It is sufficient if the quality controls take place during the key phases of the facade assembly. An experienced facade specialist should draw the attention of the permanent site manager to any faulty work on the part of the facade construction firm during joint inspections of the assembly process. Any faulty work should also be recorded in the form of site notes which can serve as a check list. Having been instructed on the technical aspects of the work in consultation with the facade expert, the permanent site manager can then supervise the making-good of defects on his own and, if necessary, undertake any legal steps that may be necessary with the expertise of the consultant as a backing.

10-41 Plan of box window for refurbishment of BML, Bonn.

The inner facade skin was designed in wood; the outer facade with all-glass pivoting casements.

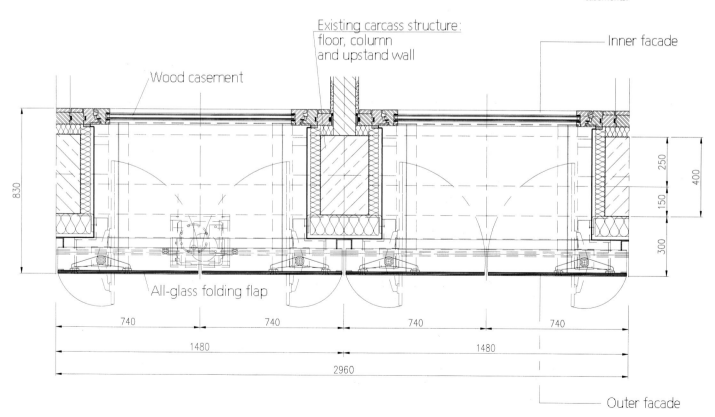

Existing carcass structure:
floor, column
and upstand wall

Inner facade

Wood casement

All-glass folding flap

Outer facade

Glass fixings in the outer facade skin

When designing double-skin facades, architects tend to concentrate on the outer layer, since that is what determines the appearance of any project: it is the visible "face" of a building. The outer skin alone is not important to users, however; they will be concerned

11-1 Diagrams of fixing strips and beads to post-and-rail and framed forms of construction respectively.

Post-and-rail construction

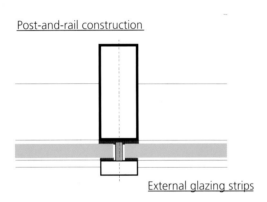

External glazing strips

Framed construction

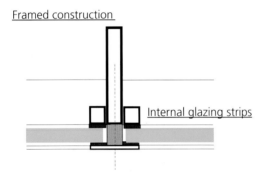

Internal glazing strips

with the construction of the inner facade as well, for their view of the outside world is through two layers. Without neglecting the details of the inner skin, an architect will understandably seek to make the outer skin as transparent as possible, depending on his design philosophy.

The means of glass fixing available and the system ultimately chosen will, therefore, be of great significance, both economically and in terms of the design.

Screw-fixed and clip-on glazing strips

The term "clamping bead" is often used in conjunction with *framed construction systems*, whereas screw-fixed glazing strips are a feature of *post-and-rail construction*. Both clamping beads and glazing strips are *linear glass fixings*. Cover strips are available in clamped form or screw-fixed as well in aluminum and can be manufactured with different cross-sections and to various depths. Usually they will be 50 or 60 mm wide. It is also possible to omit the cover strips, leaving the screw fixings visible. Since this "visually pronounced" form of fixing is very rarely used in double-skin facade construction, however, it will not be described in detail here.

Framed types of double-skin construction are increasingly favored because of the scope they allow for prefabrication. For that reason, the following glazing systems are most commonly used today:
- clamped fixings
- point fixings and
- structural glazing or quasi-structural-glazing systems.

All these types of fixing will be considered here independently of the current discussion of the relative merits of using toughened safety glass or laminated safety glass in the outer skin. This issue will be treated later in a separate section of this chapter.

To ensure a maximum degree of slenderness in the overall appearance of the facade construction, the widths of the metal sections visible externally are often reduced to the minimum allowed by building regulations. In this respect, the rebate depth (cover depth) of the glazing prescribed in codes of practice must be observed, and the relevant glazing tolerances should not be overlooked either. In designing and planning the construction and details of the glazing, it is also important to ensure a rational form of execution. Similarly, where subsequent cleaning and maintenance of the building is to be carried out by means of traveling facade cradles or cleaning robots, this should be taken into account during the design phase. In the built example shown here, the Business Tower in Nuremberg, the grooved track for the facade cradle is integrated into the main posts on every second axis.

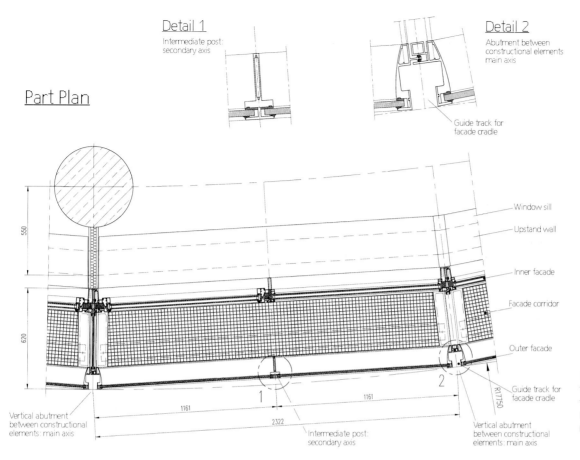

Detail 1
Intermediate post:
secondary axis

Detail 2
Abutment between
constructional elements
main axis

Guide track for
facade cradle

550

620

Window sill

Upstand wall

Inner facade

Facade corridor

Outer facade

Guide track for
facade cradle

R11750

2

1

1161

1161

2322

Vertical abutment
between constructional
elements: main axis

Intermediate post:
secondary axis

Vertical abutment
between constructional
elements: main axis

11-2 External post construction, incorporating a track for
the traveling facade cradle.
Detail from the Business Tower,
Nuremberg.

In developing the glass fixings for this scheme, the aim was to create a clamped fixing system that would be as slender as possible. Aluminum clip-on sections, clamping strips and thin sealing strips were used, all reduced to a minimum thickness.

A similar form of glass fixing with integrated grooves for traveling cradles was planned and executed by the architects Hentrich Petschnigg und Partner for their high-rise building for the Victoria insurance company in Düsseldorf (completed in 1997).

Point fixings

Point-fixed systems are often used in an effort to increase the transparency of the outer facade and to dematerialize the glass fixings themselves. By minimizing the surface area of the fixings in this way, a greater degree of transparency is obviously achieved. As a comparison,

■ the area of linear glazing strips amounts to 8 to 10% of the total facade area;

■ the area covered by point-fixing systems is less than 0.5 percent.

Point-fixed glazing systems place greater demands on the supporting structure. Tolerances can be accommodated only to a limited extent. The point transmission of loads also means more elaborate calculations; and a special calculation is required to determine the thickness of the glass: the so-called "finite element method".

In order to withstand the forces acting on the glass via the point fixings, it will be necessary to use toughened glass. This can be either *toughened safety glass* or *partially toughened safety glass*.

In most countries, glass has not yet been approved as a load-bearing material because of its special properties. In many planning developments in which point-fixed glazing is to be used, therefore, official permission will have to be obtained for each specific project. In Germany, for example, where authorization for a particular form of construction is the prerogative of the individual states (Länder), approval will be granted by the relevant higher building supervisory authority.

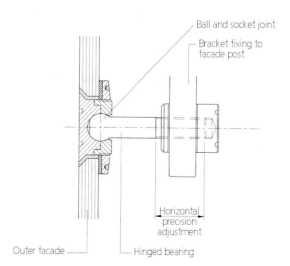

Ball and socket joint

Bracket fixing to
facade post

Horizontal
precision
adjustment

Outer facade

Hinged bearing

11-3 Diagrammatic detail of
flush-finished point fixing with
conical sunken boring in glass.

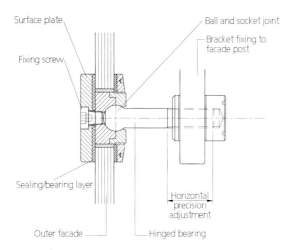

11-4 Diagrammatic detail of point fixing with clamping plate.

Surface plate

Fixing screw

Sealing/bearing layer

Outer facade

Ball and socket joint

Bracket fixing to facade post

Horizontal precision adjustment

Hinged bearing

Flexible mountings allow rotational movements and shifts in certain directions. Where point fixings are used, care should be taken to avoid strains occurring in the glass or any jamming of the panes resulting from the construction process or from glazing tolerances. Strains of this kind can cause the glass to shatter.

For surface-mounted (non-recessed) point fixings, a normal boring of the glass will be required and the pane will be *rigidly clamped* in position. The requisite flexible and rigid fixings are achieved by using different sleeves or variable socket pieces in the glass. Any minor rotational movements of the pane can be absorbed by soft, elastic bearings integrated at these points or by the glass fixings themselves.

Where flush fixings are used, conical recesses will be bored in the glass in which the point fixings are *rigidly inserted* and attached. The plastic ring integrated into the fixing will usually be conical in shape and sit on the splay-cut edge of the glass. This form of fixing is, therefore, always rigid, and there will be no real scope for absorbing tolerances at this point. Any flexibility will have to be provided by the fixing element itself or in the supporting construction.

New developments would seem to be in the pipeline, however. The aim of these is to cushion the hard-edged abutment between the glass and the conical screw fixing; for example, through the insertion of soft cast-resin bearings.

Experience shows that permission is more easily obtained when point-fixing systems are used that have been tested by an approved materials testing institute. In large-scale building projects, facade construction contractors may use their own expertise to develop individual point fixings designed for the specific needs of the scheme. In this way, the firms may also seek to circumvent the costs of standard systems available on the market and to create products tailored to an individual project. In drawing up schedules, account will have to be taken of the time needed to develop the system and to obtain permission for its use.

There are two basic kinds of stainless-steel point fixings for double-skin facade construction, the outer layer of which will generally be in single glazing:
- surface-mounted point fixings that are not flush with the surface of the glass, and
- recessed point fixings that are flush with the surface of the glass.

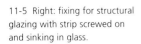

11-5 Right: fixing for structural glazing with strip screwed on and sinking in glass.

In both cases, numerous system products are available. These are manufactured by the glass industry itself or by supply firms and are obtainable in rigid and flexibly mounted forms. The authors recommend planners not to use rigid systems, since they limit permissible tolerances even further, thereby increasing the problem of ensuring a stress-free mounting and allowing for expansion and contraction. Products with ball-and-socket hinged mountings are preferable.

Where point-fixing systems are used, the difference between flexible and rigid fixings is of great significance for the construction. The entire pane of glass must be held in a statically determinate manner; i.e. where one point of support is rigidly fixed and the others are flexibly mounted. The *rigid fixing* will bear all active loads and moments, whereas the *flexible mountings* will bear loads only in certain directions.

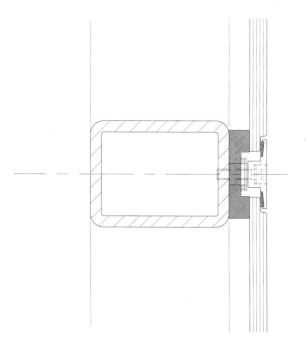

Structural glazing

The expression "structural glazing" (SG) is used to describe frameless glazing in its purest form: where there are no glazing beads or point fixings externally; in other words, where the panes of glass are fixed to the facade supporting construction solely by means of adhesives. This type of glazing is already in use in France and especially in the U.S., but in other countries, including Germany, its application above a height of eight meters has found little favor with building authorities. Where no general approval has been granted for SG at a height exceeding eight meters (above ground level), special permission will have to be sought for this form of construction in each individual case. The higher building supervisory authorities responsible for granting approval are prepared to consent to its use only when proof of reliability is furnished based on long-term experience. Alternatively, permission is often coupled with demands that are economically virtually impossible to fulfil; e.g. annual safety tests for which the client would be responsible. Tests of this kind, in which, for example, the entire adhesive fixing of the glazing or each individual pane of glass would have to be examined, imply such an enormous burden in terms of costs, labor and time that it is practically impossible to execute structural glazing under these circumstances.

The fact that the conditions imposed by German higher building supervisory authorities or their respective specialist departments are not entirely unfounded is demonstrated—quite independently of the discussion of adhesive-fixed structural glazing—by the cases of "falling glass" recorded in Hamburg, Duisburg and Berlin. According to present findings, these incidents, which endangered the lives of passers-by, had a number of causes that are not specifically related to the SG form of construction. It would be completely wrong

and unobjective, therefore, to condemn individual glass-fixing techniques; but it would be equally wrong to reject the safety requirements imposed by building authorities as exaggerated or unjustified. Guaranteeing public safety is one of the most important duties of the authorities responsible for granting building permission.

In view of the problems attached to gaining approval and acceptance of structural glazing—in part because of the purely adhesive nature of the fixings—a number of mixed forms have now been developed that incorporate some of the features of this kind of construction. In most of these mixed forms of glazing, the edges of the panes of glass are treated in various ways, for example:

■ chamfered to an angle of roughly 45°, or
■ provided with ground recesses or rebates.

In this way, a means of glass fixing has been introduced that does not rely exclusively on adhesives; the glass is secured additionally or entirely by mechanical fastenings fixed flush with the surface. The likelihood of obtaining building permission within a reasonable time for the execution of these mixed forms of glazing is much greater, provided the building supervisory authority is consulted in good time and the necessary tests are carried out and proof certificates submitted.

In order to avoid any unpleasant surprises in the planning and scheduling of glass fixing methods of this kind, one should clarify as early as possible whether tests of selected components will be necessary as part of the process of obtaining official approval for a specific scheme. Tests of this nature take a lot of time and can incur considerable costs. Tests of selected building components are carried out by a relatively small number of independent institutes that specialize in certain fields.

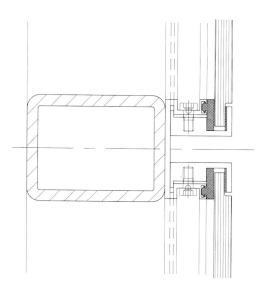

11-6 Left: fixing for structural glazing with screwed sections and sinking in glass.

Glazing to the outer facade skin

Flint glass

Greater transparency can be obtained by using flint glass. In contrast to normal glass, the visible coloration of flint glass is reduced solely to a green tint that is scarcely perceptible to the human eye. Flint glass is marketed by the glass industry under various trade names, such as:
Saint Gobain diamond,
PILKINGTON opti white, etc.

The term "flint glass" is used regardless of the type of product when a certain light transmittance is achieved in relation to the thickness; e.g. $\tau_L \geq 91\%$ for glass 12 mm thick.

In manufacturing flint glass, a different combination of raw materials is used from those contained in normal glass. A decisive factor in this respect is the minimized proportion of iron oxide in the silica sand, since this will significantly reduce the greenish tone of the end product. The glass will have a visually "white" quality; in other words, it will be perceptibly more transparent. When built into a facade, flint glass appears much more brilliant than normal glass.

When flint glass is to be used in a building, the thicknesses currently available from the glass industry should be taken into account. Up to a few years ago, flint glass was manufactured to a maximum thickness of only 12 mm. Today, thicknesses of 15 mm or even more are obtainable. If panes of this thickness are to be used, however, it is advisable to address inquiries to the glass industry at an early stage about the availability of these products. This should also be seen as a precautionary measure when drawing up the time schedule, since flint glass is not a standard product. It is usually manufactured at greater intervals of time and stockpiled for use. When flint glass is to be used in the form of toughened safety glass, one should also ascertain the available sizes and dimensional limitations in advance, especially the width of panes. The maximum width of this type of toughened safety glass available at a reasonable cost is at present between roughly 2,250 and 2,400 mm.

The higher degree of transparency provided by flint glass is an important aesthetic factor in double-skin facades, since when normal glass is used, the number of layers and the thicknesses of the panes will obviously be greater than in single-skin construction. This, in turn, increases the visible green component.

The green coloration is even greater where laminated safety glass has to be used in the outer facade skin—in response to building regulations or to meet the needs of radar damping, for example. If one looks through the corner of a building that has a slenderly dimensioned double-skin facade construction, the line of vision will pass through four layers of glazing. In this case, the coloration of normal glass will be clearly perceptible. This effect will depend partly on the form of the building, but above all on the darkness of the background (e.g. dark clouds or a neighboring building).

Specifying flint glass means higher building costs than where normal glass is used. In any discussions with clients and architects on the need for this additional outlay, it is important that the points described above should be presented. The high degree of transparency evident in the double-skin facade of the RWE tower in Essen by the architects Ingenhoven Overdiek und Partner was possible only with the use of flint glass.

Toughened, partially toughened or laminated safety glass

For various reasons, the glazing to the outer layer of double-skin facades is often executed in *toughened safety glass* or *partially toughened safety glass* rather than in *laminated safety glass*. Among the factors that are usually decisive in this respect are the use of certain kinds of glass fixing, the bedding of the glass, the need to exploit the greater admissible bending strength, or regulations requiring protection against falling glass. In this respect, the use made of the area at the foot of the facade is of great importance. If the building is located in a shopping street, for example, the statutory requirements will certainly be greater than for a facade rising above an area of water where there is no pedestrian traffic.

Since there are no generally valid rules for granting building permission for this kind of glazing, and since no general guidelines or standards exist, official approval can be granted only in specific cases.

In recent years, the large number of incidents in which damage or injury has been caused by the breakage of glass have understandably led—not only in Germany—to a tightening of requirements for granting planning permission for this type of construction. The overriding aim of the building supervisory authorities must be to prevent injury to people as a result of falling glass, whether in the form of broken pieces or entire panes.

In part, this has led to great uncertainty among planners affected by these regulations because, in view of the responsibility of the individual states for legislation within their areas of jurisdiction, the requirements are interpreted differently from one state to another. Two well-known incidents that have received widespread publicity are the fall of glass from the Galeries Lafayette department store in Berlin and the glass damage in the House for the Promotion of Trade and Industry, a technology center in Duisburg.

Generally acceptable rules in the form of standards or codes of practice that might be applied directly or indirectly to the glazing of double-skin facades cannot be expected in the immediate future. To avoid uncertainty about obtaining building permission and in view of the imponderables of planning and building costs related to this, it is advisable to contact the local building authority at an early stage to discuss the current criteria for granting approval for specific projects.

Since there can be no absolute guarantee against breakage or falling glass, attempts are being made at present to minimize the causes of failure resulting from a combination of faulty materials, incorrect assembly and inappropriate application. Of central interest in these investigations is the use of toughened and partially toughened safety glass.

Toughened safety glass is a standardized toughened product manufactured from float glass. The toughening process results in a completely different breakage behavior. The glass shatters into tiny grains, whereas float glass breaks into large jagged pieces.

The toughening process consists of refining the starting material as follows:

- heating the float glass to a temperature of ≈ 650 °C
- controlled cooling by air injection.

In the process of transforming float glass into thermally toughened glass, compression stresses are created in the surfaces of the pane, and tensile stresses are "frozen into" the interior. The compression stresses serve as a reserve safety factor that has to be reduced to zero by any negative loading before dangerous tensile stresses can occur in the surface. Toughened safety glass is, therefore, capable of withstanding greater loads than float glass.

If the balance between compression and tensile stresses within the pane is disturbed (e.g. through damage to the surfaces or edges of the glass), the stresses frozen in the pane can lead to a sudden chain reaction that will tear it into tiny pieces. The pieces will be roughly rectangular in form and have less dangerous edges.

Partially toughened safety glass is also made from float glass, which is toughened by thermal treatment. Unfortunately, no standards exist for this product yet. In contrast to toughened safety glass, partially toughened safety glass is not generally recognized by building authorities as a construction material. Official approval for its use in building must, therefore, be obtained from case to case.

The partial toughening is achieved by a process similar to that used in the manufacture of toughened safety glass, with the difference that:

- the glass is heated to a lower temperature; and
- it is subject to a slower, controlled cooling process.

The degree of toughening is not as great as in normal toughened safety glass, so that the load-bearing capacity lies somewhere between that of float glass and toughened safety glass. The behavior of the glass in the case of failure is similar to that of float glass: in other words, it shatters into larger, jagged pieces. This coarser breaking pattern is of advantage, however, when partially toughened safety glass is used in the manufacture of laminated safety glass. In this case, the glass has a greater load-bearing strength compared with float glass and a better residual bearing capacity in view of the composite, laminated structure. In the event of breakage, this results in a greater degree of mutual bonding between the individual pieces of glass in the various layers compared with a single layer of toughened safety glass. Both these properties can be effectively exploited in certain situations.

Laminated safety glass is, as its name implies, a composite material consisting of two or more layers of glass. Laminated safety glass can be manufactured from various types of glass: float glass, toughened safety glass or partially toughened safety glass.

The bonding of the layers is designed to prevent danger to life in the event of breakage, when pieces of glass would normally fall out. The bond between the individual sheets of glass is achieved with a layer of polyvinylbutyral (PVB) film. The PVB is usually as clear as the glass, but it can also be translucent or opaque if required.

The thin layers of film are pressed between the panes of glass in a heated vacuum chamber (a so-called "autoclave"). This results in an adhesive-like bonding between the panes; in other words, the effect is based on the principle of adhesion. A true adhesive bonding would be more likely to suffer damage along the lines of fracture, since it would remain hanging to the sharp broken edges. In the present case, the adhesion-like effect means that the film can easily lift from the edge of the glass in the vicinity of the fracture, but it holds the individual pieces together over the remaining area.

A further advantage of laminated safety glass is its residual load-bearing capacity, the degree of which will depend on the types of glass used and on the breakage behavior of the individual layers in conjunction with each other. The larger the pieces that are held together by the film, the greater will be the blocking effect of the composite sheet, and thus the residual load-bearing capacity. For that reason, laminated safety glass made from partially toughened safety glass will have a higher residual load-bearing capacity than that made from ordinary toughened safety glass. As a result of its greater residual load-bearing capacity, laminated safety glass made from partially toughened safety glass is recommended by building supervisory authorities for use in overhead glazing, despite the fact that no standards exist for this material.

Since the bonding between the individual panes is not resistant to shear forces, the loads to be borne should be distributed over the individual panes in proportion to their rigidity. Additively, however, the individual panes do not achieve the same load-bearing strength as a single sheet of glazing with the same overall thickness. In order to provide the same load-bearing capacity, therefore, a sheet of laminated safety glass will always have to be thicker and heavier than a monolithic pane of the same type of glass.

Toughened safety glass is the usual form of glazing in the outer layer of double-skin facades. The most common cause of failure is a fault in the material itself: so-called "nickel-sulfide flaws". A pocket of nickel-sulfide can be regarded as an impurity in the body of the glass. When the pane is subjected to heat, the enclosed pocket expands disproportionally within the glass and can cause it to shatter. This phenomenon is referred to as a "spontaneous" or "butterfly" breakage. The latter term describes the characteristic pattern of the breakage—circular forms around two central points—which resembles the shape of a butterfly.

To identify panes with impurities of this kind before they are dispatched from the works, all sheets of toughened glass have to undergo a heat-soak test, in which panes with defects are automatically destroyed. The chance of a defective pane surviving the heat-soak test is 1 in 100,000, according to Prof. Wörner of the University of Technology, Darmstadt.

To increase the safety standards of glazing with toughened safety glass, taking account of the assembly process, and to guard against possibly incorrect applications, the relevant building authority for Hamburg imposed additional requirements for the testing, control and assembly of this material in two parallel large-scale building projects. These measures were imposed early in 1999 as part of the process of granting planning permission for the schemes.

Only because the authority was prepared to explore systems of this kind and because the officials responsible for the work displayed such a high degree of professional competence—in collaboration with the clients, the architects, the specialist facade planners, and the facade construction firms—was it possible to execute a facade in toughened safety glass. This helped to avoid a much more expensive form of construction in laminated safety glass, which would have involved a number of visual disadvantages, too.

In Hamburg, the following additional requirements (given in summarized form) were made before granting permission for this type of construction.

Reports / Trials / Independent supervision

■ Compilation of a report by a specialist consultant to determine the requirements for granting approval
■ Testing of specific building components
■ Independent supervision of glass production in consultation with the German Institute for Building Technology (DIBt), Berlin, and the building supervisory authority in Hamburg
■ Independent supervision of the assembly by a testing engineer

Requirements made of the glass

■ Experimental simulation of glass cooling from warm to cold state (extreme case: cooling during a thunderstorm in summer)
■ Stricter control/supervision of heat-soak test
■ Special glass quality seal with Ü symbol and number of certificate of official approval for specific construction scheme
■ Continuous protection of all edges of glass panes during transport

Assembly requirements

■ Measurement of glass borings prior to assembly
■ Measurement of fixings (point fixings) in the facade prior to assembly of glazing
■ Detailed documentation of technical measurements and comparison of dimensional deviations between glass and facade construction over the entire facade area
■ Inspection of the glazing after one year and three years.

These additional requirements involve considerable extra costs, which have to be paid to the facade construction firm on top of the contract sum. The costs are considerably lower, however, than for a facade in laminated safety glass. In the latter case, not just the additional costs of the glass have to be taken into account, but the additional structural and constructional measures necessitated by the greater weight of the glass. These examples in Hamburg show that it is worth the effort for the facade planner to find a solution—jointly with the authority that grants planning approval—based on the use of a single layer of toughened safety glass, since this will be in the client's economic interests.

The solution often proposed by facade planners who wish to err on the side of safety and who claim that this form of construction is possible only with laminated safety glass can result in extra costs for the client that run into six figures (or seven figures in the case of large projects). In many cases, the client's representative may not even be aware that a more economical and a more transparent solution is possible. This will, however, demand a greater degree of planning and a greater commitment on the part of everyone concerned in the execution of the work.

Admittedly, the problem of falling glass can be largely overcome by using laminated safety glass in the outer skin. Laminated safety glass consists of two or more layers of toughened safety glass, partially toughened glass or float glass laid on top of each other. The layers are bonded together with a resilient PVB film during the manufacturing process under a pressure of roughly 12 bar and at a temperature of approximately 140 °C (see also page 152). In the event of breakage, the pieces of glass are held together by the intermediate layer(s) of PVB, thus ensuring an adequate residual load-bearing capacity. The synthetic PVB film, therefore, prevents the glass from suddenly falling from the building in the event of breakage, as is likely to occur with a single layer of toughened safety glass.

An adequate residual load-bearing capacity can also be achieved by applying a special film to single-layer toughened safety glass. In this respect, at least, the glass will have the same property as laminated safety glass. But that is more in the nature of an emergency measure that should be implemented only as kind of "follow-up treatment" after the work has been completed. The sheets of film that are available to date are not sufficiently resistant to scratching nor, in the long term, to the influence of UV radiation. At present, the aging of these materials in terms of brittleness and loss of adhesion at the edges is not satisfactorily proven for the required period either. Furthermore, special care and maintenance are necessary, which cannot be guaranteed by most clients.

Accommodating structural tolerances

As part of the measures to reduce the overall construction period of a building, efforts are inevitably made to shorten the facade assembly time. The optimization of the facade construction process is very advanced today, but there is still room for improvement.

The assembly of facades to high-rise buildings proceeds only a few stories behind the ongoing carcass construction; i.e. behind the climbing shuttering. The facade construction company's assembly team is shielded by protective scaffolding against any objects that may fall during the erection of the main structure. This kind of advanced facade assembly may also be used in buildings only six to ten stories in height as a means of saving valuable construction time.

Until relatively recently, it was common to construct facades based *on the actual measured dimensions of the carcass structure*. In the meantime, this method is rarely used in medium-sized or larger schemes. The process of optimization that has taken place in the work of facade contractors, which manifests itself in a high degree of prefabrication with state-of-the-art equipment, has meant that an individual manufacturing process to measured dimensions is economically scarcely viable anymore. In modern facade construction, the components are manufactured and assembled *to theoretical dimensions*.

The points of abutment with the structure have to be designed in such a way that they can accommodate the dimensional tolerances in the carcass structure allowed by building standards. This applies equally to double-skin facades, regardless whether they be prefabricated or based on traditional forms of construction.

Valid guidelines

Since the load-bearing structure has to be erected under virtually all weather conditions, whereas valuable manufacturing equipment can be used to only a relatively limited extent, it is not possible to execute the structure to the same degree of precision as the facade or the fitting out work. Dimensional deviations in the carcass structure from the theoretical measurements contained in the plans are, therefore, permissible and, indeed, quite normal. Depending on the material used, structural dimensions may vary by as much as ± 30 mm in all directions (e.g. with concrete). The permissible tolerances in each case are given in the relevant standards /CD1/, and a responsible planner should take account of these in the detailed design.

What dimensional deviations actually occur?

The necessary and unavoidable "accommodation" of structural tolerances within the facade construction can be regarded as a problem facing the planning team—one that is all too often neglected and to which too little importance is attached. The question of deviations in the dimensions of the carcass structure, therefore, will be discussed in terms of the permissible tolerances for in-situ concrete construction.

The tolerances allowed in building standards should be assumed in all directions—i.e. three-dimensionally—in terms of:
- length, width and depth
- axial and grid dimensions
- angles
- surface planes and alignment of edges.

11-7 Horizontal section through side abutment of box window, with details of structural tolerances given in the facade drawing.
Without an internal lining to accommodate variations in tolerances, an acceptable fitting of this window element is possible only if it is tailored to measurements taken on site.

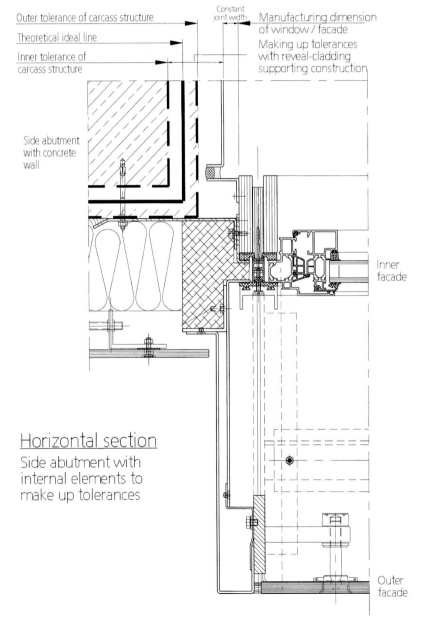

Outer tolerance of carcass structure

Theoretical ideal line

Inner tolerance of carcass structure

Constant joint width

Manufacturing dimension of window / facade

Making up tolerances with reveal-cladding supporting construction

Side abutment with concrete wall

Inner facade

Horizontal section
Side abutment with internal elements to make up tolerances

Outer facade

If the standards specify a permissible tolerance of ± 25 mm for a certain situation, planners should be aware that in extreme cases this can amount to a difference of 50 mm, without the contractor responsible for the carcass structure being obliged to remedy this and reduce the deviation.

Recommendations for practical construction

The problems associated with dimensional deviations cannot be overemphasized. As a rule, "remedial" work to concrete is scarcely possible, or only to a limited extent. The reason for this is obvious: in the soffit of a concrete floor, for example, or in the jambs of an opening, there will usually be a continuous layer of reinforcement, and the steel cannot simply be removed and refixed after the concrete is cast.

A further reason is that errors in tolerances— deviations from the planned structural dimensions in excess of permissible limits—are usually recognized only when it is too late to do anything about them; in other words, when one can no longer break out an entire concrete element, such as part of a floor slab, a wall or a column, since the next floor above has already been concreted. Common reactions on the part of planners and contractors are:

■ "We'll deal with that through the bills of quantities; the permissible tolerances will have to be reduced", or
■ "We'll work to such precision that the permissible tolerances will be undercut".

Statements of this kind can only be described as wishful thinking. The reality on site means that it is virtually impossible to implement any such intentions.

For the planner, entering the tolerances in the detail plans is a good method of checking—at the drafting table or on the screen—the feasibility of implementing them on site. In this respect, facade abutment and jointing details should be viewed with a very critical eye where the internal fittings and finishings do not allow for any accommodation of tolerances.

With details of this kind, the planner will have to accept that admissible deviations from specified dimensions will possibly remain visible. Subsequent corrections during the construction phase will be virtually impossible, unless, for example, a lining can be built in around an opening to accommodate tolerances. Since substantial extras of this kind incurred during the construction phase are not foreseen in the contract, which has already been awarded, they will possibly result in a large potential for additional costs. Measures such as this should, therefore, be regarded as only a theoretical alternative.

In the course of the construction work, the prevention of inadmissible deviations from tolerances can be achieved only with constant surveying checks, which should be implemented from the very beginning of the work. After every major phase of concreting or

structural work, dimensional deviations should be precisely measured and recorded in general layout plans. This will help to prevent an incrementation of deviations from the dimensions contained in the plans.

Controls of this kind should be carried out by an independent surveyor, or at least by a surveyor who is not involved in the project, and not by the foreman of the firm responsible for the execution of the structure or by the site manager of the general contractor. Keeping a continuous record of dimensional deviations in this way provides a neutral, written basis for all parties in the event of subsequent accusations, disputes or litigation. Above all, it is usually the only way of guaranteeing that critical dimensional deviations are recognized in time; for who willingly admits to having made an error?

11-8 Horizontal section through side abutment of box window, with details of structural tolerances given in the facade drawing.
With an internal lining to mask dimensional variations, this window can be fitted to theoretical dimensions and can accommodate structural tolerances, too.

Built example: box window construction for Savings Bank in Waiblingen.
Architects: Kist, Koop, Fehmel, Waldmann, Stuttgart

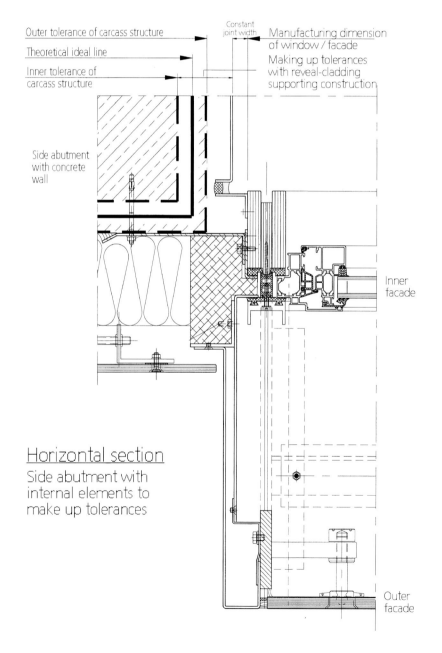

Outer tolerance of carcass structure
Theoretical ideal line
Inner tolerance of carcass structure
Constant joint width
Manufacturing dimension of window / facade
Making up tolerances with reveal-cladding supporting construction
Side abutment with concrete wall
Inner facade

Horizontal section
Side abutment with internal elements to make up tolerances

Outer facade

Fixings and forms of anchoring

All forces and loads acting on the facade construction have to be transmitted via load-bearing facade components to the structure of the building. With double-skin facades, the greater dead load of the facade itself and the cantilever moment of the outer skin have to be taken into account as well.

The load-bearing facade structure should be able to transmit all horizontal wind loads from the outer skin via the supporting construction to the carcass of the building. The wind loads that have to be assumed are given in the relevant regulations in relation to the height and geometry of the building. Since no regulations exist for double-skin facades in conjunction with the geometry of buildings—and these are unlikely to exist in the foreseeable future—it is advisable to commission a wind-loading report, especially for high-rise building projects.

Reports of this kind are compiled by specialist institutions and provide much more accurate values and safety factors for the loads that will actually occur than the calculation procedure set out in standards and regulations. To determine these values, the relevant institutions will carry out wind-tunnel tests, using scale models of the building. This approach is, in fact, expressly favored by local building authorities. The calculated statical values will then have to be accepted by the testing engineers.

The facade construction comprises an additive assembly of many small components to form a whole. This means that the loads have to be transmitted from each individual element to the load-bearing structure. Much greater wind loads occur around the corners and salient edges of buildings than in the middle of the facade.

In much of Europe, the loads to be assumed and the corresponding safety coefficients are generally comprehensible and can be calculated by experienced planners on the basis of existing national or upcoming European regulations. For overseas building projects, that will not necessarily be the case. For example, in parts of Asia, building components have to be dimensioned to withstand loads up to 10 kN/m² in trials without sustaining permanent damage.

Fixing and anchoring requirements

Unit construction systems based on a high degree of prefabrication are the building form of the future for medium- and large-scale structures. That also applies to double-skin facades. This has to be taken into account in the fixing and anchoring construction, therefore, in order to comply with the rapid assembly sequence. Facades are usually fixed to the carcass structure not in a planar fashion, but via individual plates, fin-like elements or brackets.

In view of the great loads to be transmitted to the structure, individual fixing brackets are usually attached to built-in concrete elements in the carcass structure. This kind of fixing, which is most simply executed with anchor channels, is clearly preferable to welded forms of construction.

11-9 Photo showing details of fixing bracket for ventilation box in "City Gate", Düsseldorf. The special form of the bracket allows the elements to be adjusted in all three dimensions to accommodate variations in structural tolerances.

Welded connections, such as brackets fixed to anchor plates, may be appropriate in certain situations, but they can rarely be recommended as a system solution. They result in a much more elaborate assembly process. What is more, in the event of having to adjust an error, a welded connection, once executed, can be undone only through a laborious cutting process.

The fixing and anchoring system, selected in accordance with the facade construction, should permit simple and extremely fine adjustments in all directions if it is to accommodate structural and facade-assembly tolerances.

■ It should be horizontally adjustable in four directions: to left and right; forwards and backwards.
■ It should be vertically adjustable in two directions: upwards and downwards.

Simple means of adjustment play an important role in the context of ever shorter assembly times.

Built-in concrete elements

Since the majority of load-bearing structures are executed in concrete (in Europe at least), only built-in elements in this material will be considered here. The anchor channels recommended for fixing the individual brackets can be in the form of short lengths cast into the concrete on the facade axes. Their precise position and layout should be determined at the planning stage by the architect or the facade planner. The anchor channels will be adapted to the requirements of the facade construction and situated on every axis; in other words, at roughly 1.2 to 1.5-meter centers; or alternatively on every second facade axis. The anchor channels enable horizontal adjustments to be made: for example, either to left and right or backwards and forwards.

Determining the precise construction and dimensions of the anchor channels and their structural integration into the concrete floor slabs are planning processes that should be carried out in consultation with the structural engineers.

Fixing brackets

In view of the form and execution of the fixing brackets, they are sometimes referred to as "fixing shoes". In their design and construction, they often exhibit typical stylistic features of the firm that manufactures them. For the contractor executing the facade work, this has the advantage that the assembly teams will usually be familiar with the fixing system of a certain manufacturer. This, in turn, means that the proportion of errors and the assembly time can be cut. The process of horizontal adjustment in the second dimension will usually be effected by means of a ratchet strip or similar construction incorporated in the bracket.

The principle of working with fixing shoes as a means of assembly is not new. One well-known facade construction concern has been using this form of fixing—adapted to the specific needs of each project —for nearly 20 years and with great success. This sensible and simple system has, therefore, been adopted by many progressive facade construction companies in similar if not almost identical form. Where manufactured in large batches, the fixing brackets are usually made (for cost reasons) of higher quality cast aluminum. Galvanized steel is less commonly used. Steel brackets can be made, for example, from standard channel sections in short lengths. A head plate will then be welded on to the channel, on or in which a "top-hat" section or lipped channel is integrated.

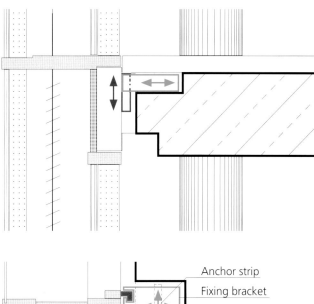

11-10 Diagram of facade fixing with anchor brackets. Tolerances are accommodated by means of various adjustable / sliding elements.

Anchor strip
Fixing bracket
Sliding shoe to post
Groove in concrete

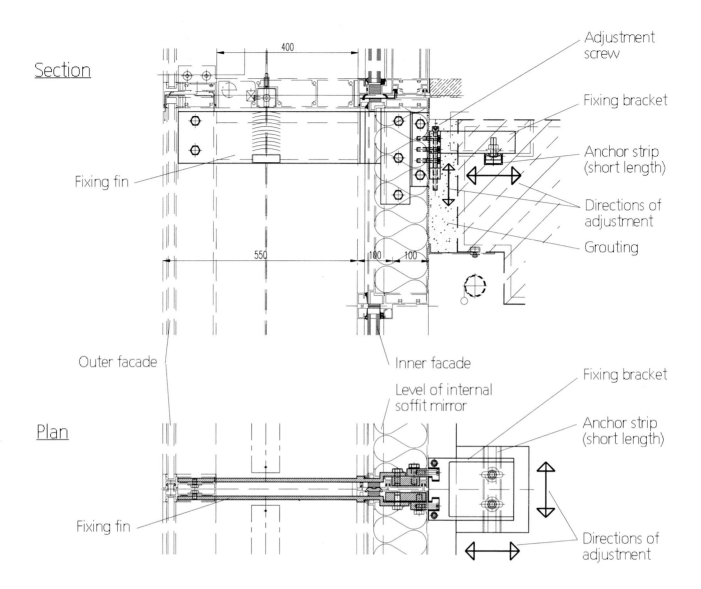

Section

400

Fixing fin

550   100 100

Outer facade

Inner facade

Level of internal
soffit mirror

Plan

Fixing fin

Adjustment
screw

Fixing bracket

Anchor strip
(short length)

Directions of
adjustment

Grouting

Fixing bracket

Anchor strip
(short length)

Directions of
adjustment

11-11 Vertical and horizontal
sections through facade support construction for tower
block at Olympic Park in Munich: system using fixing fins.

Fixing fins

Fixing fins or plates are integrated into the double-skin
facade construction and transmit the entire structural
loads from the facade to the fixing brackets. The facade element can be *vertically adjusted* via the fin construction, or by means of a head or top-hat section in
the bracket.

A provision for vertical adjustments can be planned
and executed in a simple form as an integral part of
the construction by means of an appropriately dimensioned stainless-steel screw. This method also provides
scope for simple, swift subsequent adjustments of the
facade elements. The fins are normally made of aluminum plate or sections with the appropriate structural dimensions. The required bracket form, determined
by design or structural constraints, can be cut from
aluminum plates. Steel and stainless steel are used for
fins only where this is required by fire regulations, or
where the loads to be transmitted exceed the limited
strength of aluminum.

Division of works: structure / facade construction

To take maximum advantage of a fixing system that has been optimized by a particular firm, all built-in elements and fixings should be manufactured and supplied by the facade construction firm. These include

- elements built into the structure
- fixing brackets
- fixing fins or plates.

Although elements to be incorporated into the structure may be supplied by the facade construction firm, they will be cast or built in by the general contractor. This division of work should be covered in detail in the bills of quantities for the trades responsible for the carcass structure.

This presupposes an early scheduling of all work related to the facade construction, however. The facade planning, the award of contracts, the mock-up facade, the commencement of assembly, and the various intermediate stages of work should be planned in detail and should not lag behind the carcass structure. In the opinion of the authors, an ideal division of works would be as follows.

Work to be executed by the general contractor

- Building into the structure the components supplied by the facade construction firm.
- Insertion of the components to be built into the carcass structure according to the plans of the facade construction firm.

Work to be executed by the facade construction firm

- Supplying elements to be built into the structure.
- Drawing up plans for the location of built-in elements in collaboration with the structural engineers.
- Providing proof of the load-bearing capacity in collaboration with the structural engineers.
- Submission of proof of structural fitness to testing engineer.

A slightly modified work interface is, of course, conceivable. The possible sequence of work in relation to the overall scheduling of the project should be considered in detail.

11-12 Diagrams of facade support system with fin brackets. Tolerances accommodated by means of various adjustable / sliding elements.

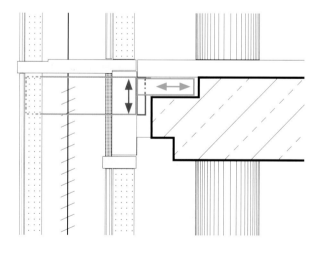

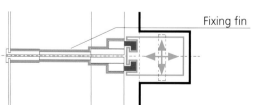

Fixing fin

Built example: Post Office Tower, Bonn

11-14 Far right: diagrammatic section through north facade and space to rear, showing ventilation and air-conditioning elements.

The proposed headquarters tower for the German Post Office was designed by the architects Murphy/Jahn as a wholly transparent structure. Situated between the two segments that house the office spaces are nine-story-high "sky gardens", at the center of which are the vertical lines of access.

The office facades were designed as slenderly dimensioned, filigree double-skin facades with automatic controls. The facade construction is suspended in nine-story-high sections. The structural concept provides for a transmission of horizontal (wind) loads via a series of so-called "wind needles" situated on every floor and every facade axis. The south face of the tower has a scale-like construction, with horizontally pivoting lights that allow an intermittent air-intake and extract and thus a natural ventilation of the offices. The north side of the tower has a smooth, planar external facade with integrated flaps. All opening lights in the external skin are operated by electric motors controlled from a central monitoring system.

The inner facade skins in each case contain narrow side-hung casements in alternate facade bays. These are also operated by electric motors and serve to ventilate the offices by natural means.

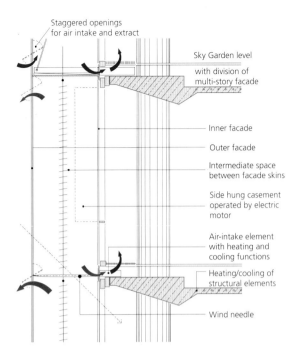

Staggered openings for air intake and extract

Sky Garden level with division of multi-story facade

Inner facade

Outer facade

Intermediate space between facade skins

Side hung casement operated by electric motor

Air-intake element with heating and cooling functions

Heating/cooling of structural elements

Wind needle

The facade is in a multistory form of construction with horizontal divisions only at the levels of the sky gardens: in other words, every nine stories. This enhances the transparency of the facade even further. In addition, the use of flint glass is foreseen for the inner and outer facade skins.

11-13 Photo of model of proposed Post Office headquarters tower.

Architects: Murphy/Jahn, Chicago
Structural engineering, design and facade construction: Werner Sobek Engineers, Stuttgart, DS-Plan

11-15 Far right: section through nine-story segment of multistory facade, showing principle of staggered air-intake and extract openings distributed over the height of the building.

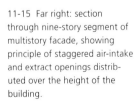

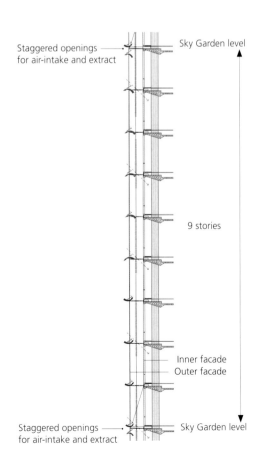

Staggered openings for air-intake and extract

Sky Garden level

9 stories

Inner facade
Outer facade

Staggered openings for air-intake and extract

Sky Garden level

Protection against birds

The development of double-skin facades repeatedly leads planners and especially clients to ask apprehensively whether the requisite ventilation openings in the outer skin do not provide birds with welcome nesting places. The question is understandable and justified, as is the wish on the part of clients to obtain reliable information on this matter. Unfortunately, it is virtually impossible to meet these expectations.

In the authors' opinion, no firm assurance can be given based on reliable facts (e.g. economic data). The exact behavior of birds depends on a number of factors that cannot be evaluated within the scope of the engineers' planning brief. The following aspects play a major role, for example:
■ Do natural feeding grounds exist for birds in the immediate vicinity of the building?
■ Are there active bird-lovers who feed birds in the vicinity of the building?
■ Do natural enemies of birds exist in the area?

In inner-city areas, the birds that create the greatest "annoyance" around buildings are usually pigeons, whose behavior is likely to be adapted to local conditions. In many cases, therefore, people may speak of precautionary measures against pigeons rather than against birds in general.

In describing the places favored by birds, the experience of the authors corresponds with the findings of ornithologists: birds prefer locations in and around buildings where they can find shelter from the wind and other elements. Typical roosting places include
■ recesses
■ roof projections (under eaves)
■ sheltered set-backs in a building.

In this sense, corridors or ventilation boxes in double-skin facades offer a great degree of protection against wind and weather.

So far, however, completed examples of double-skin facades have not proved to be especially frequented by birds. This is probably related to the fact that these areas of a building are almost always in close proximity to and directly overlooked by the users. In the facade corridors of office buildings, birds have no peace, for during the day, they are disturbed by the presence of people close to the facade. In addition, when the sun shines, the sunshading will be lowered with the accompanying noise of the motors. Users may also open the windows in their rooms, so that conversations and other noises enter the facade intermediate space.

Virtually no reliable data exists on the heights at which birds fly and roost. In the case of churches, one knows that pigeons can pose a problem up to the very tip of a building. In the areas in and around buildings where birds find a near-natural habitat, as in the well-planted "sky gardens" of tower blocks, various species have been encountered up to a height of 150 meters.

If planners wish to play safe with respect to pigeons and other birds, one answer is to install stretched wires or wire netting to prevent access. In the section of this book describing the optimization of resistance to air currents (in the chapter "Aerophysics"), reference has already been made to the serious hindrance to ventilation in double-skin facades that may be caused by preventive measures of this kind.

Nevertheless, where a potential annoyance from birds exists, it is advisable at the outset to install stainless-steel tensioned cables with integrated stainless-steel springs, or at least to provide for their subsequent installation. Stainless-steel nets, adapted to specific requirements, can also be used.

To ensure a maximum degree of safety for a specific scheme in respect of the recommended size of the mesh openings or spacing of the wires, precise information on the types of birds to be found in the location and their habitat would be necessary. Only an ornithologist with a knowledge of the actual location will be able to provide reliable data of this kind.

Radar damping

The globalization of the world economy, the flexibility of movement this requires of people in the form of business trips, and the rapid increase in tourist flights in recent times have led to a dramatic growth of air traffic. All predictions say this trend is likely to continue in the future, with a further increase in the volume of aviation. This is borne out by the extensive building activity taking place in and around major airports. The density of air traffic necessitates precise supervision, free of interference, of all airborne objects by the air-traffic-control authorities.

Interference to air traffic makes itself felt in the form of delays and is becoming increasingly common. One cause of this is the reflection of radar waves from the faces of existing buildings, or those under construction, around airports. Depending on the height of the building, the area affected by this phenomenon can extend to a radius of 10 to 15 kilometers (6 to 10 miles). Radar reflection causes not only interference,

however; under certain circumstances, it can pose a serious threat to air traffic. To eliminate this danger, it may be necessary to implement certain measures in the construction of buildings to reduce the level of disturbing radar reflection and thus comply with local aviation regulations.

Statutory background
The question of radar interference caused by buildings is regulated by legislation. In Germany, for example, §12 and 18a of the Air Traffic Law (LVG) are relevant in this respect. The need to gain planning permission is covered by §12, paragraph 2, according to which, approval has to be obtained from a state aviation authority for the erection of a building within a radius of 15 km of an airport.

If local conditions, including the height of a building, cause the aviation authority to demand a low-reflection facade, it is incumbent on the client to implement this. If interference manifests itself after the completion of the building, it will be the client's responsibility to alleviate the problem.

Officially recognized consultants
The reduced level of interference required in a building will have to be determined by a consultant recognized by the relevant aviation authority. The specialist, who will be engaged by the clients, will draw up a radar-compatibility report. This will include the requisite technical measures to be implemented to reduce the radar interference caused by the building, drawn up in the form of an authoritative report and to be submitted for planning approval. For this purpose, the risk of interference will be investigated in detail, and any necessary countermeasures described. An analysis of the local radar system will also be made in collaboration with the relevant aviation authority, since not all airports use the same systems.

The exact level of requirements for radar damping will depend on the height of the building, its distance from the airport, and the orientation of the facade to the angle of incidence of the airport radar impulses. The degree of so-called "echo damping" required as part of these measures can be between about 6 and 40 dB. In other words, between 75 and 99.99% of the radar intensity hitting the face of a building may not be reflected by the facade construction.

11-16 Diagram of airport surveillance system, using primary and secondary surveillance radar.

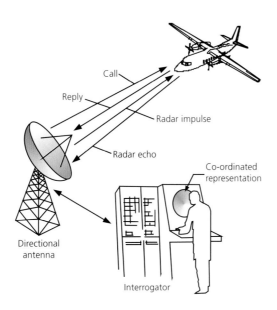

11-17 Phantom image caused by buildings that reflect radar.

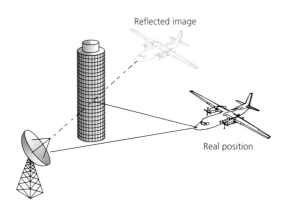

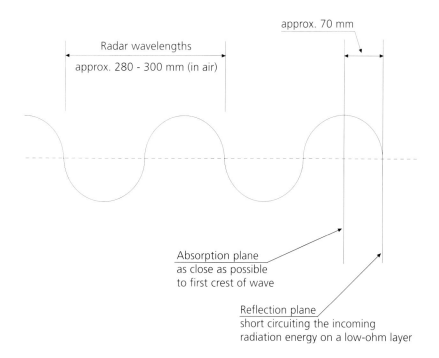

approx. 70 mm

Radar wavelengths
approx. 280 - 300 mm (in air)

Absorption plane
as close as possible
to first crest of wave

Reflection plane
short circuiting the incoming
radiation energy on a low-ohm layer

11-18 Basic principle of
Jaumann absorber.

Preliminary inquiry to aviation authority

In planning taller buildings near airports, it is advisable to address certain inquiries to the local aviation authority during the preliminary planning stage, asking whether any requirements for facade radar damping are likely to be imposed on the project in question. Only when this authority indicates the need to implement certain measures should the above-mentioned consultant be contacted and commissioned to draw up a report.

Airport surveillance system

Airport surveillance is usually the responsibility of regional or national air-traffic control authorities and is implemented in most cases using a combination of primary and secondary radar systems. Primary surveillance radar functions solely on the basis of the echo obtained from airborne objects. The principle is the same as that with which one is familiar from sea navigation.

Secondary surveillance radar (SSR) is a radio-location process based on long-term measurements and an interactive exchange of information. This system requires two components that communicate with each other:
■ the interrogator in the ground station:
the active interrogation equipment;
■ a transponder on board the airborne object:
the active response equipment.

In this system, every activity on the part of the ground station represents a question that has to be answered by the object in the air in the form of a coded reply. The position of the object in the air is plotted by measuring the time that elapses between the transmission and the reception of impulses, in combination with an evaluation of the antenna position (rotation). The interrogation is transmitted from the ground station to the aircraft via a certain carrier frequency. The reply from the transponder in the aircraft is transmitted via a different frequency. From this reply, the requisite information can be obtained with respect to
■ the precise location
■ the flight altitude
■ the flight direction and
■ the flight number
of the plane.

If the reply signal from the transponder strikes the facade of a tall building and is then reflected in the direction of the airport, the ground station or the aviation authority, will thus receive a number of signals relating to the location of the aircraft:
■ the so-called "real target" (the true position) and
■ one or more "phantom targets".

If, as a result of this, the flight controllers are unable quickly to identify the true position of a plane coming in to land, they will send the aircraft into a holding pattern for safety reasons.

Other complications that may be caused by radar reflections include:
■ the loss of the flight number, resulting from the garbling of codes;
■ an increased interrogation rate and the resultant strain this imposes on air-traffic controllers; and
■ a reduced quality in the radar image.

These aspects will not be discussed further at this point, however.

Construction principles for radar damping

The following construction principles can be applied where it is necessary to damp radar reflections from facades:

■ radar damping through absorption
(absorption of energy)
■ radar damping through interference
(elimination or reduction by means of superimposition)

Absorption facades

Where radar reflections are to be damped by means of absorption, the principle of the so-called "Jaumann absorber" is used.

By short-circuiting the radar radiation energy on its arrival in a low-ohmic layer (conductive with low resistance), a standing wave is built up in front of this layer, which is referred to as a "reflector". With this method of radar damping, the absorber, which is meant to soak up the energy, should be positioned as close to the first crest of the standing wave as possible, since the greatest amount of energy can be extracted here.

The distance between the reflector and the absorber will thus be dependent on the wavelength of the radar beams and on the media that have to be penetrated and which also exert an influence on the wavelength.

By a process of polarization (turning the vectors of the radar beams), the distance between the constructional elements (absorber and reflector) can be optimized. The true reflection plane can be assumed to lie a few centimeters further inward than the actual position of the reflector element (EADS principle, protected by international patents), a fact that facilitates a smaller constructional depth. This method of radar damping is particularly suited to double-skin facades, since a polarizing plane can be incorporated in the outer skin.

The absorption of radar radiation is achieved by means of a special radar fabric with a mesh-like structure. In areas of transparent glazing, this will take the form of a hair-fine mesh of threads. Laid between two layers of PVB film within laminated safety glass, the threads are scarcely visible. Ready-made products are obtainable as absorption systems for the non-transparent areas of facades, such as apron panels, soffits and wall cladding. Two absorption systems of this kind on the market—Radotherm by G+H Isover and Gigaram by the Oellerking company—can be used in rear-ventilated facade areas and thermally-insulated composite facades. Materials suitable for use as rear-vented facade cladding include ceramic, fibre-cement, and glass products.

When glass is employed as a cladding material, one should ensure that any coatings on the rear face do not consist of substances capable of conducting electricity.

Sunshading systems with a radar-absorbing effect are not available at present; nor is it possible to damp the strong reflection from metallic facade elements reliably—e.g. through radar-absorbent paints.

Interference facades

In this form of construction, the facade materials and elements are structured by setting back the interference plane and angling it from the vertical in such a way that an effect of superimposed layers is created, so that only diffuse reflections of the incoming radar beams will occur.

Radar damping in double-skin facades

The construction of double skin facades, with one layer set in front of the other, means that there is scope for effective radar damping in the outer skin alone; and indeed, this is the most common solution in practice. The sunshading installation, which under certain circumstances can also have a radar-reflecting effect, and the low-E glazing in the inner skin thus lose any significance they may have had in terms of radar technology.

Alternatively, a system of radar damping to selected areas can be used—a combination of damping in the outer skin and damping and reflection in the inner skin. The best solution for a particular scheme, based on visual and, above all, economic factors, should be selected through a process of consultation between the architect, the radar consultant and the facade experts. The Business Tower project in Nuremberg may serve as a positive example of the means by which a bespoke solution was achieved.

Radar damping solely in the outer facade layer

Depending on the measures to be implemented (magnitude of the return-flow damping), great glass thicknesses may be necessary where only the outer skin of glazing is used for radar damping.

The requisite absorption layer is created by an antenna structure, consisting of 0.02 to 0.20 mm metal (e.g. tungsten) threads arranged parallel to each other. This structure is embedded in the jointing film between the sheets of laminated safety glass (between positions 2 and 3). The spacing of the metal threads and the angle at which they are set should be determined by the radar consultant and will depend on the angle of incidence of the radar beams and the degree of damping required.

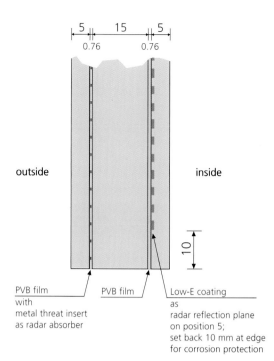

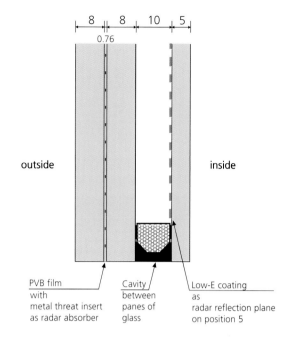

11-19 Far left: radar damping solely in the external laminated-glass skin by means of metal threads and a low-E coating inserted between the layers.

11-20 Radar damping in insulating double glazing by means of a low-E coating to the inner pane and metal threads inserted between the outer layers of laminated glass.

In addition, it may be necessary to apply a radar-reflecting layer to the rear face of the second pane of glass (position 4). Since this should also be as unobtrusive as possible when viewed as part of the facade elevation, a metal-oxide layer, as employed in low-E glazing, is sometimes used. The rear face of the glass has to be cleaned from the facade corridor, and metal-oxide or similar reflecting layers do not have a surface that is scratch-resistant or proof against damage from cleaning. As a result, this layer will have to be covered with a further—albeit thinner—pane of glass.

The various panes of glass in a three-layer laminated sheet can quickly add up to an overall thickness of 25–35 mm, which represents a considerable additional structural load on the double-skin facade construction as a whole. If it is necessary to insert a distance piece between the second and third layers of glass to achieve extra depth, the thickness of the glazing will be even greater. In addition to the problem of the glass thickness, where triple glazing is used in the outer facade, it will also be necessary to alleviate the loss of transparency that occurs. The visual problems involved may be seen in the example of the Business Tower in Nuremberg.

Radar-damping measures have to be implemented only on the side of the building facing the landing direction. However fine they may be, the metal threads cannot be considered as completely invisible. In addition, the considerable thickness of glass required where radar-damping measures are confined to the outer facade skin has a pronounced visual effect, since
■ the side of the building facing the landing direction will be glazed with three-layer laminated glass, while
■ the side turned away from the landing direction will have only a single layer of toughened safety glass.

A further visual drawback exists in the fact that, because of the relatively great distance from the airport, the radar-damping measures for this 134-meter-high building were required only from the eighth floor upward.

To avoid the negative visual effects caused by radar-damped areas within the all-glass double-skin facade of this circular building, steps had to be taken to achieve some form of visual balance. This meant finding a more even distribution of the different glass thicknesses (without the inlay of metal threads), an aspect that was investigated at the tender stage. The outcome of this would inevitably have been considerably higher costs.

Attempts to compensate for the greater thicknesses of glass solely by using flint glass did not prove as successful as was hoped. The concept of providing the required radar damping with three-layer laminated safety glass solely in the outer skin was, therefore, rejected shortly before the commencement of the main construction work, yet in good time for the facade contractor; namely, during the assembly planning phase.

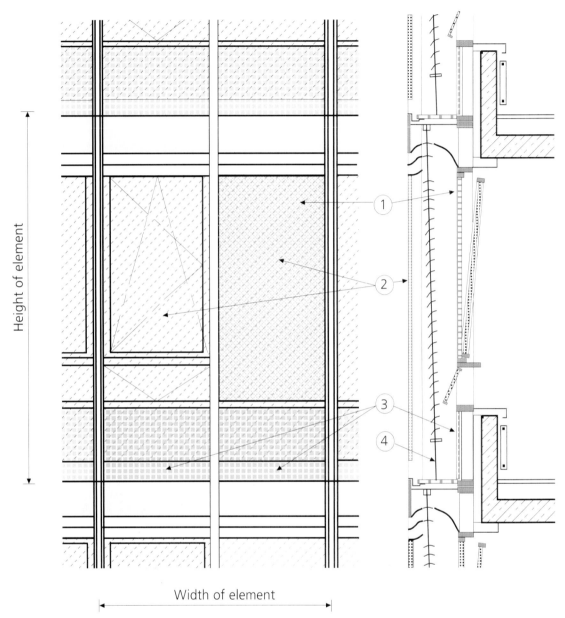

Elevation of facade element

Vertical section

11-21 Elevation of and section through radar-absorbing facade elements in Business Tower, Nuremberg.

The hatching shows the areas of radar damping.

1 Fixed glazing in inner facade skin
2 Glazing in outer facade skin
3 Apron-wall cladding
4 Sunshading tilted slightly outward.

Height of element

Width of element

Radar damping distributed over the inner and outer facade skins

Ultimately, a more economical form of damping was implemented in specific areas of both the outer and inner facade skins. The effective damping construction described below was executed on the side of the building facing the landing direction:

Outer facade skin
Single glazing, consisting of (two-layer) laminated safety glass with a metal-thread insert and without a low-E layer on the inner face.

Facade corridor
Sunshading was installed in the form of pull-up louver blinds set in an inclined position (tilted slightly outward).

Inner facade skin
Low-E double glazing, with two-layer laminated safety glass externally and with a metal-thread insert in the fixed glazing panels in every other facade bay. Fritted glass in the non-transparent apron panels with low-ohmic coating and radar-damping mesh on the rear face of the glass.

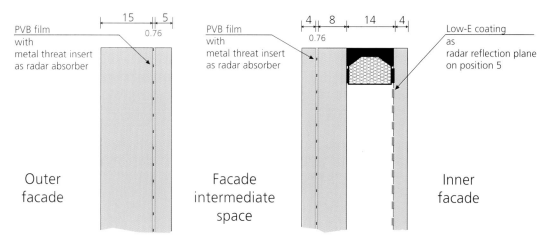

External story-height glazing
laminated safety glass, radar damped

Fixed internal glazing
low-E glass, radar damped

PVB film with metal threat insert as radar absorber

15 | 5
0.76

PVB film with metal threat insert as radar absorber

4 | 8 | 14 | 4
0.76

Low-E coating as radar reflection plane on position 5

Outer facade

Facade intermediate space

Inner facade

11-22 Radar-damping measures finally implemented in facade of Business Tower, Nuremberg.

Note:
the measures shown are a response to the specific radar conditions applicable to this development and cannot be applied to other structures.

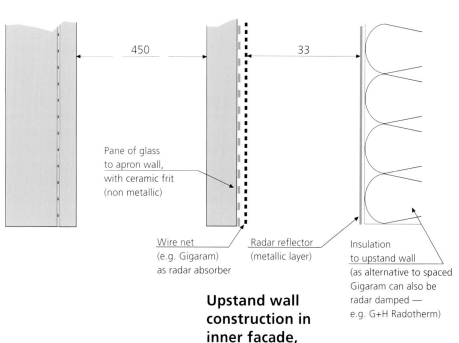

450

33

Pane of glass to apron wall, with ceramic frit (non metallic)

Wire net (e.g. Gigaram) as radar absorber

Radar reflector (metallic layer)

Insulation to upstand wall (as alternative to spaced Gigaram can also be radar damped — e.g. G+H Radotherm)

Upstand wall construction in inner facade,
radar damped

In conclusion, one can say that through a creative collaboration between all those involved in the planning, the solution finally found for the radar-damping problem represented a noticeable financial saving for the client. The design goal—to create the impression of a homogenous glass tower—was also achieved to the satisfaction of both client and architects.

The air-traffic controllers at the Nuremberg ground station will not be hindered in their work by this new 134-meter-high tower. Furthermore, the experience gained during the planning of the scheme will prove useful in the future where buildings have to undergo technical radar-damping treatment—not only to ensure unrestricted freedom for aviation, but to comply with the safety requirements necessitated by the growing volume of air traffic.

12 Air-Conditioning

Mechanical ventilation and cooling can rarely be omitted

One frequently expressed opinion is that, with the construction of double-skin facades, the air-conditioning plant (for heating, ventilation and cooling) can be reduced in size, or that certain sections can be omitted altogether; i.e. the mechanical ventilation and cooling. This cannot be confirmed as a general rule; but it cannot be dismissed either, since any such reduction will depend on the many constraints that apply in each individual case. For example, in extreme weather conditions, the lack of mechanical air conditioning in a building can result in a sense of thermal discomfort that may well prove unacceptable.

Some buildings with double-skin facades are ventilated entirely by natural means. The assessment of such systems by the users ranges from satisfactory to extremely unsatisfactory. The former applies, for example, to the refurbished Gladbacher Bank (see built example, pp. 174f. and /AC1/). Here, by providing scope for window ventilation, the degree of thermal comfort was appreciably improved in comparison with the original situation; that is to say, a single-skin facade with insulating double glazing and inadequately rear-vented louver blinds. On the other hand, there are examples of buildings where the lack of mechanical ventilation and cooling have led to serious complaints from users about overheating and what was subjectively felt to be an inadequate supply of fresh air in the occupied rooms. In some of these schemes, the conditions were improved by an elaborate and expensive supplementary program, in which mechanical ventilation and cooling were added after completion of the building. In other cases, economic considerations and lack of space prevented the addition of any such plant, with the result that user conditions remained unsatisfactory. In the opinion of the authors, double-skin facades make sense technically especially when they facilitate natural ventilation for as much of the year as possible, despite adverse external conditions such as high noise levels or strong winds. Although mechanical air conditioning can ensure very high standards of thermal comfort in internal spaces today, users in Germany still attach a very high priority to window ventilation. The reason for this would seem to lie in the fact that by opening a window one has the sensation of control-

ling the internal climate oneself and enjoying immediate contact with the outside world whenever one wishes.

Only in exceptional cases, though, will it be possible to do without mechanical ventilation and cooling in buildings with double-skin facades. Experience shows that the following conditions have to be met:

■ Adequate sound insulation against external noise should be provided even where windows are opened for ventilation purposes (see the section "Window ventilation and sound insulation").

■ Statutory guidelines for workplaces have to be met. These cover the provision of adequate opening areas in the facade and impose limitations on the depth of rooms (cf. the section "Basic principles of aerophysics —Regulations and requirements"). These constraints may rule out any possibility of natural ventilation in open-plan offices from the very outset in view of the room depth that is required.

■ The overall maximum cooling load should not exceed about 35–40 W/m^2 in office spaces (value based on authors' experience). This may mean that the proportion of facade glazing in relation to the overall area of the facade will have to be limited (no full-height glazing, for example). Furthermore, there should be a high thermal storage capacity in the rooms, and the internal heat loads should be low.

■ The double-skin facade should be constructed in such a way that contact with the outdoor realm is immediately perceptible (no aquarium effect). This means that the inner and outer skins should be of optimal form aerodynamically (see also the section "Aerodynamic optimization of resistances").

■ Outside the heating period, the inner facade layer will be opened at night to allow heat to escape from the rooms.

■ A lower degree of thermal comfort will probably be accepted in preference to mechanical forms of air conditioning.

How much mechanical air-conditioning is necessary?

If it is not possible to do without mechanical air-conditioning altogether, the question arises whether the dimensions of the installation can at least be reduced in buildings with double-skin facades, in contrast to single-skin construction. As described in the chapter "Thermal Insulation", double-skin facades do provide scope for reducing these dimensions because of the better building physics associated with this type of construction. Examples of this are the better U-values in winter and the potentially better seal provided by two skins instead of one. In summer, the advantage of a double-skin construction—especially in high-rise buildings—lies in the system of sunshading, which is, in effect, situated externally, yet protected within the facade intermediate space.

As far as mechanical ventilation is concerned, differences will occur where, in the absence of openable windows, the internal spaces would normally have to be air-conditioned. With a double-skin facade it may be possible to open the inner facade layer for the purpose of natural ventilation. In that case, it will perhaps be adequate to install a *partial air-conditioning plant* instead of a system that provides heating, cooling, humidification, and dehumidification. A partial system will differ from a *full air-conditioning installation* in the omission of the humidifying and dehumidifying functions, for example, and through a reduction of the cooling capacity. The term "supporting ventilation system with cooling" is often used for this kind of installation.

In conjunction with double-skin facades, "supporting ventilation" also means using mechanical room ventilation only at the height of summer and in winter, and managing without it entirely during the transitional seasons when the heating and cooling loads are low. In practice, external temperatures of roughly 5 °C and 20 °C have been established as parameter values in this respect. Other factors that play a role are potential heating-energy savings through heat recovery in the mechanical ventilation plant, and lower standards of comfort resulting from the ingress of cold or warm external air. When external temperatures are high, air cooling and dehumidification in particular have a positive effect on the users' sense of well-being within buildings /AC2/. Recent investigations have shown that the perception of air quality is influenced not only by the degree of pollution in a room, but by temperature and humidity; in other words, the enthalpy of the air in a given space. Users evidently prefer dry, cool air. Dehumidification would seem to be worth considering, therefore, since the technical input for this process is confined to enlarging the capacity of the air-cooling element somewhat (which will be re-

quired anyway) and possibly installing a supplementary heating device after it in the air-conditioning plant. The energy consumption will not be excessive either if the air-change rate is restricted to hygienic needs.

In winter, the situation is reversed to some extent. The greater air-moisture content that is physiologically desirable can be problematic in double-skin facade construction: there will be an increased tendency to condensation on the inner face of the outer skin if the inner skin is not kept closed. Experience gained from a number of buildings in operation shows that users do open windows sporadically in winter, with the result that warm, moist room air is able to escape in large quantities into the facade intermediate space. Any technical moisturization of the air, therefore, should be related to external temperatures, which indirectly determine the temperatures on the inner face of the external facade layer.

This applies especially where the external skin can be closed. Because of the small volume of air passing through the intermediate space for ventilation purposes in one building, the outer facade was completely obscured with condensation after the windows had been open for a longer period. Initially, it was not possible to see out of the building; and if the surface temperature had been low enough, frost could have formed. Even after the external facade had been opened, it took a number of hours before the sun was able to evaporate the condensation completely. This gives some indication of the large amount of moisture precipitated with a relative humidity of 50% at a temperature of 22 °C. By lowering the dew-point temperature of the incoming air below the external temperature, the problem was overcome immediately and completely. In this case, however, with low external temperatures, it is no longer possible to guarantee a relative humidity in the rooms of at least 30%, not to mention the 40% humidity required by Japanese regulations. If one nevertheless wishes to ensure that the recommended level of humidity is attained, the inner facade will have to remain closed in winter, as would be the case with a single-skin facade.

Built example 1:
debis headquarters at Potsdamer Platz, Berlin

Architects: Renzo Piano Building Workshop, Paris, in collaboration with Christoph Kohlbecker, Gaggenau

The main objective of the clients, the Daimler-Benz company, and the planners of this development at Potsdamer Platz was to create an environmentally sustainable and user-friendly building. Various measures were implemented with this in mind: the offices were provided with a natural system of ventilation (air-intake and extract); the air-conditioning plant was reduced to sensible proportions; the thermal insulation was optimized; and concepts were introduced for the improvement of the micro-climate (extensive roof planting, the recycling of rainwater, the creation of areas of water, etc.). To achieve these goals, large-scale investigations and research work were undertaken after the inception of the scheme and during the planning stage (cf. /AC4/).

12-1 debis headquarters at Potsdamer Platz, Berlin: view from Reichpietschufer.

Architects: Planning Group Renzo Piano Building Workshop, Paris, in collaboration with Christoph Kohlbecker, Gaggenau.

The double-skin facade

The debis headquarters, which was taken into service in the fall of 1997, was designed with a corridor facade along the south and west faces of the high-rise tract (85 m high). The inner skin consists of a strip-window facade with double low-E insulating glazing in aluminum frames. In every facade bay, there is a side- and bottom-hung casement, supplemented by a motor-operated, bottom-hung top light. The solid upstand walls on the room face are lined with insulated panels with a covering of toughened safety glass. On the west side of the building, the upstand walls are clad with terracotta elements fixed to an aluminum supporting structure, which forms the internal section of the three-bay outer facade elements. The floors to the facade corridors consist of sheets of toughened safety glass laid on metal gratings. This construction provides a smoke-proof division between stories.

The external facade, 70 cm in front of the inner skin, is divided into bays, each consisting of eight horizontal laminated safety-glass pivoting flaps or louvers per story. The louvers are operated in groups of seven via a common sliding rod with a spindel drive. The eighth louver, adjoining the horizontal story divisions, can be opened only for cleaning purposes /AC5/. This construction allows the outer facade to be opened over its full area in summer, so that users are not separated from the outside world by a fixed layer of glazing.

The excess temperatures in the intermediate space in summer remain at a minimal level. This is confirmed by experience gained in operating the system and by measurements made since the building was taken into use. Great importance was attached to the design of the sunshading. This applies not only to the screening factor z, but also to the permeability of the system for the ventilation of the offices. Instead of the fabric blinds originally foreseen, therefore, sliding louver blinds were installed in front of the inner facade. This allowed the sunshading to be located close to the inner skin, while at the same time still complying with airflow requirements into the rooms. For design reasons, the color of the sunshading to the west face was matched to that of the terracotta elements.

Acoustic tests have shown that the large proportion of joints in the glass louver construction means that there is only a very small reduction in the level of external noise when the flaps are open (roughly 1–2 dB). An appreciable reduction of external noise can be achieved only when the louvers are closed. Measurements showed a reduction of roughly 7 dB in this case.

opening the external skin to a greater degree has a positive influence on the ventilation, since it helps to remove the heat in the intermediate space. The glass louvers can be opened to a maximum angle of 70°, as required in this case by the fire department for the purpose of smoke extract.

As in all high-rise buildings, account had to be taken of the effect of wind when the windows are open. This was especially important in this project, since Berlin is subject to strong winds. To avoid unacceptable tractive wind forces on doors, a critical wind speed of roughly 7.5 m/s was derived from the external pressure distribution. Depending on the height and position of individual workplaces, this would restrict window ventilation for 15 to 40 percent of the working time. The layout, comprising a central elevator core with single-bay office wings adjoining it to east and west, facilitated a windward/leeward separation of the building in this direction. The atrium of the lower-rise structure adjoins the tower on the north side up to a height of about 30 m. Only above this level is the north face of the high-rise block exposed to winds. Strong cross-currents of air may therefore be expected only on the upper floors in a north-south direction. Northerly and southerly winds are not so common in Berlin, however, and they are usually of a lower velocity than west-east winds. If one calculates the periods when excessively strong winds prevail and deducts the times when temperatures are either below 5 °C or above 20 °C, the scope for natural window ventilation is approximately 50 percent of the operating time in the upper part of the building and 60 percent in the lower part. These figures have been confirmed in practice.

12-2 South face of debis building, showing the opened louvers in the outer facade skin.

12-3 West facade of debis building: view along intermediate space.

Window ventilation improves comfort

The possibility of providing window ventilation for the rooms was also investigated. In a closed position, there is a 1 cm peripheral gap around the louvers (with an overlap of 5 cm). This therefore meets the requirements for a minimum opening area of 200 cm^2 per m^2 of office area laid down in German guidelines for workplaces. In a thermal airflow trial carried out with a 1:7 scale model, the influence of the opening angle of the external glass louvers and the internal casements was investigated. When the external louvers were opened at an angle of 10°, the rooms already enjoyed a good supply of external air with a specific hourly air-exchange rate of 1.35 1/h $\sqrt{K}$. As ill. 12-4 shows, opening the louvers to a greater angle results in only a small increase in the air-exchange rate. This can be explained by the role played by the resistances in the inner facade skin. On the other hand,

12-4 Graph of specific air-exchange rate measured by Prof. Ruscheweyh, RWTH Aachen, in simulation trials with a model.

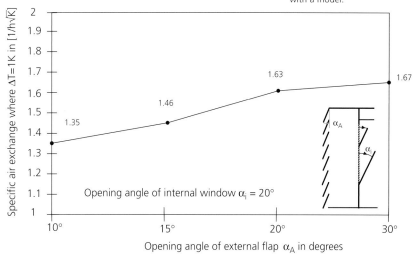

Built example 1: debis headquarters at Potsdamer Platz, Berlin

Small-scale air-conditioning plant

A mechanical ventilation plant was installed to provide partial air-conditioning for those periods in winter and summer when extreme weather conditions prevail. The conditioned air is either cooled or heated and is injected continuously into the rooms, ensuring a threefold air change every hour. No other cooling facilities, such as cooling soffits, were provided in the offices, but provision was made for their subsequent installation, should the need arise. The air-conditioning plant, reduced in scale, is designed to operate when external temperatures drop below 5 °C or rise above 20 °C. The efficient sunshading system, the upstand walls and the floor slabs, which can be used in part as thermal-storage mass, help to ensure a high degree of thermal comfort in summer. These conditions were calculated on the basis of preliminary simulations and have since been confirmed in practice. A further important factor in this context is the scope for controlled night-time ventilation in the form of an electrically operated top light.

To combine the advantages of natural and mechanical ventilation, while at the same time taking account of fire regulations, an integrated control concept was drawn up for the facade and the air-conditioning. Special care was taken to ensure that during the operation of this system, the facade is not subject to constant changes and movements for reasons that may not be evident to users. The system is operated separately for the west and south facades via a central control unit. The controls are also activated individually for each story from a joint switchboard. The switching panels on each floor are connected via four busbars to the control center, where the parameters can be adjusted as required, and where a manual intervention is possible as well. Also linked to the control center are a series of external sensors, which transmit data on external temperatures, wind speed and direction, and precipitation, as well as warning signals from the fire-alarm center.

The control program triggers the following reactions:
- in the event of fire, the external skin opens to its maximum extent
- with gale-force winds, the facade closes; with high wind speeds (> 16 m/s), the facade openings are reduced to narrow slits (10° opening angle) to protect the sunshading
- in the event of rain or hail, the facade openings are reduced to narrow slits
- in summer nights, the facade opens to allow the rooms to cool
- when external temperatures sink below 10 °C, the facade openings are reduced to narrow slits; below 5 °C, the facade is closed altogether and the mechanical ventilation comes into operation.

Up to now, the reactions of users to this program have been positive. The only criticisms have concerned the frequent movements and changes of position that occur in the facade—an aspect that has since been corrected. To date, there have been no reports of drafts or excessive door-opening forces caused by wind pressure.

This example shows that, with a coordinated approach to building physics, double-skin facades and air-conditioning, the plant for indoor climate control need not be an elaborate installation. Based on a floor area of roughly 10 m² per person and heat loads of 15 W/m² resulting from the communications equipment, the overall concept applied here guarantees users a good level of thermal comfort.

In planning the partial air-conditioning plant, great care was taken to provide scope for extensions to upgrade the equipment into a full air-conditioning installation, should higher internal heat loads or greater comfort requirements render this necessary.

A further example of a high-rise building with a double-skin facade and a smaller-scale air-conditioning plant is the tower block at Potsdamer Platz 1, Berlin, described in the chapter "Types of Construction" (page 14). Here, too, the appropriate building physics (a moderate proportion of glazing in a facade with conventional rectangular openings; floor slabs with a thermal-storage capacity; night-time ventilation via the box windows) provide the right conditions for this form of construction.

12-5 Standard office in debis building.

Built example 2:
DB Cargo administration building, Mainz

Architects: Rhode, Kellermann, Wawrowsky + Partner, Frankfurt am Main, in collaboration with Infra Gesellschaft für Umweltplanung mbH, Mainz

The west-facing double-skin facade of this building was discussed at length in the section on "Modern double-skin strip-window facades" (page 128). The facade has a simple form of construction, but is extremely effective acoustically and aerophysically. The decision to use a double-skin facade was made in response to the high external noise levels from Federal Highway B9, which runs along one side of the building. At this point, the road forms one of the main access routes into the city center of Mainz.

The construction of a double-skin facade made window ventilation possible, thereby overcoming the problem of a non-openable facade with inevitable air-conditioning of the adjoining rooms. A partial air-conditioning system was installed, providing a 2.2-fold hourly air change. A single-skin facade with adequate window ventilation would not have been able to achieve the maximum admissible acoustic level of 55 dB(A) for workplaces.

The building was taken into operation in March 1998. Experience of its functioning to date shows that the indoor climatic conditions have been completely accepted by users. Furthermore, the degree of sound insulation achieved permits permanent window ventilation of the offices without disturbance to the working atmosphere, despite external noise levels of more than 70 dB(A). The numerous open windows in the facade during working hours are evidence of the way the building has been accepted by users. Measurements made on the finished building show that the outer facade skin improves the sound insulation by 6 dB. The level of sound in the rooms when the windows are open remains constant around 50 dB(A). This represents a good standard of acoustic comfort.

Viewed in an overall context, taking account of the savings made in the air-conditioning, the simple form of construction and the high degree of prefabrication of the facade resulted in an economical solution.

In the late summer of 1998, measurements were taken at various points of the facade to determine its temperature behavior. Under conditions of diffuse sunlight, the temperature in the intermediate space followed the same pattern as the external temperature without the space heating up significantly. As soon as the afternoon sun reached the facade and the sun-shading was activated, the temperature of the air in the upper part of the intermediate space rose by 4–5 kelvin. The air supply to the rooms, on the other hand, showed an excess temperature of only 1–2 kelvin.

12-6 Top: diagram of mechanical ventilation to room in debis building, Potsdamer Platz, Berlin, in winter.

12-7 Bottom: diagram of natural ventilation to room with open windows in debis building, Potsdamer Platz.

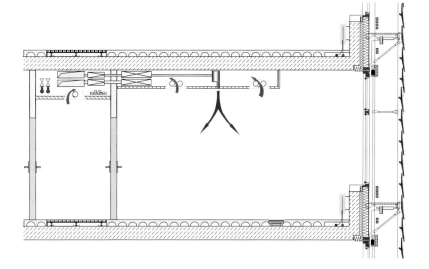

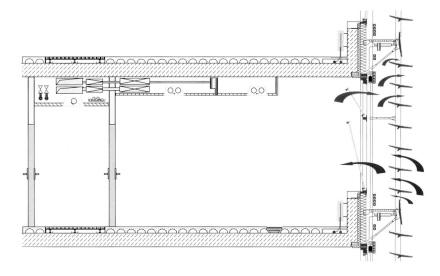

Built example 3:
Gladbacher Bank, Mönchengladbach

Double-skin facade without mechanical ventilation and cooling

Architects: Schrammen und Partner, Mönchengladbach

The existing windows to the south face of the Gladbacher Bank were inadequately insulated. As part of the refurbishment of this facade, the windows were to be replaced with new ones /AC1/, and the thermal insulation and acoustic insulation against external noise were to be appreciably improved. At the same time, the intake of fresh air exclusively via the facade was to be retained. In view of the projecting balconies and the high external noise levels (roughly 70 dB(A)), the addition of a second facade layer seemed the appropriate solution.

A double-skin facade was developed, the outer layer of which was designed as a virtually frameless glass construction, articulated into a series of horizontal stepped-back planes. Aerophysically, the concept is based on the shaft-box facade principle. A vertical section through the facade in diagrammatic form is shown in illustration 12-11. The thermal uplift over the three upper stories and the appropriate dimensioning of the air-intake and extract openings ensure a satisfactory supply of external air for the rooms when the inner facade is open. It was thus possible to do without a technically complex and expensive air-conditioning installation.

Protection against overheating within the facade in summer was greatly improved by inserting a single layer of reflecting, sun-screen glazing in the outer skin and installing adjustable sunshading in the intermediate space. Prior to refurbishment, the sunshading consisted of clear glass to the windows and an inadequately rear-vented louver blind on the balcony side, which often led to uncomfortably high room temperatures in summer. The new double-skin construction, in combination with an effective sunshading system, has resulted in an appreciably greater degree of thermal comfort in summer, despite the fact that the artificial lighting is turned on for somewhat longer periods.

When the windows in the inner skin are open, the improvement in acoustic insulation against external noise is about 10 dB (measured results), which means that the internal spaces can now be permanently ventilated via the windows, despite the high level of traffic noise. An improvement of the thermal conditions in the rooms is also possible by exploiting the new scope for night-time ventilation afforded by the openings in the outer facade and the horizontally pivoting casements in the inner facade.

12-8 Top:
Gladbacher Bank before refurbishment of facade, showing former balcony construction.

12-9 Bottom:
Gladbacher Bank after refurbishment, with double-skin facade.

The present example shows that even with a double-skin facade, the air supply for occupied rooms can be guaranteed entirely by natural means, provided the building physics and aerophysics follow the right concepts, and the internal heat loads occurring during use are not too great.

The facade refurbishment was executed in 1995.

12-10 View along facade, showing the openings on the underside of the stepped bands of glazing.

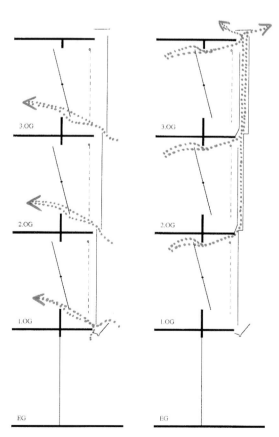

12-11 Diagrammatic vertical section through double-skin facade.
Left: air-intake route on the balcony axes;
right: air-extract route in intermediate shafts.

Built example 3:
Gladbacher Bank, Mönchengladbach

New approaches: air-conditioning without radiators

The excellent thermal insulation that double-skin facades provide in winter means that only small heating loads occur with this form of construction. The cooling loads, however, may be considerable. In combination with mechanical ventilation, increasing use is being made of low-temperature panel-heating systems such as underfloor heating, heating soffits or the heating of individual constructional elements. These systems can also be employed for cooling purposes. The question arises whether and under what conditions one can forgo static radiators situated near the windows.

Down to the present day, room heating has been installed almost exclusively in the form of underfloor convectors, or radiators placed in front of the inner facade. Neither of these methods provides an ideal solution functionally or formally, but there will usually be no alternative. In 1993, during the planning of the "City Gate" in Düsseldorf, the idea evolved of using the proposed radiant cooling soffits for heating purposes as well. One condition for this was that the heating soffit could be operated with surface temperatures low enough not to interfere with user comfort. Decades ago, attempts were made to meet the heating needs in rooms by means of heating soffits. These aims were frustrated by the high water temperatures (40–50 °C) that were necessary in view of the thermal insulation standards for buildings applicable at that time. The one-sided nature of the heat source meant that the so-called "radiation temperature asymmetry"

/AC3/ within a room was so great that users complained of thermal discomfort. One knows that people prefer to have warm feet but a cool head. With the system described above, this was turned upside down, with the result that the concept was not able to assert itself on the market.

Today, with the aid of low-E glass, heating requirements can be reduced to such an extent that the use of heating soffits with a maximum flow temperature of roughly 30–35 °C is possible. Moreover, the radiation temperature asymmetry both vertically (≤ 3.5 K) and horizontally (≤ 8 K) is so small that no sensation of thermal discomfort occurs. To achieve this with single-skin facades and room-height glazing, one would need to use triple low-E glazing and frames with a high insulation value (e.g. in wood). For the inner layer of a double-skin facade where the outer layer can be closed, double low-E glazing would be adequate. A U-value of roughly 1.0 to 1.15 W/m²K can thus be achieved. The discomfort caused by cold-air drop near the inner face of the inner facade when external temperatures are low is then prevented to a large extent.

After laboratory tests had been carried out, the concept was implemented in practice. The cooling soffits are divided into segments that are connected to both the hot- and cold-water systems and can be switched from one to the other. For a depth of 1.50 m along the facade, the cooling-soffit elements are also used for heating. Behind this strip is a second bay of similar size, which is available throughout the year for cooling purposes. Data obtained from simulation trials carried out during the planning stage shows that in

12-12 Corner room in "City Gate", Düsseldorf, with view of peripheral facade corridor. The heating / cooling-soffit panels can be seen at the top of the picture.

various rooms, both heating and cooling needs may occur in the same space during the transitional periods, depending on the internal heat loads and the degree of insolation.

The concept has proven most successful in practice. Measurements of the radiation-temperature asymmetry taken in the winter of 1998/1999 provided values that lie well below the thermal-physiological limits cited above. Even when the external temperature fell below 0 °C, the surface temperatures on the inner face of the internal facade skin were only 1–2 kelvin below room temperature, thus ensuring ideal conditions of thermal comfort. Systems of this kind also make sense in terms of the energy balance of a building: even when it is extremely cold outside, the rooms can be heated by a low-temperature water supply.

To round off the subject, it should be mentioned that in the glazed corner rooms, additional underfloor heating was also installed to meet the greater thermal needs in these positions.

If the thermal insulation in a double-skin facade is further improved for winter conditions (e.g. by means of non-transparent elements in the inner skin with much lower U-values than in the case of windows with double low-E glazing, and by making the outer skin closable), it may be possible to do without a conventional heating system altogether. In this case, the rooms could be heated, for example, by *thermal activation of the storage mass of the concrete structure* /AC6/ in combination with a mechanical ventilation system. Thermal activation of the mass of the structure means that the reinforced concrete floor is directly cooled or heated by water-bearing pipes laid within the slab. The pipes are usually spaced at between 10 and 30 cm centers and placed in the mid-depth of the floor, in the structurally neutral zone. Where a system of this kind is used, the daytime surface temperatures of the concrete floor will be between 21 and 25 °C. In energy terms, this is particularly effective, but the actual heating or cooling effect that can be achieved is quite limited because of the small differences that exist between the room temperature and that of the structural element. As described in /AC6/, a cooling capacity of up to about 50 W/m² and a heating capacity of up to about 30 W/m² can be achieved.

Story-height glazing and thermal activation of the concrete core are compatible only to a certain extent, therefore. The reason for this is not just the limited heating/cooling capacity, but above all the sluggishness of the system. In the event of sudden solar heat gains in winter, this can lead to an overheating of the rooms. Today, this technology, also known as building element heating or cooling, is generally used to cover only basic needs and is frequently applied in conjunction with systems that can react to changing conditions more swiftly.

12-13 Graph showing range of radiation-temperature asymmetry for "City Gate", Düsseldorf, measured under extremely cold conditions when heating / cooling soffits in operation.

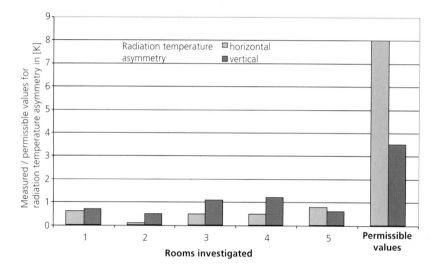

12-14 Prefabricated reinforcement element with pipe runs for thermal activation of concrete core.

13 | Economic Viability

The economic viability of double-skin facades is usually a controversial topic among planners. Views range from "a waste of money" to "economically viable because of energy savings". Opinions of this kind are very often generalizations that take account only of the capital outlay and energy costs. No one would dispute that double-skin facades are more expensive than single-skin forms: the construction of the outer layer and the space between the two skins makes the former type far more elaborate. The decisive question, however, is whether the savings accruing from the use of a building with a double-skin facade can compensate for the higher investment costs. Investigations of this aspect rarely provide detailed conclusions. As yet, neither comprehensive, conclusive cost calculations nor generally applicable methods of assessing cost effectiveness exist. In this chapter, the authors wish to introduce a greater degree of objectivity to the discussion and establish a basis for an overall assessment of the economic viability of double-skin facades.

Procedure for economic analysis

The limited availability of resources in the world compels us to husband them and to consider alternative uses. At the same time, economic activity is subject to the general principles of rational behavior, which require that a particular goal be achieved with a minimum of means. Economic analyses are often undertaken, therefore, to obtain reference data for planning decisions, the ultimate goal being to determine the most economical solution. To this end, alternatives have to be drawn up and studied according to an appropriate method. Studies of economic viability require a systematic approach and should lead to some form of ranking. Drees and Höh /E1/ recommend that the following eight steps be followed in the planning of buildings:
1. The purpose of the study should be determined.
2. A list of alternatives should be drawn up.
3. The investment costs should be determined.
4. The follow-up costs should be determined.
5. The effective costs for the use of the building should be determined.
6. The differential costs should be determined and analyzed.
7. A ranking should be made and alternative proposals drawn up as a basis for selection.
8. The above steps should be supplemented with a cost-benefit analysis.

Step 1: Determining the purpose of the study
This comprises a description of the objectives.

Step 2: Listing the alternatives
The scope of the study should be confined to a typical section of the building. The alternatives should offer a variety of solutions and reveal significant differences in the results.

Step 3: Determining the investment costs
The costs should be divided up in accordance with the relevant national standards, such as DIN 276 (Costs of buildings) in Germany. The unit numbers and unit costs should be calculated. The basis for pricing (i.e. at the time of calculation) should be determined.

Step 4: Determining the follow-up costs
Follow-up costs are the annual costs resulting from an investment. In Germany, these are described in DIN 18960 (Effective operating costs for buildings) and consist primarily of the operating and maintenance costs (see step 5).

Step 5: Determining the effective costs for the use of the building
DIN 18960 (Effective costs for the use of buildings) /E2/ is an appropriate instrument for a comprehensive assessment of the economic viability of a structure, since it takes account of both investment costs and the resulting follow-up costs. The costs are calculated according to a predefined cost structure and converted into annual amounts, the sum of which gives the effective operating cost in monetary units (e.g. €, $) per year. This figure will be required when comparing the various alternatives. The most economical solution is the one that results in the lowest effective costs for the use of the building.

Categories 1 (capital costs) and 2 (amortization) depend entirely on the investment costs of a building. Categories 3 (administrative costs), 4 (taxes), 5 (operating costs) and 6 (maintenance costs) are referred to as follow-up costs. Investigations of cost-effectiveness are usually confined to categories 1, 2, 5 and 6, since administrative costs and taxes are largely independent of the variables to be assessed.

Operating costs include the costs of

- cleaning the building
- water supply and sewage
- heating and cooling (costs for heating and cooling energy, and for electricity for the circulation of air and water)
- electricity (e.g. costs for operating computers and for lighting)
- operation, maintenance and inspection
- parking and planted areas
- sundry items (e.g. supervision and security staff / services, building insurance, etc.).

In making an economic analysis of buildings with double-skin facades, the major elements of the operating costs will be for maintenance and cleaning the building, heating and cooling, and electricity.

Maintenance costs are the costs of all measures necessary to keep the building in its intended state. These include the maintenance of the structure, the facade and the technical installations.

In September 1998, a new draft of DIN 18960 (Costs for the use of buildings) was prepared, in which the cost categories are regrouped and amortization / depreciation disappears altogether. Since this standard has not yet come into effect and further revisions cannot be excluded, reference will be made to the existing contents of the standard for the time being.

Step 6: Determining and analyzing differential costs
The differentials in operating costs and other cost categories are determined. Cost reference values are established. The factors that influence cost differentials are defined. Where calculations are based on uncertain assumptions, a sensitivity analysis should be carried out.

Step 7: Establishing a ranking and making recommendations
Recommendations are made on the basis of the ranking, and possible improvements will be indicated that may be considered in the further course of planning.

Step 8: Supplementary cost-benefit analysis
An underlying assumption of cost-effectiveness studies is that the function or value of the alternatives to be examined is equal in all cases. This will ensure that the common scale for the ranking of alternatives is the cost. There are cases, however, where the functions or values of the alternatives differ so greatly that an assessment of the function itself will have to be integrated into the study. Where the value can be expressed in monetary terms (e.g. leasing a building), the assessment will be simple. Where the function or value does not conform to a monetary scale, but is an expression of comfort, aesthetics, or functionality, for example, the situation will be more problematic. In this case, a different scale of comparison will be required, such as a points system. An analysis of the functional value of the alternatives will be necessary, so that the costs can be set in relation to the utility. The general procedure for such an analysis is as follows:

- the criteria to be assessed should be listed;
- the criteria are weighted by assessing the degree to which they fulfill their designated function;
- a functional value is calculated by adding the respective items in terms of their weighting and the degree to which they fulfill the required function;
- the various alternatives are ranked according to the resultant functional value;
- a sensitivity analysis is conducted. A check is made whether the ranking of the alternatives should be changed; for example, if individual weightings change.

Analyses of functional value can be extremely subjective, since the criteria, their weighting and the assessment of the degree to which they meet requirements are determined by the person conducting the analysis. It makes sense, therefore, to determine the parameters within a team. This will ensure a maximum degree of objectivity in the process. Experience shows that the person responsible for making a value analysis often opts for the alternative he or she believed to be the best solution from the very beginning.

In investigations of the cost-effectiveness of double-skin facades, non-monetary factors such as comfort, the aesthetics of a building, and efficiently functioning window ventilation under adverse external conditions play a major role.

A comparison of double-skin facade concepts shows that the same function will generally exist in all alternatives, thus obviating the need for an analysis of functional value. Differences may occur, however, in the field of aesthetics; for example, when comparisons are made between double-skin facades with or without parapet walls, or with great differences in the depth of the intermediate space. In such cases, it may be worthwhile making an analysis of the functional value (cost-benefit analysis).

A comparison between concepts for single-skin and double-skin facades will reveal great differences in the functional value of the alternatives. Double-skin facades offer the architect greater design scope, which can manifest itself in a marked improvement in the aesthetics of a building. The transparency of a building can be greatly increased with a frameless form of construction to the outer skin, a deep cavity between the facade layers, and room-height glazing. Similarly, the avoidance of external sunshading, which a double-skin facade construction allows, can also improve the outward appearance of a building.

Where comfort is concerned, mention should be made of the scope for natural window ventilation that double-skin forms of construction provide, even under adverse weather conditions. The saying that "a person who can open a window is a king" expresses an idea to which the users of buildings still attach enormous importance. Opening a window not only facilitates a direct exchange of air; it establishes a vital link between the workplace and the outside world, an aspect that is of great importance to the well-being of users. Improving the level of comfort in spaces for human occupation generally leads to greater satisfaction on the part of users and, in most cases, to increased productivity—an aspect that may possibly balance out the higher costs of a double-skin facade.

Methods of calculating the costs for the use of a building

According to Drees and Höh /E1/, there are three ways of calculating the effective costs for the use of a building.

1. Simplified calculating method

The capital costs change as the period of amortization advances, since the capital sum subject to interest decreases progressively in the course of time. To simplify matters, a mean value is calculated, based on a uniform consumption of capital and employing a simple interest calculation. The *interest payments V* will be:

$$V = \frac{K}{2} \bullet p \quad [\text{€}] \quad (E1)$$

where
K is the capital invested in [€] and
p is the rate of interest in [%].

The *amortization A* is assumed to be a linear progression when calculating operating costs, as is also foreseen in tax legislation for buildings.

$$A = \frac{K}{n} \quad [\text{€}] \quad (E2)$$

where
n is the period of use in [years].

When calculating the operating and maintenance costs, the prices in effect at the time of planning are used. No attempt is made to extrapolate current price developments into the future.

2. Calculation on the basis of annuity

With this method, the simplified calculation based on amortization and interest payments is replaced by one based on annuity; in other words, a regular annual payment comprising interest on the capital not yet paid off and partial repayment of the capital sum. The *annuity a* can be calculated, using the following equation:

$$a = K \bullet \frac{(q^n \bullet p)}{(q^n - 1)} \quad [\text{€/a}] \quad (E3)$$

where
q = 1 + p is the interest factor.

The calculation of operating and maintenance costs can be made as in the simplified method described above.

3. Dynamization of costs for the use of a building

This much more elaborate method is based on the full investment costs in the form of the outlay at the time of making the calculation. The date at which payment is made is covered by the calculation of interest. A schedule of payments is drawn up for this purpose, and the payments are adjusted with the aid of a discount factor to the time of calculation. Accrued interest will be added to payments dating from before this time. Payments scheduled subsequently to the time of calculation will be subject to a discount.

Operating and maintenance costs are subject to a discount during the period of use of a building. In other words, with this method, all expenses of any significance are evaluated in conjunction with the date when they are incurred.

What is the appropriate method of calculation?
After assessing the various methods, Drees and Höh come to the conclusion that it is usually immaterial which one is used for comparing alternatives: given comparable conditions, a cost-efficiency ranking will be independent of the method of calculation. The method used is of significance, however, if the investment costs and the operating and maintenance costs differ significantly. In this case, the simplified method will result in a different ranking from the other methods.

Greater differences between the investment costs on the one hand and the operating and maintenance costs on the other are most likely to occur in cost analyses involving a comparison of single- and double-skin facade concepts. For comparisons between different forms of double-skin facade, however, the simplified method of calculating will usually suffice, as long as the other subsystems within the overall concept are more or less identical.

Further methods of calculating cost effectiveness exist, of course. In Germany, for example, they are described in detail in VDI guidelines 6025 /E3/ and 2067 /E8/.

Covering the costs of alternatives in their entirety
When comparing the costs of alternatives in economic analyses of this kind, it is important to consider the systems in their entirety where the component parts are interrelated. Restricting the comparison to individual elements or subsystems of a building is acceptable only when these have no significant influence on the cost of other parts. For example, in comparing alternative forms of facade construction where thermal and acoustic insulation, natural window ventilation and air-conditioning are involved, the costs for these systems should also be taken into account. The reciprocal relationship between the various subsystems can be so great that a modification of one may lead to changes in others that will have serious implications for the costs of the scheme as a whole. A simple example may serve to illustrate this.

A single-skin facade with room-height glazing and internal sunshading will result in a much greater external cooling load than a single-skin solid facade with conventional openings and external sunshading—providing the contingent conditions are otherwise identical (e.g. internal heat loads). The former will require a more elaborate air-conditioning system to reduce the cooling loads, however, and that, in turn, will affect the investment costs as well as the operating and maintenance costs. On the other hand, the cost of electricity for lighting will be higher for the building with the solid facade because it has a greater opacity than a facade with room-height glazing. One sees that it would be wrong to consider only the costs of the facade construction in drawing a comparison, since not all the costs affected by the alternative forms would be taken into account.

In general, economic analyses of facade alternatives should take account of the following cost components:

Investment costs
■ facade (construction, glazing, and any controls that form part of the concept)
■ sunshading
■ air-conditioning
■ fire protection
■ sound insulation against external noise and in office partitions

Operating and maintenance costs
■ facade cleaning
■ energy costs for air-conditioning and lighting
■ operating, inspection, servicing and maintenance costs for the facade, sunshading, air-conditioning plant, fire protection, and lighting installations.

Cost determinants for double-skin facades

Each of the cost components listed above is dependent on numerous determinants.

The range of cost components that have to be considered shows how complex economic analyses of this kind are. It would be beyond the scope of this book to describe all the possible forms of construction and the related cost determinants. Taking double-skin facade construction as an example, we shall discuss the most important components and the influence they have on costs. The division reflects the cost determinants affecting the outer skin, the inner skin, the intermediate space and other elements. *The costs given below are based on average west European standards and prices in the year 2000 and do not include value-added tax.*

Outer facade skin

The following construction elements in the outer skin have an influence on costs:
■ type of glass fixings
■ type of glass (toughened safety glass, laminated safety glass, etc.)
■ type and size of opening (partially openable, whether closable or not, completely openable outer facade skin)
■ size and width of panes

The most economical kind of *glass fixings* are linear types to two or four sides in the form of screw-fixed glazing beads or clamped strips. Fixings that require special processing of the glass are much more expensive. These include point fixings, where holes have to be drilled through the panes, and fixings analogous to those used in structural glazing.

The type of *glass* used will be influenced to a large extent by the authorities responsible for granting planning approval, who increasingly insist on laminated safety glass. The costs of glazing with this type of glass are more than twice as high as those for simple toughened safety glass. In addition to the higher costs of the laminated safety glass itself, the supporting structure and fixings will also be more expensive in view of the greater weight of this type of glass. If, instead of 12 mm toughened safety glass with linear fixings, the glazing has to be executed in a comparable thickness of laminated safety glass, the price for panes of glass of identical dimensions (ordered in large quantities) will increase from about €25–€40 to about €40–€60 per square meter. This does not include possible additional costs for the supporting construction.

The type and size of the *openings* also have a major influence on the costs of the outer facade skin. The most economical form of construction is with non-closable fenestration; the most expensive is that consisting of story-height elements with fully openable glass louvers or flaps. These can cost as much as €1,000 per square meter of facade area.

The *size and width of panes* also affect the cost of the outer facade skin. For structural reasons, the width of the panes (facade axes) has a greater influence on costs than the height. Furthermore, in high-rise buildings, the greater wind-loads affect the thickness of the glass and thus the cost.

Inner facade skin

The costs of the inner facade skin are influenced primarily by the following determinants:
■ the type of opening element (side-hung casement, bottom-hung tipped casement, top-hung flap, vertically pivoting casement, cranked sliding casement, etc.)
■ the proportion of glazed to closed areas in the facade
■ the type of glass.

The most economical *opening elements* are mass-produced casements. All the above-mentioned types can be manufactured in this way, with the exception of the cranked sliding casement, which is significantly more expensive than the others (up to €2,000 per casement light where the facade consists of room-height glazing) because of the elaborate furniture required. These casements are not available as mass-produced items, but have to be designed and constructed specially for each project. In comparison, the additional cost (over a fixed glazed facade) of a side- and bottom-hung casement approximately 1.80 m high is roughly €350–€450 per casement when purchased in large quantities.

The advantage of cranked sliding windows is the scope they provide for finely controlled ventilation, and the fact that, in view of their parallel sliding movement, no space is wasted when they are opened. This means that a room can be freely furnished even in the areas near the facade. This special kind of sliding casement also has better sealing qualities than normal sliding windows. The cranked sliding casement has distinct formal advantages, too: the minimal elevational width of the frame means that it can be accommodated flush with the surround when in a closed position.

The greater the *proportion of glazing* in the facade, the higher the investment costs will normally be. An aluminum facade with glazing strips costs roughly €350–€500 per square meter. The costs are not determined by the glazing alone, however. Further related costs may be incurred, for example, when the requisite fire-stop height is not observed in a building with room-height glazing, thus necessitating additional measures such as an intensified sprinkler system in the rooms. The location of static heating elements in the room may also result in higher costs in a building with room-height glazing; for example, if these elements take the form of underfloor convectors instead of conventional radiators set in front of the facade. The most economical form of facade construction consists of solid, closed wall areas with thermal insulation and rear-ventilated cladding. Simply worked rear-vented cladding, such as aluminum sheeting, costs about €175/m^2 for facades of this kind.

The *type of glass* used will influence the cost of the inner facade as well. If, instead of the usual two-layer low-E glazing, triple low-E glazing is specified, the glass price for larger quantities will increase by about €50–€100/m^2.

Facade intermediate space

The following factors influence the construction costs of the intermediate space:
- depth
- structural considerations (accessible or not)
- type of sunshading
- form of ventilation boxes that may possibly be required (whether load-bearing or not; with or without integrated air-deflector plates).

The *depth of the space* between the facade skins and the *live loading* that has to be borne obviously have an effect on the load-bearing structure and the cost of construction. The deeper the space between the facade skins and the greater the load to be borne there, the greater the load-bearing capacity will have to be and the more expensive the construction becomes. Permanent access to this space will impose a live loading of 5 kN/m^2. Where only occasional access is necessary, for example for cleaning and maintenance of the two skins, the live loading will be reduced to between 1.5 and 2.0 kN/m^2.

The effect on the price of a double-skin facade of *ventilation boxes* and any air-deflector plates that may be installed will largely depend on the number of different types of construction and the quantity of such elements. The greater the number of construction types and the smaller the number of ventilation boxes, the higher will be the price.

The cost of *sunshading installations* will depend to a great extent on whether the products are mass-produced, custom-made or indeed protected by patent. The cost relationship between mass-produced systems and other types of sunshading can easily range from 1:3 to 1:5. Where large quantities of identical elements are ordered, louvered blinds can be obtained for about €75 to €100/m^2. Those with an inbuilt light-deflecting function can easily cost between approximately €200 and €375/m^2. External sunshading to a single-skin facade costs significantly more than a comparable system in the intermediate space of a double-skin facade. This can be explained in part by the less complicated form of the fixing brackets and the sunblind casing in the sheltered cavity. For blinds of standard design, the cost difference can easily be between €25 and €50/m^2.

Other factors influencing costs

Further important cost factors include:
- the number of different types of construction
- the overall area of the facade (size of project)

Individual *construction types* consist of facade components of identical shape and size. In order to produce an aluminum ventilation box, for example, a number of new pressing or molding tools will be required. The money spent on planning and manufacturing these tools is independent of the quantity of items they will be required to produce. The portion of the costs attributable to each ventilation box will vary inversely with the quantity. In other words, the greater the number of identical ventilation boxes manufactured with these tools, the lower will be the unit cost. The goal of cost-effective planning must, therefore, be to use as few different constructional types in all sections of the facade as possible. This will ensure considerable advantages in the logistics of the preparatory work as well as during the assembly phase, and it will have a decisive effect on prices.

The positive effects of using only a small number of constructional types should be seen in relation to the *area of the facade* and the size of the project as a whole. Beyond a certain number of identically sized facade components (e.g. several thousand units), the cost gains from increasing the number even further will be negligible. Once the quantity of individual facade components has reached a certain level, the number of different constructional types will no longer be so crucial.

Investment costs for double-skin facades

Practical experience in recent years has shown that investment costs for double-skin facades cover a very large range. The authors are aware of prices (including sunshading) of between €650 and €1,500 per square meter. A medium price level of between €750 and €1,000/m^2 may be cited for larger projects.

The additional costs for story-height double-skin facades lie between €175 and €750/m^2, depending on the type of construction. In estimating the costs of double-skin facades, there is a great risk attached to using lump-sum estimates without sufficient knowledge of the relevant cost determinants or without giving them adequate consideration. Practical examples are known where there was a difference of nearly 50% between the estimated cost and the tender price. Cost estimates should, therefore, be made only by competent and experienced professionals. A common mistake made today is to base the cost estimate for a double-skin facade for a new building on the prices of projects already executed, even though the pricing determinants differ greatly, or certain market forces prevailing at the time of the initial scheme are no longer relevant. One of the problems is the comparatively small number of projects of this kind that have been realized to date.

The costs of double-skin facades can be reduced if this type of construction allows the sound-insulation quality of the inner facade to be lowered. If, for example, instead of requiring a sound-insulation of 42 dB for a single-skin facade, 37 dB for the inner layer of a double-skin facade is acceptable, it will be possible to do without cast-resin panes, which cost about €50/m^2 more than normal insulating double glazing. Where, on the other hand, a sound-insulation value of 37 dB is acceptable for a single-skin facade, and the requirement for the inner layer of a double-skin facade is reduced to 32 dB, this would technically mean no more than a reduction of the thickness of the glass panes, resulting in a cost saving of about €20/m^2.

A blanket budget to limit investment costs

If one wishes to limit the costs of double-skin facades, this can be done by fixing a lump-sum or blanket budget. The architect and the facade consultant will then have the task of developing a double-skin facade concept that will ensure the greatest degree of functional efficiency and aesthetics for a predetermined sum. This approach can be problematic, however, because it means that full-size details have to be drawn up at an early stage of the planning. The architect will not have the usual period at his disposal in which to develop these aspects of the construction, or only to a limited extent.

What are the typical features of an economical double-skin facade?

From the above description of the cost determinants, certain conclusions may be drawn about what goes to make an economical double-skin facade. This is a purely functional analysis that takes no account of non-monetary factors such as the aesthetics of a building. Double-skin facades can be constructed economically if the following basic principles are observed:

■ use of mass-produced or largely mass-produced, prefabricated elements;

■ avoidance of opening elements operated by electric motors;

■ the outer facade skin should contain non-closable openings;

■ the facade intermediate space should not be too deep (approx. 30–50 cm);

■ the floor of the intermediate space should not be accessible, or only for cleaning purposes;

■ the spread of fire from one floor to the next should be prevented by self-contained segments of the outer wall;

■ a minimum number of constructional types should be used;

■ in larger building projects, prefabricated construction should be specified.

With these factors in mind and employing a competent planning, it should be possible to achieve specific costs for a double-skin facade of €600 to €750/m².

Operation and maintenance costs for facades

A comparison between the operating and maintenance costs for double-skin facades and those for single-skin facades shows that the former result in higher cleaning, operating, inspection, servicing and maintenance costs.

Cleaning costs

The cost of cleaning facades is generally calculated separately for the outer surfaces, the inner surfaces and the frames. Dividing the cost in this way allows account to be taken of the different frequencies of cleaning and unit prices for the various sections. When comparing systems, the cost of cleaning the sunshading should be considered as well.

In calculating the costs, one should differentiate between cleaning from within the building, from a hydraulic lifting platform, or from a traveling facade cradle. In difficult situations, robots may be used for cleaning large, inaccessible surfaces. The size of the areas of glass also plays a role in calculating cleaning costs. The cost of cleaning windows with glazing divisions, for example, will inevitably be higher than for large, undivided panes because of the smaller areas of glass and the larger proportion of framing in the former case. The frequency of cleaning will depend mainly on the degree of soiling and the comfort and convenience expected by the users.

Glazed facades

As a guide to cleaning costs for glazed facades, the following prices apply for large areas:

a) cleaning from inside the building

■ glass without frames, internally and externally: approx. €0.55/m²

■ glass with frames, internally and externally: approx. €0.80/m²

b) cleaning from a lifting platform (up to a height of 28 m)

■ glass with frames, one side (externally): approx. €0.75/m²

■ rental cost of hoist: approx. €250/day (cleaning capacity approx. 1,000 m²/day)

■ external blinds, both sides: approx. €2–3/m²

In cleaning high-rise buildings from a traveling facade cradle, the above variables are not the only aspects to be considered. The time lost as a result of high winds and the geometry of the building are also important factors. No approximate values can be given for this case.

Metal and stone facades

The cost of cleaning metal and stone facades will depend on the surface character of the materials. In general, one can assume costs of roughly €1/m² for cleaning a metal facade from a lifting platform, plus the rental of the hoist itself.

Comparison of costs between
single- and double-skin facades

The cost of cleaning double-skin facades is inevitably higher than that for single-skin facades because of the two additional surfaces involved:
- the inner face of the outer skin and
- the outer face of the inner skin.

It is often asserted that the cleaning costs for double-skin facades are also higher than those for single-skin types because of the condensation that can form on the inner face of the outer skin /E4/. In the authors' experience, this is true only if condensation occurs very frequently over longer periods of time. If the double-skin facade is well ventilated and the right air-conditioning concept is implemented (see the chapter on "Air-Conditioning"), this will not occur. Experience shows that the frequency at which double-skin facades have to be cleaned is not greater than that for single-skin types. Similarly, there is no evidence to confirm the assumption that the space between the facade layers will be subject to heavy soiling from the external air flowing through it.

Even on streets with heavy traffic, double-skin facades do not have to be cleaned more frequently than single-skin types. There is also a small additional advantage in placing the sunshading in the space between the facade layers. Compared to sunshading fixed externally to single-skin facades, an installation in the intermediate space of a double-skin construction will, as a rule, be less subject to soiling, since it is not immediately exposed to the outside air. This, too, can influence the frequency of cleaning. Conclusive data on the influence of cleaning costs is not yet available, however.

Example calculation
For a building project with a double-skin facade on a street with heavy traffic, the following cleaning is undertaken:
external skin (including frames)
- outer face   twice a year
- inner face   once a year
internal skin (including frames)
- outer and inner faces   once a year
- blinds in the intermediate space   every 4 years

If one compares this with a single-skin facade with external blinds, where all other factors are equal (surface area of facade, frame proportion by area, etc.), the following data may be used as a basis for calculating the cleaning costs:
- outer face (including frames)   twice a year
- inner face (including frames)   once a year
- blinds   every 3 years

In both cases, the cleaning of the outer face is assumed to take place from a hydraulic hoist. The remaining areas are cleaned from within the building.

The cleaning of the external blinds to a single-skin facade is executed from a hydraulic hoist and costs €3/m² (area of blinds in extended position). Access for cleaning blinds in the facade intermediate space (60 cm deep) is from within the rooms. The cleaning cost is €2/m².

The following increased and reduced costs thus accrue.

The extra costs for cleaning a double-skin facade are the outcome of the additional surfaces adjoining the intermediate space. The following additional costs will be incurred for cleaning areas of glass:
- the inner face of the external skin
  0.5 x €0.80/m² once a year
  = €0.40/m² per year
- the outer face of the internal skin
  0.5 x €0.80/m² once a year
  = €0.40/m² per year
- total
  = €0.80/m² per year

In the case of a single-skin facade, higher costs will be incurred for cleaning the external blinds. Calculated for an entire year, the cleaning costs will be
€3/m² ÷ 3 (years) = €1/m² per year

For a double-skin facade, the costs will be
€2/m² ÷ 4 (years) = €0.50/m² per year

The cost of cleaning the outer and inner surfaces of both types of facade construction will be the same and can be omitted from this comparison.

If one draws up a balance of costs for cleaning both types of facade, the double-skin construction results in additional costs of €0.30/m² per year. Assuming a glass facade 3.0 m high per story with an office space 5.40 m deep to the rear, the additional costs for one square meter of office area will amount to no more than €0.17/m² of floor area per year.

If one assumes that the surfaces adjoining the facade intermediate space are cleaned twice instead of once a year, the additional cleaning costs for a double-skin facade will be €1.10/m² of facade area per year, or €0.61/m² of office area per year.

The example shows that the additional cost of cleaning is largely dependent on the frequency at which it is carried out. In most projects on which the authors have worked to date, the glazed surfaces adjoining the facade intermediate space have been cleaned once a year.

Costs of inspection, servicing and maintenance

The work involved in the inspection, servicing and maintenance of facades depends mainly on whether and to what extent the construction contains moving parts. Where facades have no moving parts, clients usually dispense with inspection and servicing. During the guarantee period, the servicing of the facade will, as a rule, be covered by the original contract. Only when damage occurs outside the guarantee period will steps be taken to restore the facade to its proper state (maintenance and repair work). In practice, where a facade is well planned and executed to a high level of quality, this approach can be perfectly economical. For larger projects and facades with moving parts, however, contracts will normally be made with the construction firms to cover inspection and servicing, and—to a limited extent—maintenance work.

The cost of maintenance and repairs is often limited to a percentage of the sum for inspection and servicing. After the expiry of the guarantee, costs exceeding this are usually paid separately by the client.

During the guarantee period, the defective constructional elements will be replaced free of charge, provided the defect was not caused by incorrect use or operation by third parties or by an act of God. When contracts of this kind are concluded, the contractor will usually allow the client to extend the guarantee period if he wishes. For fixed, unmoving components, for example, the period might be extended from five to ten years; for movable sunshading elements, from two to five years; and for other moving parts, from one to five years.

The annual costs of inspection, servicing and maintenance range from 0.5% to 3% of the investment costs. The percentage may vary considerably, depending on the quantity of the moving parts in the construction and the quality of the work. Moving parts include manually or motor-operated side-hung, and bottom- and side-hung casements, flaps, push-pull rods, electric motors, etc. The greater the proportion they represent in the overall facade construction, the higher the costs for inspection, servicing and maintenance will be.

Does the facade intermediate space form part of the floor area of a building?

When exploring the cost-efficiency of double-skin facades, the question is often raised whether the horizontal floor area of the intermediate space between the facade skins has to be considered part of the effective floor area when calculating the *floor area factor*.

The floor area factor defines how many square meters of floor area are permitted per square meter of site area. This helps to determine the dimensions of a building and regulates the density of development in a planning zone. In the authors' experience, there is no consistency in the way various local authorities treat the area of the facade intermediate space. If it is counted as part of the total floor area in determining the floor area factor of a particular development, the building will lose valuable space, which may result in a lower income from rents. This would considerably reduce the cost-efficiency of double-skin facades from the outset. The additional costs of the double-skin construction itself would be compounded by the reduced revenue resulting from a smaller floor area. This aspect has no influence on the costs for the use of a building, but it does affect subsequent theoretical calculations of the return on capital.

Air-conditioning plant

The interaction between the various subsystems of a building was described in the chapter on "Air-Conditioning," where, from the vast range of options and permutations that exist, a number of practical examples were presented and evaluated.

The calculation of investment costs plus the operating and maintenance costs of the air-conditioning installation will be closely related to the particular concept used and the type of building. Only very approximate basis values can be given for these costs. Individual values can be found in the relevant literature on this subject /E5, E6, E7/.

Given a concept with mechanical ventilation and air filtering, plus the thermodynamic functions of heating, cooling and dehumidification (partial air-conditioning plant), with room heating via radiators, and assuming

■ a volume of air of 7.0 m^3/h m^2

(constant air-change rate) and

■ a heating demand of 40 W/m^2 for the radiators, then the investment cost will be in the order of €170/m^2 of office space. With a system of this kind, a cooling load of approximately 20–25 W/m^2 can be extracted.

If significantly greater cooling loads have to be removed, the installation of cooling ceilings might be recommended. These cost between about €150 and €350/m^2 of active surface area and can cope with a cooling load of approximately 60–120 W/m^2.

If elements of the building structure are to be activated for cooling purposes instead, a cooling load of up to 50 W/m^2 of active surface area can be provided. The costs for the entire system will be between €60 and €75/m^2 of active surface area. In view of the lower efficiency of this form of cooling, the installation will usually extend over the entire area of the element.

In investigating the *operating and maintenance costs* for air-conditioning installations, one should differentiate between the various systems available. The operating costs will consist largely of the outlay for energy and the costs of controlling, inspecting and maintaining the plant. If the costs of inspection, servicing and maintenance are added together, one arrives at what German standard DIN 31051 defines as the *care and upkeep* of the system. Empirical values exist for the overall and individual costs of these services. They are expressed as a percentage of the investment cost. The annual costs for the upkeep of air-conditioning installations lie between roughly 2% and 4% of the investment cost, depending on the form of construction and operation. For further details, see VDI guideline 2067 /E6, E7/, for example, which gives values for individual elements or subsystems as percentages of the investment cost for upkeep (= maintenance costs) of the heat supply systems or of the upkeep costs for the ventilation and cooling systems.

To determine the energy costs for air-conditioning plant, one must first calculate the energy demand. The most reliable method of doing this is to assess the annual requirements by means of simulations for the building based on reference weather data. In many countries, this can be obtained from local meteorological authorities.

Fire-protection measures

The additional fire-protection measures that may be required as a result of a double-skin facade construction can be divided into active, passive and organizational components. Active measures include, for example, sprinkler plant, pressurized ventilation of staircases, and fire-warning installations. The term "passive components" is applied to constructional measures involving elements with a higher degree of fire resistance. Organizational measures include, among other things, fire drill and the presence in the building of staff trained in fire-fighting and protection techniques.

Active measures affect not only investment costs, but also operating and maintenance costs. Passive measures do not result in operating or maintenance costs, with the exception of fire-resisting doors and gates. Organizational measures, on the other hand, lead to operating costs for training personnel and their exemption from other duties.

Since operating and maintenance costs for active measures are incurred continuously over the functional life of a building, it is preferable to provide fire protection as far as possible by passive means. Organizational measures are generally avoided in office and administration buildings as well as in housing. They are encountered principally in industrial construction.

The measures described in the chapter on "Fire Protection" are mainly active ones and include the provision of sprinklers, fire alarm systems, etc.

If it should be necessary to install a sprinkler system in the double-skin facade of an office building, for example, investment costs of about €15 to €25/m^2 of gross floor area may be expected. If a sprinkler system has to be installed anyway, but a greater density of sprinkler heads is required, the additional cost will be about €5 to €10/m^2 of gross floor area, depending on the spacing of the axes. If the double-skin facade construction necessitates a fire-alarm system, investment costs of approximately €10 to €12.50/m^2 of office area should be reckoned.

The operating and maintenance costs resulting from fire-protection measures will be largely for statutory tests and inspections which have to be carried out by independent experts at regular intervals. The annual operating and maintenance costs for sprinkler plant amount to roughly 2–3% of the investment costs.

Office partitions

As described in the chapter on "Sound Insulation", the high degree of acoustic screening provided by double-skin facades can, in some cases, require greater sound insulation in the partitions between offices. For example, instead of stud walls lined with a single skin of plasterboard, two layers may be necessary on each face. This will improve the sound insulation of the partition by about 5 dB. The additional costs for this form of construction will be about €7.50/m².

Where a high standard of sound insulation is specified for a building, acoustic improvements to the walls alone may not be adequate. Additional measures may be necessary to hollow floors, to suspended soffits and to facade abutments. In conjunction with the installation of ducts for mechanical services, it may be necessary to provide additional sound-insulating cladding or larger sound absorbers to prevent noise traveling over long distances. The costs of these measures are specific to an individual project and must, therefore, be calculated for each scheme separately.

As a rule, no significant operating or maintenance costs are incurred by such measures.

Effects on lighting installations

In the chapter on "Daylight", mention was made of the fact that in double-skin facade construction, the projecting horizontal divisions at floor level and the additional outer layer of glazing can result in appreciably less natural light entering the internal spaces. This, in turn, means that, under otherwise identical conditions, the artificial lighting will be turned on for a longer period than it would be in a building with a single-skin facade. The result is a greater consumption of electricity and a shorter life for the lighting elements. The related costs will, therefore, be higher for double-skin than for single-skin facades.

The additional costs for power, new light bulbs and the work of changing them will depend largely on the depth of the space between the two facade skins. The deeper this space is, the longer the lighting will be switched on, and the shorter will be the life of the bulbs. These drawbacks can be offset partially or completely if light-deflecting elements are inserted in the facade space.

The annual cost of new light bulbs K_{nb} and changing the bulbs K_{cb} can be calculated as follows:

$$K_{nb} = \frac{t_{AL} \cdot n_z \cdot K_{LB}}{t_L} \quad [\text{€/a}] \quad (E4)$$

or

$$K_{cb} = \frac{t_{AL} \cdot n_z \cdot K_{LC}}{t_L} \quad [\text{€/a}] \quad (E5)$$

where

K_{nb} is the annual costs for light bulbs in [€/a]
K_{LB} is the cost per light bulb in [€/each]
K_{cb} is the annual cost of changing bulbs in [€/a]
K_{LC} is the cost of changing each light bulb in [€/each]
t_{AL} is the annual amount of time the artificial lighting is switched on [hours per year]
n_z is the number of light bulbs
t_L is the life of a light bulb in [hours].

Example of economic analysis

In planning a roughly 20-meter-high office building in a noisy location (76 dB(A) relevant external noise level), the question arises whether the facade should be designed with a single or double skin. Two possible forms of construction are shown in the diagrams below. Calculations made by the acoustic engineer show that natural ventilation via the windows is not possible with a single-skin facade, because the perceived noise level internally would be too high. If a double-skin facade were used, however, the additional sound insulation afforded by the outer layer ($\Delta R = 7dB$) would make window ventilation possible. In this case, the total sound insulation would be about 21 dB with the windows in the inner skin in a tipped position. The acoustic design for the facades ensures that within the rooms the noise level caused by external sources is roughly the same for both alternatives when the windows are closed.

The planning team will then recommend the client to have a detailed calculation made—in the form of an integrated economic analysis—of the difference between the investment and operating costs for the facade on the one hand and those of the related subsystems of the building on the other. This will then provide a reliable basis for making decisions.

Single-skin facade

Facade
- aluminum post-and-rail construction
- side-hung casements in every other facade bay (cleaning lights)
- frame $U_f = 2.0$ W/m^2 K
- combined low-E and sound-insulating glass 12 (16) 9 GH, $U_g = 1.5$ W/m^2 K
- window $U_w = 1.6$ W/m^2 K
- rear-ventilated (fritted) glass cladding with 12 cm thermal insulation ($U_{AW} = 0.32$ W/m^2 K)

Sunshading
- external aluminum louver blinds (standard quality)
- raised and lowered on tensioned wire guides
- extruded-aluminum blind box

Office space
- hollow floor construction
- sound-absorbing, suspended metal soffit panel, flexible from bay to bay
- ceiling slab with 50% thermal storage area

Maximum heating loads
Contingent conditions:
- joint permeability coefficient of the cleaning lights: $a = 0.3$ m^3/(m h Pa$^{2/3}$)
- area subject to high winds
- floor layout type I
- story-type building

Maximum heating load of static heating, calculated in accordance with DIN 4701: 34 W/m^2 of office area

Maximum cooling loads
Mean value of four rooms facing south, north, east and west.
Contingent conditions:
- energy transmission of glazing g = 58%
- sunshading coefficient z = 0.15
- internal heat loads by people and PCs: 18 W/m^2
- internal heat loads caused by lighting (operation coupled to daylight levels): 15 W/m^2

Maximum cooling load (calculated in simulation trials): 54 W/m^2 of office area

13-1 Elevation of a single-skin facade.

13-2 Section through office space with single-skin facade, showing air-conditioning installation.

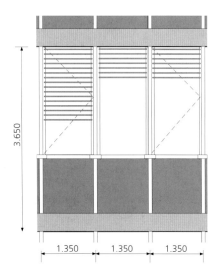

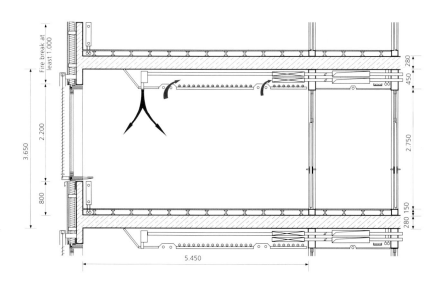

Air-conditioning plant
The following concept is chosen:
▦ panel radiators for static heating
▦ air-conditioning plant providing heating, cooling, humidification and dehumidification with a constant airflow volume (7.5 m³/h m²)
▦ suspended soffit with cooling soffit (cooling capacity: 35 W/m² of office area)

Double-skin facade
Facade
Outer skin:
▦ aluminum curtain-wall construction with vertical posts and toughened safety glass
▦ linear fixing of glazing on both faces, with permanent rear ventilation
▦ staggered air-intake and extract openings in alternate bays

Facade corridor:
▦ accessible for cleaning; grating walkway on supporting structure

Inner skin:
▦ aluminum post-and-rail construction
▦ side- and bottom-hung casement or all-glass flaps in alternate bays
▦ frame U_f = 2.0 W/m² K
▦ combined low-E and sound-insulating glass 8/12/4, U_g = 1.5 W/m² K
▦ window U_w = 1.47 W/m² K
(inner and outer facade skins)
▦ ventilation box in area of parapet wall with 12 cm thermal insulation (U_{AW} = 0.32 W/m² K)

Sunshading
▦ aluminum louvered blinds (standard quality)
▦ raised and lowered on tensioned wire guides

Office space
As for single-skin facade

Maximum heating loads
Conditions as for the single-skin facade, but with
▦ area of low wind speeds (assumed), since the inner facade skin is not directly exposed to wind currents
▦ natural ventilation where external temperatures ≥ 0 °C. Where external temperatures sink below this, the mechanical ventilation should be activated.
Maximum heating load of static heating, in accordance with DIN 4701: 33 W/m² of office space

Maximum cooling loads
Mean value of four rooms facing south, north, east and west.
Contingent conditions:
▦ Function: as for single-skin facade
▦ Secondary heat emission from sunshading and solar heat transmission is calculated dynamically in simulation trials together with the flow of air through the facade intermediate space.
Maximum cooling load (calculated by means of simulation): 53 W/m² of office area

Air-conditioning plant
The following concept is chosen:
▦ panel radiators for static heating
▦ partial air-conditioning plant, providing heating, cooling and dehumidifying services, with a constant airflow volume (7.5 m³/h m²)
▦ suspended soffit with cooling soffit (cooling capacity: 35 W/m² of office area)

13-3 Internal elevation of double-skin facade.

13-4 Section through office space with double-skin facade, showing air-conditioning installation.

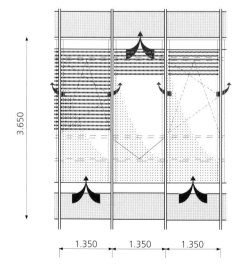

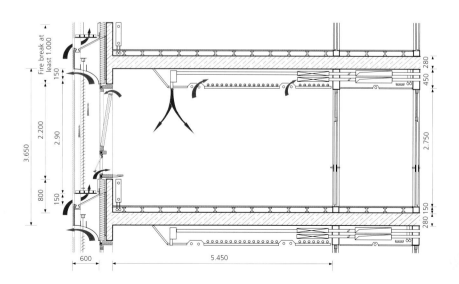

Discussion of maximum heating and cooling loads

The maximum heating load for static heating is about the same in both alternatives. Various effects cancel each other out. In the case of the single-skin facade, the thermal transmission factor will be higher than with a double-skin facade because of the poorer U-value (see the chapter "Thermal Insulation"). On the other hand, the thermal requirements for ventilation will be much lower in the single-skin alternative because only the heat losses through the joints have to be considered (windows are opened solely for cleaning purposes). With a double-skin facade, natural window ventilation is designed to occur only when temperatures rise above 0 °C, so that heat losses caused by ventilation via the open inner facade skin are the dominant factor here. These losses are significantly greater than the heat losses through the joints of the single-skin facade. On balance, the heat losses will be roughly equal. To reduce the risk of condensation on the outer layer of a double-skin facade, the use of mechanically humidified air should be avoided with this form of construction.

The maximum cooling load is also about the same for each alternative. In the case of the single-skin facade, the absence of a second, outer layer means that solar transmission through the glazed areas will be higher than in the alternative case. What is more, a "night purge"—the escape of heat through open windows—will usually not be possible. On the other hand, with double-skin facades there will be a greater heat gain within the rooms as a result of thermal transmission. This occurs because the temperatures in the intermediate space are higher than the external temperature. On balance, if the space between the inner and outer layers of a double-skin facade—including the sunshading—is well ventilated, these two effects will more or less cancel each other out.

Fire protection

Klingsch recommends that an automatic early-warning fire-alarm system be installed in the facade corridor (see the chapter on "Fire Protection"). According to relevant guidelines in Germany, a fire-alarm element is necessary about every ten bays of the facade. Other measures are not required for a building of this height and use.

Calculation of investment costs

Only costs that serve to draw a comparison between the two alternatives are discussed here. Costs that are the same in both cases are not considered.

Single-skin facade
The estimated costs apply to an overall facade area of at least 3,000 m². The costs are calculated for two adjacent bays.
- glazed facade (as described above):
2.20 m x 2.70 m x €425/m² = €2,525
- additional cost of sound-insulating glazing (R = 45 dB instead of R = 37 dB):
2.20 m x 2.70 m x €75/m² = € 445
- additional cost for side-hung casement:
1 no. x €450/each = € 450
- rear-ventilated (fritted) glass cladding:
1.45 m x 2.70 m x €250/m² = € 980
- sunshading:
2.40 m x 2.70 m x €125/m² = € 810

total €5,210

That amounts to costs of around €530/m² of facade area or €354/m² of office area.

Double-skin facade
The estimated costs apply to an overall facade area of at least 3,000 m². The costs are calculated for two adjacent bays.
- inner skin:
Individual cost components for the inner skin (glazed facade with additions for side-hung casement and rear-ventilated cladding) can be calculated in the same way as for the single skin facade.
Total = €3,955
- additional costs for the all-glass flaps: = € 475
- outer skin with supporting construction
3.20 m x 2.70 m x €250/m² = €2,160
- grating to support personal access:
2.70 m x €175/m = € 473
- sunshading:
3.05 m x 2.70 m x €88/m² = € 725

total €7,788

That amounts to costs of around €790/m² of facade area or €530/m² of office area.

Air-conditioning plant

The costs for static heating, cooling soffits and low-temperature plant are similar in each case and may be excluded from the calculations.

Single-skin facade
In the single-skin facade concept, the approximate costs given below can be assumed for the service installations for two office bays.
- air-conditioning system (heating, cooling, humidification and dehumidification):

110 m³/h x €17.50/(m³/h)	= €1,925

- dynamic heating:

0.80 kW x €225/kW	= € 180
total	€2,105

Double-skin facade
- part air-conditioning plant, providing heating, cooling and dehumidification (without humidification):

110 m³/h x €15.50/(m³/h)	= €1,705

- dynamic heating:

0.60 kW x €225/kW	= € 135
total	€1,840

The amount of dynamic heating required for heating the air differs in the two concepts. In the building with a single-skin facade, an air-conditioning system was specified that allows the air to be humidified in winter to provide additional comfort (the windows cannot be opened for ventilation). In contrast to the system with a partial air-conditioning plant with no humidifying facility, additional heating is required. The dynamic heating capacity will thus have to be greater for the single-skin facade concept. This, in turn, has an influence on the investment costs.

Early fire-warning system (double-skin facade)

One fire-alarm element is installed every ten bays along the facade intermediate space. The cost for two bays is therefore €35.

Overall costs relevant to a comparison between the two systems

Single-skin facade

facade and sunshading	€5,209
air-conditioning plant	€2,105
total	€7,314

This represents a cost of about €500/m² of office space.

Double-skin facade

facade and sunshading	€7,780
air-conditioning plant	€1,840
fire alarms	€ 35
total	€9,655

This represents a cost of about €655/m² of office space.

Calculation of costs for the use of the building

1. Calculation of capital costs and amortization costs on annuity basis. The following assumptions have been made:

- rate of interest = 7% per annum
- life of element = n
  - single-skin facade: n = 30 years
  - sunshading to single-skin facade: n = 15 years
  - inner layer of double-skin facade (only limited exposure of the sealing to the weather): n = 35 years
  - gratings: n = 30 years
  - sunshading within double-skin facade (protected from wind): n = 20 years
  - outer layer of double-skin facade: n = 30 years
  - air-conditioning plant: n = 15 years
  - early fire-warning system: n = 10 years

This results in the following annuity costs:
single-skin facade:
    approx. €46/m² of office area per year
double-skin facade:
    approx. €57/m² of office area per year

Difference:
    approx. €11/m² of office area per year

The capital costs and amortization costs for a double-skin facade are, therefore, about 24% higher than those for a single-skin facade. This is accounted for largely by the additional construction costs of the double-skin facade. The lower costs for the air-conditioning plant and sunshading do not balance out the additional costs.

Operating and maintenance costs

Costs of cleaning the facade
The following cost data is based on a single bay.

Single-skin facade
Surfaces to be cleaned
- glazing and frames: each face 3.00 m²
- sunshading: 3.25 m²
- apron wall panels: 1.95 m²

Frequency of cleaning
- outer face of windows: twice a year
- inner face of windows: once a year
- sunshading: every 3 years
- apron wall panels: every 5 years

The inner face is cleaned from within the building.
The outer face and the sunshading are cleaned from a hydraulic hoist.

Costs
- cleaning from within the building
(glass and frames): €0.40/m²
- cleaning from a hydraulic hoist:
  – windows (glazing and frames) €1.15/m²
  – apron wall panels €1.40/m²
  – sunshading €3.00/m²

This amounts to a sum of about €1.63/m² of office area per year.

Double-skin facade
Surfaces to be cleaned
- outer skin, glazing and frames: each face 4.30 m²
- inner skin, glazing and frames: each face 3.00 m²
- sunshading: 4.10 m²
- external (fritted) glass panels: 0.60 m²

Frequency of cleaning
- outer face of outer skin: twice a year
- inner face of outer skin: once a year
- outer face of inner skin: once a year
- inner face of inner skin: once a year
- glass panels: every 5 years
- sunshading: every 5 years

The inner facade skin, the inner face of the outer skin, and the sunshading are cleaned from within the building. The outer face of the outer facade skin is cleaned from a hydraulic hoist.

Costs
Data as above, except for the sunshading, where a price of €2.00/m² is applicable.

This amounts to a cost of about €2.15/m² of office area a year.

Energy costs
The energy costs for air-conditioning and lighting also have to be determined. Energy needs for these functions are calculated on the basis of simulation trials for the building.

With a double-skin facade construction, one should assume that the partial air-conditioning plant will not be in operation when external temperatures are between 5 °C and 20 °C. Within this range, adequate thermal comfort can be achieved by means of window ventilation and cooling soffits. When external temperatures lie outside this range, the partial air-conditioning plant should be operated.

In a building with a single-skin facade, the air-conditioning will be in operation all year round, since the windows cannot be opened.

The lighting in the rooms of buildings with a double-skin facade will be switched on for longer periods than in buildings with a single-skin facade. This is because the corridor between the facade skins has a shading effect and because the additional facade skin reduces the amount of natural light that enters the building.

The following assumptions may be made.
Monday–Friday operation
- air-conditioning: 6:00 a.m. to 7:00 p.m.
- partial air-conditioning (when the outdoor temperature is below 5 °C or above 20 °C): 6:00 a.m. to 7:00 p.m.
- cooling soffit, year round (according to needs): 6:00 a.m. to 7:00 p.m.

Energy prices
- electricity: €34.7/GJ
- heating energy: € 6.9/GJ
- cooling energy: €11.1/GJ

- A detailed description of contingent conditions is contained in the chapter "Thermal Insulation" ("Case study: contingent conditions relating to thermal simulations").
- The figures for energy needs are mean values, based on rooms in an intermediate story facing south, north, east and west.
- The cost of water used in the air-conditioning plant for humidification is ignored.

Alternative	Energy demand for				Energy demand for				Sum
	Heating	Cooling	Fan power	Lighting	Heating	Cooling	Fan power	Lighting	
	[MJ/m² of office area per year]				[€/m² of office area per year]				
Single-skin	285	112	79	61	1,97	1,25	2,75	2,13	8,10
Double-skin	238	76	36	72	1,65	0,85	1,25	2,50	6,25

Data obtained in simulations to determine the energy needs and annual energy costs of the two forms of facade.

In view of the fact that the air-conditioning is not in constant use, but comes into operation only when the need arises, the double-skin facade functions more economically than the single-skin construction. The costs are about €1.85/m² of office area per year (i.e. 23%) lower. Part of these gains, however, are lost as a result of having the room lighting on for about 200 hours longer in the building with the double-skin facade. The reason why the difference in heating-energy requirements is not greater is that static heating in conjunction with window ventilation when temperatures are above 5 °C requires more energy than is needed with a closed single-skin facade. This can be attributed partly to heat recovery from the mechanical ventilation plant and partly to the greater air-change rate that occurs with window ventilation. The energy requirements for heating a building with a double-skin facade when the external temperature is above 5 °C were realistically calculated, based on technical measurements of the relationship between internal and external air temperatures and the respective air-change rates (cf. the chapter on "Aerophysics").

Inspection, servicing and maintenance costs
Data for calculating annual costs.

Facades
1.0% of investment costs:
■ single-skin facade, including sunshading
0.01 x €5,210/14.72 m²
= €3.54/m² of office area per year
■ double-skin facade, including sunshading:
0.01 x €7,788/14.72 m²
= €5.29/m² of office area per year

Air-conditioning plant
In view of the great differences in the operating times of the air-conditioning plant in the two alternatives (single-skin facade: approx. 3,100 hours per annum; double-skin facade: approx. 1,400 hours per annum), different costs will inevitably accrue for inspection, servicing and maintenance. These costs can be reduced only if one departs from the usual preventive strategy based on cyclical intervals and goes over to a strategy that takes account of the actual conditions prevailing at any given time /E9/. In the latter case, emphasis is laid on maintaining certain predefined conditions (e.g. the standard of air-conditioning or the availability of the installation). With this strategy, it is not important to implement certain measures on the installations at regular intervals. The goal is to ensure that they meet the requirements made of them. Because of the relatively low degree of wear and tear to which the HVAC is subject, the maintenance costs should be lower. It is assumed that the costs of servicing the air-conditioning plant will be identical in both cases.

The *Taschenbuch für Heizung + Klimatechnik*, a manual for heating and air-conditioning technology /E5/, gives standard values for the servicing, inspection and upkeep (maintenance) of an air-conditioning plant in relation to the length of time it is in operation per annum. If one adopts these values and assumes that the costs for the cooling soffits and the static heating in both alternatives are the same, the following values can be obtained.

■ Single-skin facade
operating period of air-conditioning plant:
3,100 hours per year
costs of inspection, servicing and maintenance:
approx. 2.5% of the investment costs per year
0.025 x €2,105/14.72 m²
 = €3.58/m² of office area per year

■ Double-skin facade
operating period of partial air-conditioning plant:
approx. 1,400 hours per year
costs of inspection, servicing and maintenance:
approx. 1% of the investment costs per year
0.01 x €1,840/14.72 m²
 = €1.25/m² of office area per year

Lighting installations
One can assume that the inspection, servicing and maintenance costs for lighting will be the same in both cases, with the exception of the costs for replacement and renewal of light fittings. The longer period in which the lighting is turned on in buildings with double-skin facades means that the costs for the renewal of light bulbs will be higher than in buildings with a single-skin facade.
Assumptions:
■ life of light bulbs, etc.: 7,500 hours
■ for every office bay, 4 bulbs will be required for two light fittings
■ costs per light bulb: €5.00
■ time required for changing bulbs: 0.25 hours
■ wage costs: €27.50 per hour

The costs of lighting replacements and renewals can be calculated using formulas (E4) and (E5). A rough estimate of the annual number of hours during which the lighting is likely to be turned on was made as part of the simulation trials carried out for the building.

■ Single-skin facade
annual lighting period: 1,100 hours
costs for replacement and renewal of light fittings:
approx. €0.95/m² of office area per year

■ Double-skin facade
annual lighting period: 1,300 hours
costs for replacement and renewal of light fittings:
approx. €1.13/m² of office area per year

Early fire-warning system
The inspection, servicing and maintenance costs can be ignored in this case, in view of the small amounts involved.

Comparison of operating and maintenance costs
The table at the top of the opposite page shows a breakdown of the individual operating and maintenance costs for the two alternatives.

The figures for the double-skin facade are roughly 10% better than those for the single-skin construction. That is attributable largely to the lower energy costs and the lower costs for inspection, servicing and maintenance. This data is based on two assumptions: firstly, that in the case of the double-skin alternative, the partial air-conditioning installation is consistently turned off when external temperatures are between 5 °C and 20 °C; and secondly, that an "actual state" upkeep strategy is applied. Otherwise, the double-skin construction will have no advantages over a single-skin facade.

Comparison of costs for the use of the building
The overall costs of the building in use can be obtained by adding together the sums for the various cost groups for the two alternatives—capital costs and amortization, operating and maintenance costs (cf. the table at the bottom of the opposite page).
    The single-skin facade proves to be roughly 15% (or approx. €9.28/m² of office area per annum) more economical than the double-skin alternative. The somewhat lower operating and maintenance costs of the double-skin facade are not enough to offset the higher capital costs and costs of amortization resulting from the initial investment.

Individual cost categories	Operating and maintenance costs		Cost differences favoring double-skin facade construction
	Single-skin facade	Double-skin facade	
	[€/m² of office area per annum]		
Facade cleaning	1.63	2.15	-0.52
Energy costs	8.10	6.25	+1.85
Inspection, servicing, maintenance costs: - facade - air-conditioning plant	3.55 3.57	5.30 1.25	-1.75 +2.32
Lighting installation	0.95	1.13	-0.18
Total	17.80	16.08	+1.72

Schedule of operating and maintenance costs for a building, excluding those elements that are the same in both alternatives.

Cost group	Costs of building in use	
	Single-skin facade	Double-skin facade
	[€/m² of office area per annum]	
Capital costs and amortization	45.50	56.50
Operating and maintenance costs	17.80	16.08
Total	63.30 100%	72.58 115%

Schedule of costs of use of building, excluding those elements that are the same in both alternatives.

Possible reduction of rental income through double-skin facade construction

If one assumes that the corridor between the two facade skins has to be included in the calculation of the floor area factor (total floor area as a proportion of the site area), this would imply a serious reduction of the leasable space. Where a building is to be used by third parties and not the client's own employees, this will mean an actual loss of rental income.

In the example we have been investigating, this would amount to about 0.60 m^2 per meter length of facade in the office areas. If one assumes a monthly rent of €15/m^2 of office floor area, this would amount to a rent loss of €108 per meter length of facade on each floor per annum. With a room depth of 5.45 m, this represents roughly 11% of the rent obtainable for the office space. In relation to office floor area, this is about €20/m^2 per year. This sum is almost twice as great as the difference between the user costs of the building in our example.

Cost-benefit considerations

In comparing double- and single-skin facades, one should always ask the question whether the two forms allow the same use. Even if modern air-conditioning of rooms with non-openable windows can provide a high degree of thermal comfort, there remains a psychological drawback that should not be underestimated: the reaction of users to permanently closed windows. In other words, contact with the outside world is cut off, and the level of satisfaction will be lower than in rooms where it is possible to open the windows—notwithstanding the strong winds or high noise levels that may prevail outside. In our example, the advantage to users of openable windows would have to be worth the additional costs (the difference of the costs of the building in use). If one assumes, as in the present case, an office area (main functional area) of 11 m^2 per person, the additional costs for a double-skin facade over a single-skin form are approximately €120 per annum per workplace. On the other hand, assuming labor costs of €50 per hour per user, the additional sum is equivalent to roughly 2.5 working hours per person per year. If the greater sense of satisfaction on the part of users resulting from the option of window ventilation were to lead to an improved working performance amounting to 2.5 hours per year, the additional costs of the double-skin facade would be amortized. If the area of the facade corridor is included in the calculation of the floor area factor, roughly seven additional working hours per person per annum would be needed to balance out the additional costs.

Since there is a great element of subjectivity in assessments of this kind, a vote will have to be taken on the merits of each individual scheme. That also applies to the aesthetic aspects of a building, of course. The potentially better design that a double-skin facade allows can mean that the value of a building will be increased, and this may easily compensate for the difference in maintenance costs and possible rent losses (where the area of the facade intermediate space is included in the calculation of the floor area factor).

Conclusion

The example of a cost-efficiency analysis described above shows how vast and complex comparisons of this kind are. In the authors' experience, double-skin facades are economically viable only when they help to reduce the costs of the air-conditioning plant and its operation—and therewith, the investment costs—to a minimum. Whether this is conducive to thermal comfort in offices and at the workplace is questionable. The possibility of creating acceptable conditions should not be precluded entirely, however, as examples like the Gladbacher Bank in Mönchengladbach, the DB Cargo building in Mainz and the debis headquarters in Berlin demonstrate (see the chapter on "Air-Conditioning"). In these cases, it proved possible to reduce the air-conditioning plant to a minimum by building a double-skin facade, while at the same time achieving a high level of satisfaction among users. In at least one case, it was possible to prove the economic viability of the double-skin facade.

Before embarking on elaborate investigations of the economics of double-skin facades, one should ascertain whether the facade offers an appreciably greater functional value than a single-skin form, and whether the intermediate space between the skins has to be included in calculations to determine the floor area factor. If this is the case, and if there is no increase in functional value compared to a single-skin facade, there will be little chance of implementing a double-skin form of construction. In that case, an economic analysis will usually be superfluous as well. If one of the two questions can be answered in favor of a double-skin facade, an investigation of the cost-effectiveness will be informative and can be of considerable help in reaching a decision.

Appendix

Expression of thanks

It would not have been possible to elaborate the subject of double-skin facades in such detail and to compile this book without the commitment and indeed courage of those architects and clients who were filled with enthusiasm for this new form of construction. The positive outcome of these joint efforts may be seen in the 13 built examples contained in this book. We should like to express our thanks at this point for permission to publish these schemes.

Others who played a decisive role in preparing the extensive specialist material contained in this volume include:

■ The assistants in the department for facade technology at DS-Plan, and in particular Valentin Balog, Heinz-Ulrich Bentzin and Jochen Schindel, as well as Helmut Langthaler and Herbert Natterer, who have collaborated with us over a long period of time. They were responsible for most of the CAD drawings and for developing many of the constructional details.

■ The assistants in the department for energy management at DS-Plan, and in particular Peter Mösle, Andreas Niewienda and Dr. Michael Schwarz, who provided invaluable help in analyzing measurement data and in carrying out the thermal, daylight and airflow simulations.

■ The assistants of the Institut für Bauphysik Horst Grün, Mülheim, and in particular Dr. Christian Fischer, Ralph Kettenis and Jan Penkala, who provided measurement data and the theoretical basis for the chapter "Sound Insulation".

■ Hans-Walter Bielefeld of the Schüco company, whose measurement data on double-skin facades, compiled over a period of many years, was utilized in this book.

We should also like to extend our thanks to the many specialist colleagues who, in the course of numerous conversations and discussions about double-skin facades, contributed valuable ideas—often by expressing opposing or critical views—which helped us to comprehend our role as planners on an integrated basis and to come up with new solutions.

Finally, thanks are due to our editors Bettina Rühm and Christopher Wynne, whose persistent questioning helped make the specialist chapters more accessible to persons not familiar with the subject, as well as to our translator Peter Green, who is always in search for the better expression.

Photo Credits

The photos, illustrations and drawings not included in the following list are by the authors of this book.

Michael Barthelme on behalf of the Götz company, Würzburg: ill.12-2

DIFA, Hamburg: ill. 10-4

Hans Günther Esch, Cologne, on behalf of the Schüco company, Bielefeld: ill. 4-1

Christian Höhn, Nuremberg/Munich, on behalf of Dürschinger & Biefang, Nuremberg: ill. 10-1

Institut für Industrieaerodynamik I. F. I.
College for Applied Science, Aachen, Prof. Gerhardt: ills. 8-18, 8-19

Holger Knauf, Düsseldorf, on behalf of the architects Ingenhoven Overdiek und Partner, Düsseldorf: ills. 3-01, 10-11, 10-12, 10-18

Holger Knauf, Düsseldorf, on behalf of Murphy/Jahn, Chicago: ill.11-13

Holger Knauf, Düsseldorf, on behalf of the architects RKW, Düsseldorf: ill. 1-11

Prof. Hans Kollhoff, Berlin: CAD simulation, ill. 1-5

Lederer, Ragnarsdóttir, Oei, architects, Stuttgart: ills. 10-8, 10-9

Vincent Mosch, Berlin, on behalf of DS-Plan: ills. 1-6, 9-7, 12-1 and front title, 12-5

Nürnberger Beteiligungs AG, Nuremberg: ill. 10-2

Tomas Riehle © Tomas Riehle artur, Cologne, on behalf of Engel Projektentwicklung, Düsseldorf: ill. 1-18

RWTH Aachen, Department for Steel Construction, division for wind-engineering technology, Prof. Sedlacek: ill. 8-15, diagram 12-4

Dr. Schrammen + Partner, architects, Mönchengladbach: ill. 12-10

Ezra Stoller © esto: ill. 10-17

Thomas van den Valentyn, Cologne: drawing 1-24; ill. 1-26

Wolfgang Ziegler, Stuttgart, on behalf of the architects Müller / Djordjevic / Krehl, Stuttgart: ill. 10-5

Gartner company, Gundelfingen: ill. 1-25; drawings 10-32, 10-34. 10-35

Geilinger company, Winterthur, Switzerland: drawing 5-3

Götz company, Würzburg: ill. 12-3

Zent-Frenger company, Leonberg/Heppenheim: ill. 12-14

From: Prandtl, Oswatitsch, Wieghardt, *Führer durch die Strömungslehre*, published by Vieweg-Verlag: ills. 8-2, 8-6

Literature

Cited Literature

Chapter 1: Types of Construction

/C1/ Oesterle, Eberhard, *Doppelschalige Fassaden – Konzepte der Zukunft?*, CCI 7/1993

/C2/ Blumenberg / Zöllner, *Doppelfassaden und Technische Gebäudeausrüstun*g, Conference proceedings compiled by the FIA-Project of the *Fachinstitut Gebäude-Klima e.V.*, Bietigheim-Bissingen, 1998

Chapter 4: Sound Insulation

/S1/ VDI 2714, *Schallausbreitung im Freien*

/S2/ VDI 2058 Blatt 1, *Beurteilung von Arbeitslärm in der Nachbarschaft*

/S3/ Knaust, *Auch die Norm schützt nicht vor Planungsfehlern*, DIB, issue 1/2 99, p. 28 ff.

/S4/ Research report of the German *Dachverband der Ziegelindustrie* on the frequency of complaints regarding wrong building details

/S5/ VDI 2058 Blatt 3, *Beurteilung von Lärm am Arbeitsplatz unter Berücksichtigung unterschiedlicher Tätigkeiten*

/S6/ Schmidt, H., *Schalltechnisches Taschenbuch*, Düsseldorf, 1989

/S7/ Knaust, *Auch die Norm schützt nicht vor Planungsfehlern*, DIB, issue 1/2 99, p. 28ff.

/S8/ VDI 2058 Blatt 1, *Beurteilung von Arbeitslärm in der Nachbarschaft* and
   VDI 2058 Blatt 3, *Beurteilung von Lärm am Arbeitsplatz unter Berücksichtigung unterschiedlicher Tätigkeiten*

/S9/ VDI 2719, *Schalldämmung von Fenstern und deren Zusatzeinrichtungen*, section 10

/S10/ VDI 2058 Blatt 3, *Beurteilung von Lärm am Arbeitsplatz unter Berücksichtigung unterschiedlicher Tätigkeiten*

/S11/ *Arbeitsstättenverordnung* § 15, Schutz vor Lärm—protection to noise

/S12/ VDI 2719, *Schalldämmung von Fenstern und deren Zusatzeinrichtungen*, table 6, row 3

/S13/ H. Schmidt, *Schalltechnisches Taschenbuch*, Düsseldorf, 1989

/S14/ EN ISO 717-1:1997, *Acoustics. Rating of sound insulation in buildings and of building elements. Airborne sound insulation*

/S15/ VDI 2719, *Schalldämmung von Fenstern und deren Zusatzeinrichtungen*

/S16/ Fasold / Veres, *Schallschutz + Raumakustik in der Praxis*, Berlin, 1998

/S17/ Fasold / Veres, *Schallschutz + Raumakustik in der Praxis*, p. 117 ff.

/S18/ Fasold / Veres, *Schallschutz + Raumakustik in der Praxis*, p. 35 ff.

/S19/ VDI 2714, *Schallausbreitung im Freien*

/S20/ EN ISO 717-1:1997, *Acoustics. Rating of sound insulation in buildings and of building elements. Airborne sound insulation*

/S21/ Gertis, Bauphysik 21, issue 2/99, p. 54 ff., in respect to Koch, Weber, not yet published

/S22/ VDI 2081, *Geräuscherzeugung und Lärmminderung in raumlufttechnischen Anlagen*

/S23/ VDI 2081, *Geräuscherzeugung und Lärmminderung in raumlufttechnischen Anlagen*, section 8.5.2

/S24/ VDI 2081, *Geräuscherzeugung und Lärmminderung in raumlufttechnischen Anlagen*, section 7

/S25/ VDI 2081, *Geräuscherzeugung und Lärmminderung in raumlufttechnischen Anlagen*, see appendix A2

Chapter 5: Thermal Insulation

/T1/ EN ISO 6946:1997 Building components and building elements. Thermal resistance and thermal transmittance. Calculation method

/T2/ EN ISO 13789:1999 Thermal performance of buildings. Transmission heat loss coefficient. Calculation method

/T3/ EN ISO 10077-1:2000 *Thermal performance of windows, doors and shutters. Calculation of thermal transmittance. Simplified method*

/T4/ DIN 67507, *Lichttransmissionsgrade, Strahlungstransmissionsgrade und Gesamtenergiedurchlaßgrade von Verglasungen*

/T5/ DIN 5036 part 3, *Strahlungsphysikalische und lichttechnische Eigenschaften von Materialien, Meßverfahren für lichttechnische und spektrale strahlungsphysikalische Kennzahlen*

/T6/ VDI 2078, *Berechnung der Kühllast klimatisierter Räume* (VDI-Kühllastregeln)—Calculation method of cooling loads in buildings

/T7/ German *Wärmeschutzverordnung 1995*, §7 in conjunction with appendix 4, table 1

/T8/ EN ISO 10077-1:2000 *Thermal performance of windows, doors and shutters. Calculation of thermal transmittance. Simplified method*

/T9/ EN 12207:2000 *Windows and doors. Air permeability. Classification*

/T10/ DIN 4701 part 3, *Regeln für die Berechnung des Wärmebedarfs von Gebäuden, Auslegung der Raumheizeinrichtungen*—Calculation method of heating loads in buildings

/T11/ German *Wärmeschutzverordnung 1995*, appendix 1, paragraph 1.6.4.2

/T12/ André P. Faist, *La Façade Double-Peau*, Façade 2/99, research results of the EPFL CH-Lausanne

/T13/ Duffie, Solar *Engineering of Thermal Processes*, 2nd edition, Wiley & Sons, New York, 1991

/T14/ EN ISO 6946:1997 Building components and building elements. Thermal resistance and thermal transmittance. Calculation method

/T15/ VDI 2067, *Berechnung der Kosten für Wärme-versorgungsanlagen*—calculation of cost for heating supply
/T16/ German *Wärmeschutzverordnung 1995*, app. 1
/T17/ EN 832:2000 *Thermal performance of buildings. Calculation of energy use for heating. Residential buildings*
/T18/ VDI 6020, *Gebäude- und Anlagensimulation*—computer simulations of buildings and air-conditioning systems, under preparation
/T19/ Oesterle, Eberhard, *Wirtschaftlichkeit bautech-nischer Energiesysteme von Büro- und Verwaltungs-bauten*, Bauverlag, Wiesbaden, 1985
/T20/ DIN 1946 part 2, *Raumlufttechnik, Gesundheits-technische Anforderungen*—hygienic requirements for air-conditioning plant
/T21/ *Seminar sommerlicher Wärmeschutz*, seminar proceedings of the *Institut für Fenstertechnik*, Rosenheim

Chapter 6: Daylight
/D1/ DIN 5034 part 1, *Tageslicht in Innenräumen, All-gemeine Anforderungen*
/D2/ Bartenbach in: *Seminar sommerlicher Wärme-schutz*, seminar proceedings of the *Institut für Fenstertechnik*, Rosenheim

Chapter 7: Fire Protection
/F1/ Wolfram Klingsch, *Brandschutztechnische Beurteilung von Doppelfassaden*. Referat auf der Jahresfachtagung des vfdb (Vereinigung zur Förderung des Deutschen Brandschutzes e. V.) in Frankfurt, 1995

Chapter 8: Aerophysics
/A1/ DIN 1946 part 2, *Raumlufttechnik, Gesundheits-technische Anforderungen*—hygienic requirements for air-conditioning plant
/A2/ VDI 2083 part 5, *Reinraumtechnik, Thermische Behaglichkeit*
/A3/ DIN 33403 part 3, *Klima am Arbeitsplatz und in der Arbeitsumgebung, Beurteilung des Klimas im Erträglichkeitsbereich*—evaluation of climatic conditions at workplaces

Chapter 9: Highrise Buildings
/H1/ DIN 4710, *Meteorologische Daten zur Berech-nung des Energieverbrauchs von heiz- und raumluft-technischen Anlagen*—meteorological data for calculating the energy consumption of air-conditioning plant
/H2/ *European Wind Atlas*, Meteorology and Wind Energy Department, Risø National Laboratory, Roskilde, Dänemark, 1990
/H3/ Davenport, *The application of statistical concepts to the wind loading of structures*, Proc. Inst. of civil engineering, 1961, vol. 19, p. 449-472

Chapter 11: Special Constructional Details
/CD1/ Some of the more important standards applica-ble in everyday planning practice in Germany are listed below for orientation:
DIN 18 201 Tolerances in building construction
DIN 18 202 Tolerances in building construction; tolerances not related to specific materials.
DIN 18 203 Part 1 Tolerances in building construction: precast concrete elements
DIN 18 203 Part 2 Tolerances in building construction: prefabricated steel elements
DIN 18 203 Part 3 Tolerances in building construction: prefabricated elements in wood and other natural materials
DIN EN ISO 13 920 Tolerances in welded construction

Chapter 12: Air-conditioning
/AC1/ Fischer, C.; Schrammen, W. *Fassadengestaltung am Beispiel der Gladbacher Bank in Mönchengladbach*, DBZ 3/97
/AC2/ Fanger, P.O. *Enthalpy and Perceived Air Quality—a Paradigm Shift*, HLH 11/97, Springer / VDI Verlag
/AC3/ DIN 1946 part 2, *Raumlufttechnik, Gesund-heitstechnische Anforderungen*—hygienic require-ments for air-conditioning plant
/AC4/ Joule II Contracts Jou – CT93-0426, *The overall conception and integration of active and passive solar technology within the energy budget in general use.* Coordinator: Renzo Piano Building Workshop, Paris. Contractor: debis Gesellschaft für Potsdamer Platz Projekt und Immobilienmanagement mbH, Berlin. Sub Contractor: Drees & Sommer AG, Stuttgart. Associated Contractors: Dipl.-Ing. Christoph Kohl-becker, Gaggenau; Ove Arup & Partners, London.
/AC5/ Doleschell; Lödel, *Energetik und Ergonomie. Die Glasdoppelfassade des debis-Gebäudes C1 am Potsdamer Platz in Berlin.* Proceedings of GlasKon98
/AC6/ Oesterle, Eberhhard; Koenigsdorff, Roland, *Thermische Aktivierung von Bauteilen zum Heizen und Kühlen von Gewerbebauten*, HLH 1/99, Springer / VDI Verlag

Chapter 13: Economic Viability

/E1/ Drees, Gerhard; Höh, Gerhard, *Entwicklung einer Methode für Wirtschaftlichkeitsuntersuchungen bei Baumaßnahmen des Bundes*, Schriftenreihe Bau und Wohnförderung des Bundesministers für Raumordnung, Bauwesen und Städtebau, 1983

/E2/ DIN 18960, *Baunutzungskosten von Hochbauten*

/E3/ VDI 6025, *Betriebswirtschaftliche Berechnungen für Investitionsgüter- und Anlagen*

/E4/ Gertis, *Sind neuere Fassadenentwicklungen bauphysikalisch sinnvoll? Teil 2: Glas-Doppelfassaden*, Bauphysik 21, issue 2/99, Ernst & Sohn

/E5/ Recknagel / Sprenger / Schramek, *Taschenbuch für Heizung + Klimatechnik 2000*, Verlag Oldenbourg, München, 1999

/E6/ VDI 2067 Blatt 1, *Berechnung der Kosten von Wärmeversorgungsanlagen, Betriebstechnische und wirtschaftliche Grundlagen*, 1983

/E7/ VDI 2067 Blatt 3, *Berechnung der Kosten von Wärmeversorgungsanlagen, Raumlufttechnik*, 1983

/E8/ VDI 2067 Blatt 1 Entwurf, *Wirtschaftlichkeit gebäudetechnischer Anlagen, Grundlagen und Kostenberechnung*, 1999

/E9/ Braun / Oesterle / Haller, *Facility Management, Erfolg in der Immobilienbewirtschaftung*, Springer Verlag, 1996

Recommended Reading:

■ Bächlin, *Belastung von Gebäuden durch den windinduzierten Innendruck*, Dissertation, Karlsruhe 1985

■ Institut für internationale Architekturdokumentation (ed.), *Glasbau Atlas*, Birkhäuser Verlag, Basel, 1998

■ Knaack, *Konstruktiver Glasbau*, Verlag Rudolf Müller, Cologne, 1998

■ Oesterle, Eberhard; Lieb, Rolf-Dieter, *Die doppelschalige Fassade des Düsseldorfer Stadttors*, TAB, Technik am Bau, 7/97

■ Oesterle, Eberhard; Lieb, Rolf-Dieter; Fischer, C., *Die doppelte Haut unter der Lupe*, CCI 3+4/97

■ Wigginton, Michael, *Glass in Architecture*, Phaidon, London, 1996

■ Ziller / Sedlaczek / Ruscheweyh / Oesterle / Lieb, *Natürliche Belüftung eines Hochhauses mit Doppelfassade*, Ki Luft- und Kältetechnik, 8/96

Index

List of projects

Bold printed page numbers indicate a project description. All project examples are situated in Germany.

SI-Unit Conversion

As all physical properties in this book are given in international standard units, to which the reader might not be accustomed, the main conversions are given below:

length, area, volume, air flow, air-change rate

1 m	3.28 feet
1 m^2	10.76 square feet
1 m^3	35.31 cubic feet
1 liter = 1 dm^3	0.264 gal
1 m^3/s	35.31 ft^3/s
1 m^3/h m^2	3.28 ft^3/h ft^2

weight, density, density change, pressure, acceleration, earth gravity

1 kg	2.2 lb.
1 kg/m^3	0.0623 lb./ft^3
0.004 kg/m^{3}K	1.38 10^{-4} lb./ft^3 °F
1 Pa = 1 N/m^2	0.093 N/ft^2
	= 0.0208 lb./ft^2
1 m/s^2	3.28 ft/s^2
9.81 m/s^2	32.18 ft/s^2

energy, specific energy consumption

1 MJ	948 Btu
1 kW	3412 Btu/h
1 MJ/m^2	88.09 Btu/ft^2
1 kWh/m^2 a	317.11 Btu/ft^2 year

temperature

1 K = 1 °C	1.8 °F = 1.8 R

with temperature in [°F] = 9/5 • x [°C] + 32, some examples:

-40 °C	-40 °F
-17.8 °C	0 °F
0 °C	32 °F
20 °C	68 °F
37.8 °C	100 °F

thermal transmission, heat transfer, heat capacity

1 W/m^{2}K	0.176 Btu/h ft^2 °F
1 m^{2}K/W	5.68 h ft^2 °F/Btu
1 kJ/kg K	0,24 Btu/lb.°F

money, specific cost

1 € = 1 Euro	≈ 1 US-\$
	(value is subject to change)
1 €/m^2 a	≈ 0.09 US-\$/ft^2 year

First published in German in 1999 by
Verlag Georg D.W. Callwey GmbH & Co., Munich.
Translated from the German by Peter Green, Munich
Edited by Rolf-Dieter Lieb, Stuttgart

Prestel Verlag
Mandlstrasse 26, 80802 Munich
Tel.: +49 (89) 38 17 09-0
Fax: +49 (89) 38 17 09-35;
4 Bloomsbury Place, London WC1A 2QA
Tel.: +44 (020) 7323-5004
Fax: +44 (020) 7636-8004;
175 Fifth Avenue, Suite 402
New York, NY 10010
Tel.: +1 (212) 995-2720
Fax: +1 (212) 995-2733

www.prestel.com

Die Deutsche Bibliothek CIP-Einheits-
Aufnahme data is available

Project coordination: Stella Sämann
Typography, cover, production: Matthias Hauer
Typesetting: Rolf-Dieter Lieb, Stuttgart
Lithography: Kösel Druck, Kempten
and Wilhelm Vornehm, München
Printing: Sellier, Freising
Binding: Conzella, Pfarrkirchen

Printed in Germany on acid-free paper

ISBN 3-7913-2504-3

A